First edition

CONTENT WARNING

This memoir contains depictions of childhood neglect, abuse, manipulation, poverty, addiction, grief, mental health struggles, self-harm and predatory behavior. Some readers may find these topics distressing. Please take care while reading.

I

THE GERMAN DREAM

1

THE DARKNESS

I am known as "the corpse." At least in Regensburg, the city in Germany where I live.

That was the nickname the kids in school gave me. How could such small bodies, no older than my age of seven, with big, unknowing eyes, closer to having left God than I was to returning to him, be so cruel?

I knew what I looked like. My long, tangled brown hair cascading down my back, eyes the color of a storm, and my skin so pale, the blue veins beneath my eyes showed through like cracks in porcelain. Where they laughed and played, I lingered on the edges of their world in my lanky form. I wasn't dead or anything, but the feeling haunted me, a persistent ache in my chest, a gnawing certainty that soon enough I would be, if something didn't change. It wasn't rational, just the relentless pounding of my heart as I lay awake at night, convinced it would implode before morning. Maybe the children could see it too: the gloss in my eyes, the way I drifted somewhere far away.

Still, I didn't have it as bad as the girl who sat in front of me. Her name was Jessica, and she had only one finger on one hand, so they called her the One-Finger Monster. I'll take "Corpse" over that any day.

There was a sense of safety and order in Regensburg that made life predictable. Children marched to class in neat lines like little ants, their house slippers shuffling quietly. Even the way we wrote our cursive was scrutinized, as if one wrong loop would tip the whole delicate balance of the town. Something about the culture here seemed confining, and I could see it in Mother's eyes when she sat by the windowsill with a cup of coffee, condensed milk swirling in the dark brew like storm clouds. She affectionately called me "Nanya," a nickname born from my toddler attempts at saying my own name.

Her eyes were distant, as if she could see all the way back to Kazakhstan, where my family is from, where the winds cut sharper and the mountains towered higher.

Regensburg was a place of routines, of quiet suffering tucked beneath the surface of comfortability. No one asked questions here; they simply shuffled forward, heads down, trying not to disturb the stillness. But beneath that stillness, I could feel something trembling. Something was waiting to unravel in my home.

Before Mother got sick, she was the epitome of grace. She moved with a quiet elegance, always conscious of the eyes of God. Her blonde hair, twisted into a chignon, glistened under the kitchen light. Pearl earrings peeked from behind stray wisps of hair, and an apron hung neatly from her neck. She bustled about the kitchen, her every movement a dance of quiet efficiency. With a gentle smile, she attended to every request: more butter, more spoons, another helping of dessert. She never missed a beat. She rarely took a seat, instead flowing seamlessly between the kitchen and dining room. Her sleeves bore the evidence of her labor: flour prints and smudges, proof of the care she poured into every meal, every moment. For many years, our dinner table was a bustling center of warmth and chatter. Cousins, distant relatives, Russian friends, and neighbors gathered around, their voices a lively symphony against the backdrop of freshly baked cookies and pelmenis (a sort of dumpling) wafting through the air. I sipped blue soda from a tall glass, my pink silk dress rustling softly, feeling a swell of pride and joy. As I surveyed the scene with wide, gleaming eyes, I felt like a princess in her low-income castle, blissfully unaware of what was to come.

FAME OR DEAD

Mother's ambition knew no bounds. Even as a teenager, she played life like a chess master, always calculating, always several steps ahead. She never hesitated to sacrifice anything or anyone for the win. I was like her, she told me. I was drawn to the glitz and glamour of the screen.

I didn't have any remarkable talents, but I'd dance to whatever crackled through the CD player, giving it a smack now and then to keep the music going. In my mind, I was always on a stage. I had performed ballet once, not particularly well, but I loved the feeling of being seen. Mother remembered watching movie stars and singers flickering on a retro television, their lives so different from hers. Her own dream of becoming a star grew bigger than the tiny house she lived in. Her ambition surged past the broken roof and straight up to the open sky. Even through all the discouragement, she didn't waver back then. She was determined. She would sneak into town, walking miles for the faint chance of auditioning for the smallest of local roles or singing in festivals.

"Everyone said it was a waste," she admitted. Her voice softened, and she looked at me with a faint smile as she finished her last piece of chocolate.

She won my father's affection not through fate, but through careful, calculated moves. Perhaps that was exactly how it needed to be. I can't blame her for refusing to wait on destiny, not after all it had dealt her. Why trust in fate when it had only betrayed her time and again? All those nights spent hungry growing up, watching other functional families gather around warm meals in her hometown.

She knew better than to leave her future to chance. She became the hand of God.

She had whispered into Father's ear that his girlfriend had lost interest, then told the girlfriend the same thing about him. She didn't wait for destiny to unfold. She had engineered it, like a puppet master pulling invisible strings. When she told me the story, the brilliance of her deception had left me stunned. But what haunted me most was her laugh as she recalled the story, a gleeful, melodic sound like the sweet tinkling of a music box in the dead of night. Sometimes her ruthlessness frightened me.

Mother's relationship with her parents had always been tense, laced with unspoken disappointments and complicated further by her sisters' jealousy of the things Mother managed to earn. She was forever striving to prove her worth, to earn their elusive approval through grand gestures and small kindnesses. When she flew our grandparents from Kazakhstan to visit us, she made sure they returned with bags of candy, small but tangible symbols of her success in Germany. But as she sealed the package, a pang of jealousy gnawed at me. "Why don't I get any?" I murmured.

Mother looked at me, her gaze softening. "Things are different in Kazakhstan," she said gently, a reminder of the scarcity there that, at my age, I could only barely understand. It would be years before I fully grasped what it meant to grow up with nothing.

Over time, she confided in me, unraveling fragments of her family's history. She told me about her father, Ivan, and his complicated relationship with faith. After witnessing his best friend die in the war despite his desperate prayers, Ivan had lost all belief in a higher power. In the days leading up to his passing, his lung infected from a bullet that had lodged there long ago, tensions within the family grew even darker. Arguments flared between my grandfather, Ivan, and my aunt. Their exchanges were bitter and escalating. The final straw came when, in a fit of anger, my aunt scrawled an upside-down cross on the wall. "It's her fault he died," Mother said tearfully. She blamed a curse of black magic, something she believed had haunted our family for generations, tied to an old book of spells that had long since been destroyed.

Back in Kazakhstan, my three brothers, all under ten at the time, became expert hunters out of necessity. Pigeons, frogs, whatever they could catch with their small hands and makeshift traps became dinner. Andy, the youngest, fell sick. The hospital wouldn't allow our parents to visit him, so Mother, desperate, stood outside feeding him through the iron bars of a window, her fingers slipping bits of bread and a spoon of soup through the narrow gaps. I remember hearing the story of my cousin, his hands shaking, his eyes wide with horror after accidentally shooting his brother with a gun he'd found hidden in a bush. In our world, tragedies like that didn't shock anyone. My father, exhausted from welding all day, would come home with soot-streaked hands. But his real work came after dark. He'd steal supplies from the factories, scraps of metal, parts that no one would miss, things with hidden value. Mother took those stolen bits and transformed them. What was junk to others, she made into something worth selling at the market. She was clever like that, turning scraps into survival, bending the rules when they bent against us. She'd slip bribes to police officers with one hand and sell with the other, always staying two steps ahead of anyone who might try to stop her. Once, when the night was especially still, she whispered to me about the men who had found her in the cornfields and pulled down her pants. Her voice caught in her throat, and she never finished the story, but she didn't need to. That was life where we were from. Either you learned to be ruthless, or you didn't survive at all. I knew she didn't want that life for me.

My paternal grandmother, Oma, with her unyielding German grit, fought relentlessly to secure citizenship for our family, pulling them out of Kazakhstan two years before I was born. By then, life wasn't unbearable. My parents managed to buy their own apartment in a high-rise building that swung like a pendulum during the massive earthquakes. But Mother was restless. She wanted to see a different life elsewhere, so she convinced Father to sell it and move. She would've moved without him.

My aunts and uncles came along and were grateful for the move. Germany's healthcare system offered what Kazakhstan couldn't, especially for my cousin who had lost the ability to walk. Germany was more disability-friendly.

But Mother? She despised Oma for it. Even though she recognized life was better here in Germany, the struggle was her heartbeat. Without it, Mother felt numb.

Here it was safe. Predictable. Too quiet for someone like her. There were no fires to put out, no schemes to unravel. Nothing pushing her forward.

Still, they managed to find one, at least for a little while.

The plan was simple: steal clothes from the roadside donation bins and resell them at the flea market. A hustle is a hustle, no matter the country. But it didn't last.

German police are sharp, orderly, and ask too many questions.

And my father, lugging around giant trash bags full of mismatched jackets and forgotten jeans, didn't exactly fly under the radar. It wasn't like

Kazakhstan, where a few bills could smooth things over. In Germany, the rules held. And they held tight.

And so Mother stood in this strange country, the language foreign, a jumble of sounds she couldn't make sense of. The people stared through her like she wasn't even there. An outsider. Germany definitely made us aware of that, even though half our bloodline was German.

Now, in our modest apartment, delicate porcelain figurines lined the shelves, and a Russian carpet added a touch of elegance, even though we lived in a low-income neighborhood known for its immigrant population and higher crime rates.

Dishes towered like a precarious Leaning Tower of Pisa, and flour prints smeared her sleeves. Mother lost herself in midnight shopping sprees on late-night television, spending the government-provided financial assistance for her children. Her eyes, glazed in the light of the television, seemed lost in a world she could only touch through a screen.

She hid on the balcony to smoke cigarettes, the orange glow of the tip flickering in the dark like a firefly. The bitter smoke curled around her like a shroud. The echoes of old Hollywood movies, the glamorous life she dreamed of as a child, still haunted her every day. She would hum tunes from those movies while scrubbing the bathroom floor, her voice barely audible over the drone of the washing machine.

Then, it all happened in a swift, brutal descent. Mother grew ill, her once-unstoppable vitality fading in a matter of days. She was confined to her bed, clutching her chest as if trying to keep her very life from slipping away. Her face twisted in pain, crumpling like a receipt left too long in a pocket.

I sat by her side, only four years old, my little hands trembling as I brushed her straw-like blonde hair away from her eyes. My heart felt like it was being crushed with every ragged breath she took. I was terrified at the thought of losing her.

"God has other plans," she whispered, her voice barely more than a breath. "One day, you will have a new mother and live as though I never existed."

The thought struck panic deep within me. For a fleeting second, I noticed a glimmer of satisfaction in her eyes, as if my reaction reassured her of something I couldn't yet understand.

FAME OR DEAD

"I don't want a stepmother," I sobbed, my voice breaking, raw and bitter with anger toward my father. How could he even think of replacing her?

As the days went on, she began saying that something evil had wormed its way into our home. It was seeping through him.

2

THE DINNER

One afternoon, out of nowhere it seems, Mother started referring to Father as "Satan."

It was disorienting. I had always imagined Satan as a beast: Father didn't ricochet off surfaces with cloven hooves or spew fire. There were no horns. No pitchfork. Just a man.

A man who sat across from me every night, eating buckwheat, ground beef, and salad with impeccable manners. Elbows never on the table. A crown of black hair. Eyes the color of a clear sky—eyes that mirrored mine.

He didn't growl. He didn't rage. He just existed, quietly, like something waiting.

Just like a fallen angel.

Maybe that's how Satan fools you.

He wears the face you trust. He comes in familiar skin.

Yet, the thick black mustache was a true devilish touch. It quivered with every laugh, and despite the disconcerting resemblance to my childhood imaginings, we couldn't help but laugh along. His expressive sign language and animated gestures could light up the room, offering us a temporary reprieve from the relentless shadow of mother's mystery illness.

Our evenings at the table were a swirl of stories and laughter. My father would spin tales from his childhood of his days stealing corn from the fields and getting chased by wild dogs, his hands moving like a conductor orchestrating a symphony. But every so often, when his laughter would pause, I glimpsed something deeper in his eyes—a shadow of pain, swiftly hidden behind the next joke. It was as if, while he worked tirelessly to shield us from his own turmoil, he was grappling with something that remained just out of sight.

Father loved to take candid film shots of us eating, his old camera clicking away, capturing grainy moments. He leaned in to kiss Mother, but she dodged, mumbling something about his prickly mustache. Unfazed by her reaction, he stuck a toothpick in his mouth and chewed, the wood splintering with a terrible sound. The gap between his teeth, worn from years of chewing on various objects, made the noise even more grating. I couldn't help but cringe.

"What?" Father asked in a muffled tone. He was deaf.

"Why are you chewing on a toothpick?" I asked.

His eyes narrowed as he struggled to read my lips. "Who said it's a match? I chewed down a giant tree stump into the size of a stick." He winked, then let out a boisterous laugh that echoed through the room. Slava, the second oldest of my teenage brothers and a blond replica of Father, looked up from his plate, his fork halfway to his mouth. "So . . . what do you think of the buckwheat?" he asked, his voice a mix of earnestness and mischief.

I stifled a giggle. "It looks like Andy's freckles."

"No, it does not!" Andy fretted. He was the youngest of the brothers, but still nine years older than me. He glanced at his plate and then at his shoulders, where brown dots were sprinkled all over his skin. His eyes, wide with embarrassment, darted back to his untouched buttered buckwheat. He seemed to lose his appetite and didn't touch his food for the rest of the meal.

As Mother's illness deepened, the lively dinners and joyful snapshots of our family life began to degrade. The dining room, once brimming with laughter, turned into a somber space haunted by the relentless wail of ambulances and the weight of unanswered questions. Sometimes she begged us to call the paramedics in the middle of the night, convinced something was terribly wrong. But when they arrived, she would storm out of the ambulance in frustration, her fear tangled with embarrassment, asking us why we'd called them in the first place, before returning to bed. When she went to hospitals, the doctors insisted there was nothing wrong, dismissing her symptoms of dizziness, racing heartbeat and shortness of breath as if they were figments of her imagination. Feeling abandoned by medicine, she sought solace in whispered prayers and conversations with God, yearning for divine intervention where science had failed her.

After school, I would pour my heart into creating paintings for her, using sunshine and vivid colors as my arsenal against the encroaching darkness. I'd sit next to her on the bed in her room, its emerald green walls decorated with floral prints and porcelain dolls that stared with unsettlingly long lashes. I would offer her my latest artwork of bright colors and happy faces, the sun's rays barely reaching the bed through the narrow window. Each drawing was my desperate attempt to infuse some light into the growing shadows, to offer her a fleeting escape from the reality that had begun to encircle us with its relentless grip.

"What is this?" she asked, her voice barely a whisper.

"Medicine," I replied with conviction. "If you put it on your chest, it will heal you like a balm."

For the first time in weeks, her face brightened with a genuine smile. "Thank you, my sweet little girl."

Slowly, Mother began to find her way back to us, but the recovery came with a peculiar shift. By day, she threw herself into her old routines with renewed fervor. She cooked with a passion, her culinary creations of blueberry pie and mascarpone cakes once again filling the kitchen with enticing aromas. Her paints and brushes returned to her hands, and she licked the tips of her pencils, turning them into a creamy paste of color as she obsessively painted. Her hair was neatly pulled back with a French barrette, and in those moments, she seemed almost like her old self. Yet, as night fell, she changed.

As the sun dipped below the horizon, our once cozy apartment took on a disquieting aura. The warmth of the day dissipated, replaced by an unsettling silence. Shadows from the porcelain dolls on the shelves seemed to stretch and elongate, their eyes appearing to follow anyone brave enough to look their way. I would hear Mother moving about the apartment, her footsteps soft yet persistent, as if she were searching for something elusive. Unable to resist, I crept down the hall and found her standing by the window, her outline sharp against the fading light. She stood motionless, her gaze fixed on the deepening dark, her shoulders tense and drawn. "Mother?" I whispered, barely loud enough to break the quiet.

She turned slowly, her face pale and distant, eyes a little glazed as if pulled from someplace far away. She held my gaze, then managed a soft, almost weary smile. "Go back to bed," she murmured, voice steady but hollow, as if it was meant more for herself than for me. I wanted to ask, Are you all right? but the words lodged in my throat, swallowed up by the thick quiet between us. I backed away, watching her turn again to the window, her figure fragile yet unyielding against the night.

Her nightly rituals grew stranger, taking on a life of their own. She would light candles in the dim light, shadows flickering around her as she whispered prayers, her voice low and urgent, each word spilling out like a secret shared only with the darkness. Her notebook became her constant companion; she'd fill its pages feverishly, her pen moving in bursts, eyes wide and unblinking, as though trying to pin down something trying to escape her.

Once, I dared to ask what she was writing, but she only clutched the notebook closer, shaking her head. So when she wasn't home I snooped, flipping through the pages to find disjointed scribbles, scattered sentences, fragments that felt like pieces of a puzzle I couldn't quite solve. When I asked my siblings what it meant, they only shrugged—it was just Mother being Mother. I was still a child, more focused on toys, novels, and candy than anything else. I didn't have the words for what was going on, just a weird feeling in my chest I couldn't explain. Whenever that strange feeling crept in, like the room had tilted just slightly, I'd glance at my brothers to see if they felt it too. They weren't fazed; I realized maybe I wasn't supposed to be either. By then, her rituals had woven themselves into the fabric of our home, something we accepted without question.

Mother said she was gifted, that she had to do things other families didn't. And so, I came to believe her rituals were part of a world I was too young to understand, yet somehow bound to by blood.

We were strolling home one quiet evening after a trip to the supermarket when Mother suddenly stopped and gazed upward at the sky, which was as dark and profound as the depths of an ocean. A shiver ran down my spine as the thought crossed my mind: What if gravity itself were to fail, and, weightless, we drifted into the endless void above?

The moon, emerging from the darkness with its ghostly, ethereal glow, seemed to captivate Mother entirely. She tilted her head slightly and whispered to it, a soft clack of her tongue breaking the stillness. "The moon is speaking to me," she said in a secretive tone, pointing to its cratered surface, which she saw as a face staring down at us. Despite my attempts to decipher the words of the moon, the only sounds I could hear were the soft rustlings of our plastic bags, teased by the gentle night breeze.

"Mother, I don't hear anything." I said, tightening my hand around hers.

"It has chosen me. Only I can hear it," she declared, her voice filled with an awed reverence. She leaned down and kissed my forehead, her touch both tender and reassuring, before we resumed our walk home. She draped her arm protectively around my shoulders as we moved along the path, bathed in the moon's silvery light. I stole glances at Mother, her eyes still fixed on the moon, her expression a mix of wonder and resolve, as if she were on the cusp of some profound revelation.

I didn't have any magical powers or inclination aside from a recurring nightmare that had haunted me since I was four, around the same time Mother's mysterious illness began. In this dream, the drone of the television buzzed in the background, a muffled symphony of laughter and conversation swirling around me, yet I was ensnared in darkness. My desperate calls of "Hello?" echoed unanswered, swallowed by the persistent hum of conversations that went on as if I were invisible.

I would struggle in vain, feeling the crushing pressure of what I realized were couch cushions enveloping me. I realized with a jolt that my entire family was unknowingly seated on top of me. I was within the couch. The suffocating weight seemed to press the very life from me. Then I would wake up abruptly, gasping for air, my heart pounding. I stared into the darkness of my room, my eyes straining to make sense of the shadows. The moonlight, filtering through the window, illuminated the bare tree branches outside, twisted and skeletal, like gnarled fingers scratching at the night sky.

I had finally been given my own room, an unexpected privilege after my eldest brother, Dima, was kicked out of our home to go live with Oma because of some hoodlum mischief he caused. Slava and Andy shared the larger bedroom next door.

The door was always left ajar; I was paralyzed by a deep fear of being alone in the dark. And for good reason: Each night, something was watching me as I tried to sleep. A fleeting ray of light would cut through the darkness, slipping through the crack in my open door before disappearing entirely. I lay frozen, my heart pounding, straining to catch any sound that might reveal what was lurking about. The light flickered once more, casting unsettling, shifting patterns across the walls. I held my breath as deliberate footsteps approached. I clutched my blanket tighter, desperate for its fragile comfort against the encroaching darkness. The footsteps halted just outside my door, and the light vanished abruptly, plunging my room into blackness once again.

Once, when the hallowed glow in my room grew brighter in the night and awoke me, I peeked through the crack of my door. The light reflected off Mother's face. She wasn't looking at me, but down at the white candle she held between her hands, her white nightgown billowing softly around her. She passed from my view, the candlelight growing dimmer as she moved towards the end of the hallway where her bedroom was situated, guided by something unseen.

The following day unfolded as ordinarily as ever. Slava, the second oldest sibling out of us four, seventeen years old and my protector, was in the kitchen preparing savory and sweet pastries for my lunch before walking me to school. Andy bustled by me in a hurry, a guitar bag slung over his shoulder as he rushed to the bicycle carried him to his high school. Father had long departed for his welding job at the crack of dawn, leaving before the world was fully awake. Mother remained in her bedroom, still asleep.

Slava handed me a golden pastry, still warm from the oven, the scent of fresh dough and tangy jam enveloping the kitchen. "Ready for school, little mouse?" he asked, his grin wide and comforting. His heterochromatic eyes—one green, one brown—sparkled with a blend of mischief and concern.

"Yeah," I replied, trying to muster a smile that didn't quite reach my eyes.

The morning air was crisp and invigorating, and the cheerful chirping of birds provided a soothing contrast to the unease that clung to me. I loved school, despite the torment I faced from the other children. It probably didn't help my reputation that for last year's talent show I stood on stage and ate cat kibble as my talent.

As we approached the school gates, Slava knelt down to meet my gaze. His voice was gentle but firm. "If anything happens with those kids, you let me know. I'll always be here for you."

After school, Father was waiting for me at the gates. As I approached, he took my backpack off my shoulders, his eyes bloodshot. His shoulders were hunched, as if carrying a weight far heavier than his tired body could bear. He signed, his movements slow and deliberate, "Do you want to come with me to work or go home?"

"I want to come with," I signed back eagerly, my heart swelling at the chance to spend time with him. Our signs were rough around the edges, a makeshift language born out of necessity rather than formal training. Mother disliked Father's sign language, her embarrassment growing if strangers stared. And here, where every gesture seemed to draw unwanted attention, they stared constantly. I never felt any hatred toward my father; if anything, I was trapped in a quiet war within myself, torn between the deep affection I still held for him and the unyielding loyalty I felt toward Mother.

On the bus ride into the "old city," Father's exhaustion became more evident. His head drooped against the window, the rumbling of the bus lulling him into a shallow sleep. His hand, warm and heavy, rested lightly on mine. When our stop neared, I reached out, my fingers brushing his arm as I gently shook him awake.

Street lamps cast pools of orange light onto the rain-slicked cobblestones, softly illuminating the steady drizzle. Medieval buildings of cafes, family-owned shops and offices huddled close, lined the narrow streets, broken only by the occasional shadowed alleyway. Office workers bustled out of the bank we entered, shielding themselves with briefcases, coats pulled tight against the damp chill. Father, always moving between jobs to keep up with our family's endless expenses, had just finished his shift as a welder and now prepared for his night role as a janitor. He unlocked the supply closet, handed me a bucket filled with cleaning supplies, and gave me a tired smile.

I began wiping down the handrails with a disinfectant-soaked rag while he mopped the marble floors with practiced precision, pausing every now and then to check his watch or press a hand to his aching back. We worked our way to the third floor, where Mother was scheduled to clean tonight as well, but, as usual, she hadn't shown up, leaving Father to pick up her duties. As I worked, one of the office doors opened. A well-dressed man stepped out, his round belly stretching over a polished leather belt. He paused on the white marble steps, rummaging through his briefcase, then looked up and approached me. "Keep up the good work," he said, placing a two-euro coin in my hand. Father, who couldn't hear the exchange but caught the gesture, gave me a proud smile from across the hall and signed, "That's my boss."

Afterward, we approached an ice cream vendor. The vendor's hands spread over the chilled glass like sea stars. "A scoop of watermelon, please," I said, handing over my two euros with a self-satisfied smile.

"Don't tell," Father signed, extending his pinky to interlock with mine. "Mother would've taken it from you."

We sat down and I devoured the scoop while Father stole a few bites. He wetted a napkin with his tongue and rubbed the stickiness off my cheeks. "Did you eat it or just smear it all over your face?" he signed, laughing. He leaned in for an Eskimo kiss, our noses touching, and shook his head with a smile.

The wind picked up as we headed home, howling through the narrow streets and echoing off ancient stone walls built by the Roman Empire long ago. I clung to Father's arm, and he wrapped his jacket around me, shielding me from the gusts that I feared could blow me away.

In the stillness of evening, our dining room would transform into a sanctuary for creativity, where my brothers and I gathered to sketch and paint. The wooden table, typically cluttered with schoolbooks and remnants of family meals, now became a canvas for our imaginations—strewn with paper, paints, and colored pencils. Together, we embraced the simple joy of creation, our laughter and the soft scratch of pencils blending into the warmth of the moment. Yet, amidst this harmony, I felt it—a subtle, unsettling presence creeping from the shadowed edges of the adjacent living room.

In countless cultures and ancient folklore it is whispered of as a creature of darkness, a sinister being that preys on the vulnerable, luring them toward despair. Some say it speaks to those teetering on the brink, softly coaxing them to places where death had already cast its shadow. For me, that entity had a name: Kop Kop. I was just a toddler when the first prickles of fear crawled up my spine, but my family waved it off as nothing more than a child's overactive imagination.

"It's right there!" I cried, pointing with a trembling finger into the shadowy depths of the living room.

"Where?" Slava, my blond brother, walked in, his steps deliberate and cautious. He checked all the corners, his silhouette tall and reassuring in the dim light.

"There's nothing here. No need to be scared," he said softly, though I caught the subtle tension in his voice.

Despite his reassurances, I couldn't shake the feeling that the darkness was alive, beckoning me closer like quicksand ready to swallow me whole. The shadows pulsed and shifted, their inky tendrils curling toward me. The hairs on the back of my neck stood up. Once it had me, I knew I'd never escape.

Slava returned to the table, his smile tight but comforting. "See? Just shadows. Nothing to worry about."

I nodded, though my gaze drifted back toward the living room where the darkness seemed to stare back, watching, waiting. As we sat down to draw again, I tried to focus on the bright, colorful strokes on my paper, but the sensation of being observed lingered.

Sensing my unease, Andy, my other brother with the buckwheat freckles, grinned. "Maybe we should draw something scary," he suggested. "To show the darkness we're not afraid."

I hesitated, then nodded, reaching for a black crayon. Together, we sketched monstrous figures and eerie scenes, daring Kop Kop to come closer. Our laughter returned, the warmth of our shared creativity pushing back the creeping cold. For a time, our defiance seemed to work. But when bedtime arrived, the dread returned. I reluctantly packed away my drawing supplies and followed my brothers to our rooms. Slava gave me a tight hug, his presence a temporary shield. But once I was alone in bed, staring up at the ceiling, the walls of my room seemed to pulse, and the dark corners throbbed with life.

I pulled the covers up to my chin, listening intently to the night sounds: the creak of the home settling and the soft whisper of wind against the window. In the silence, I whispered, "Go away, Kop Kop. You can't have me."

3

THE PSYCHIC

My parents' swift glances exchanged at home were like paper cuts. Father signed something to her with sharp, deliberate movements, his hands tight with frustration. Mother's hands, though, moved slowly, stiff and cracked from years of cleaning chemicals, the fingers that once painted so gracefully now rigid and brittle.

"You didn't show up for your shift again," he signed, his expression pleading and firm.

"These are artist's hands," she signed back, her gestures slow and final. Her gaze returned to her painting, a silent dismissal that severed the connection between them as she couldn't see anything else he signed.

I pretended to fiddle with pencils on the dining table, silently watching their exchange. Mother was always right; everyone in the family had learned that it was her way or no way. We all tiptoed around her moods, smoothing over any edges in her path. Yet, the way she looked at Father—disapproving, tired of his needs—made me wonder if he wasn't as supportive as I'd once thought. He complained often. I felt a flicker of doubt about him.

They rarely fought in front of me, but they didn't need to. I could sense the unease behind the closed doors, beneath my brothers' blaring American pop music like Britney Spears and Michael Jackson, and in those strained glances. I was quiet, small, like a little mouse always lurking in the shadows, watching.

It wasn't long before Mother confided in me. She had found a note in Father's pocket—another woman's phone number scrawled across it.

I had only seen her this angry once before, when I told her Father had spanked me lightly for misbehaving. That time, she locked him in their bedroom as punishment. After she stormed off to the kitchen, I lingered outside their door, peeking through the keyhole. "I'm sorry," I whispered, but he couldn't hear me.

Mother continued her nightly practices that she swore had healed her mystery illness. One night I heard the soft patter of footsteps. Rising from my bed, I crept to my door, the memory of Mother's nocturnal rituals fresh in my mind. As I moved closer, it was not Mother as I had expected, but Slava. He was hunched over some papers in his hands, illuminated by the faint glow of the hallway light.

"Slava?" My voice was barely a whisper.

He turned, surprised. "You should be sleeping," he said, glancing around as if worried someone else might hear.

"What are you doing?"

"Just . . . a project for Mother," he said, but his eyes told me there was more he wasn't saying. He folded the papers quickly, tucking them into his pocket.

"What project?" I asked.

Mother had always favored Slava. She would often say, with a strange light in her eyes, that if she could marry him she would. This favoritism created an invisible barrier between us, a silent understanding that he was different, special. He was the only one to know what she was up to.

"Nothing you need to worry about, little mouse," he said. "Go back to bed."

Reluctantly, I nodded and turned to go back to my room. As I lay back down, the sense of unease deepened. What was Slava hiding? And why was Mother involving him in her strange rituals? I listened intently, straining to hear anything that might indicate what was happening. But all I heard was the rustle of papers from Mother's room and a low-voiced conversation.

The next day, I watched Slava and Mother closely, trying to pick up on any clues. At breakfast, Mother seemed more animated than usual, her eyes alight with a strange fervor. Slava, on the other hand, looked more tired and distracted, his gaze distant.

"Are you working on another project, Slava?" I asked casually, hoping to draw out some information.

He glanced at Mother before nodding. "Yes, something like that."

Mother gave me a smile. "Slava is helping me with some important work."

"What kind of work?" I pressed.

"Nothing you need to worry about, dear. Grown-up things." Her tone was playful, but her eyes had sharpened, daring me to question further.

That evening, I resolved to find out what was going on. Mother spent most of her time in her room, the door firmly closed. I waited until the house was silent, then slipped out of bed once more. I crept to Mother's room, pausing outside the door. The light was off, but I could hear the soft rustle of papers and the murmur of voices. I took a deep breath and gently pushed the door open, peeking inside. Mother and Slava were huddled over a table, papers spread out before them.

"What are you doing?" I whispered, unable to contain my curiosity any longer.

They both looked up, surprise and alarm flashing across their faces. Mother quickly gathered the papers, hiding them from view.

"Nothing you need to worry about," she said, her voice tight. "Go back to bed."

"But I want to know," I insisted, stepping into the room.

Mother shook her head. "You're too young to understand."

"No, I'm not." I held my ground, a defiant surge rising in me.

She gasped, her voice sharp as she chided, "What a bad girl, not listening to her mother!"

The words hit me hard, embarrassment washing over me. And I knew what she'd say next: girls who didn't listen to their mothers became ugly. That was her warning, one she'd repeated until it felt carved into me.

The shame and fear of her words forced me to nod and back out of the room, closing the door behind me. My mind churned with questions. What could be so urgent, so secretive? Lying in bed, I knew I couldn't just let it go. I'd wait until they were out of the apartment, search their room, and find those papers. If this was something big, something about us, then I had to know.

In the course of weeks, I'd find out that they would sit for hours, poring over pages filled with writings from a renowned psychic in Switzerland. An older lady, in her eighties. Slava, ever the dutiful son and golden child, lent his skills to translate the dense text to mother, who didn't understand German very well, into Russian. At home, we spoke German—clumsy, patched-together German when it came from Mother's mouth. She insisted on it, though. Said Russian reminded everyone of drunks and criminals.

Maybe it was just something she believed, or maybe it was our neighborhood of foreigners we were placed in—too many shouting voices, too many vodka bottles clinking on front doorsteps. In Germany, there was a special kind of disdain for them: Russians weren't just foreigners; they were trouble. She wanted distance. She wanted elegance. And language, to her, was a kind of disguise of who we were.

Mother's obsession grew like a vine, twisting around our lives. All of Mother's questions circled endlessly around one thing: our purpose in life. She disappeared one morning, boarding a train to Switzerland, driven by the promise of truth from the so-called psychic. By the time she had returned, the truth she sought had unraveled like loose thread from a sweater. The address led to an empty lot—just another lie. She had been ensnared, her desperation preyed upon by a man hiding behind a spiritual facade, charging a lot of money.

Her silence upon return was thick, punctuated by the quiet crackle of defeat. It didn't take long for her resolve to harden into something new. She turned inward, transforming our home. The dining table, once a place of family dinners and laughter, became a temple of flickering candlelight, séances, and whispered invocations. Mother declared herself the medium now, determined to find the answers she craved through her own hands. I was both fascinated and frightened by her, drawn to the mysteries Mother sought.

I didn't fully understand what she was searching for or why it consumed her so completely. She performed her rituals late at night, during the hours when Father was either at work or asleep, shielded from witnessing just how deeply her obsession had taken root.

When he did notice traces of her nightly rituals—the faint scent of smoke, the melted candle wax—he'd tighten his jaw, his disapproval clear but unspoken. He'd learned that questioning her would only provoke her anger. It was this resistance, this perceived obstruction, that earned him the nickname "Satan" on her lips.

Andy and Slava were forced to join her, staying up late on school nights, their faces bathed in candlelight as they watched Mother slip into her trances. They swore she spoke in tongues, her voice shifting like the winds. My curiosity grew unbearable, the mystery beckoning me like a whisper in the dark. One night, I was finally allowed to join them. The room was dense with the scent of wax and the strange energy that seemed to coil around the shadows. But no spirits came. Mother, her eyes distant, turned to me with a frown. "Your energy disrupts the channel," she said, her tone final, as though I had failed some unseen test. I left the room feeling small, not understanding what was wrong with me, why I had strange dreams, why I didn't belong at the table.

On other nights, I would creep down the hall and strain to hear the sounds of their rituals—fragments of chants, voices that didn't seem to belong to anyone, the shuffle of papers covered in scribbled notes I wasn't allowed to read. Slava became the bridge between worlds, caught in the balance of Mother's dreams and reality, carrying the weight of both on his shoulders.

4

THE SEANCES

More and more, people began calling our home, wanting Mother's help. She promoted her services in the newspaper around town. A man who had stopped by earlier in the week was now on the other end of the line on the phone, pouring out his anger and despair at his illness not improving. Mother encouraged him to persist, to trust the process. She knew, better than anyone, the profound impact faith and perseverance could have in the face of adversity. She bet people's lives on it.

Her services consisted of cupping, acupuncture and urine therapy she claimed to have mastered from a book. That last one always made people pause. She believed in the healing properties of the body's own fluids, especially after a healthy diet, swore on drinking the first stream of morning urine, or rubbing it onto the skin to cure everything from rashes to bad energy. "Pure medicine," she'd say, holding a glass of it like it was holy water. Most people just nodded and tried not to look too horrified.

Father remained a silent observer in the face of Mother's intensifying beliefs, choosing instead to escape when he could, often spending time with his best friend Igor, who was also deaf and his work colleague. But even his friendships didn't escape her suspicions. One night, during a tense

37

family dinner, she fixed him with a cold stare and accused him outright of having an affair with his friend. The accusation shocked us kids, leaving us stunned and silent around the table. Father denied it, yet Mother only scoffed, saying, "Of course you'd deny it. You're a liar."

The final straw was a dried plum discovered beneath Mother's bed. She stood there frozen, holding it between her fingers like it might burn her. To her, it wasn't just a piece of forgotten fruit, it was an omen. A curse. She was certain Oma had planted it there during her brief visit. And worse, she believed Father had helped her, an unwitting pawn in some dark ritual meant to bring her harm. I remembered eating plums on Mother's bed a while back, but I stayed silent. Mother was so worked up and I didn't want to get blamed.

"Take this plum to the basement and burn it," she insisted. My brothers struggled with the task, the moisture inside the fruit resisting their attempts to set it aflame. I watched them trying to ignite the stubborn plum. The flickering flame reflected in their eyes.

Mother's words echoed in my mind, heavy and inescapable. "All they do is come over, drink, gossip, and smoke," she'd sneer about Oma and the rest of our extended family. Her voice was sharp, painting them in jagged strokes, people who wasted time, spread bad energy, and brought nothing but trouble. I couldn't forget the night Uncle Serg sat at the dinner table, strumming his guitar for us kids. His music had been soft, almost kind. But then, without warning or reason, he slammed the guitar over his wife's head. The guitar split in two and his wife acted like it didn't hurt, laughing it off. The sound of the impact, more violent than any chord he'd played, echoed through the room. I hadn't seen him in years. He was in prison now, locked away for serious crimes, possibly even murder. And so I understood Mother's fear. I understood why she shut them out, why we hardly had any visitors any more.

Finally, we gathered for a family meeting; Andy, Slava, and I on one side of the living room table, our parents on the other. The TV sat silent, casting faint shadows across the room, and we mirrored its stillness, waiting for what would come next.

"I don't want your father in my life any more," Mother said, her voice flat yet piercing. I felt a jolt of shock. Then, as though she'd questioned her own resolve, she added, "But maybe I should give him another chance. What do you kids think?"

I sat frozen, trying to grasp what she was asking of us. Did we choose Mother, with her steadfast faith, or Father, who had worked tirelessly for us but now, in her eyes, seemed tainted? I looked to Slava, the oldest sibling at home, hoping he'd say something to make sense of it all.

Slava spoke up, voice steady. "No," he said firmly. "Father has to leave."

I felt a mixture of sadness and certainty. Deep down, I knew we had to do this—that Father had betrayed Mother somehow. Maybe she was right; maybe there really was something dark in him, something hidden. I loved him, yet I trusted her instinct. She wouldn't lead us astray. Slowly, I nodded, knowing that from here on, everything would be different.

For weeks after, Father became a ghost outside our door, lingering in the twilight. I'd peer through the peephole sometimes, just to see him sitting on the cold ground, staring up at the wall. His quiet vigil became a constant, haunting presence. Each knock on the door was like the echo of an old wound tearing open again. But Mother made it clear—I was never to answer. Never to talk to him again. She'd wave him off with a sharp flick of the wrist like brushing away a fly that kept returning. As the days blurred into weeks, weeks into months, father's once-familiar figure faded from sight. First, the photos came down from the walls, his smiling face disappearing from our home. Then, the shadowy figure outside of our door vanished. Slowly, the laughter that had once filled our home disappeared. It wasn't long before Mother noticed the absence and filled the empty space with something completely unexpected.

5

THE BAND

Mother wore her grief like a pressed blouse: neat, buttoned, and carefully smoothed. But the silence around her spoke louder than words: the quiet hum of late-night movement, the flicker of light beneath the bathroom door when I'd hear her sniffle.

This is usually the point of pain where some women reach for dye or scissors. Mother reached for something deeper: a choice that would change the course of the rest of our lives. Her eyes would glaze over as she leaned in her armchair with a cup of tea and launched into one of her fantasies— grand escape to America. It wasn't a new idea. She'd floated it before: if Germany didn't tickle her fancy, she'd pack up and try America. If America didn't deliver, she'd head to Australia. Her escape plans shifted like weather, but the core remained: anywhere but here to face the life she currently had and hated. Each country was a stage, each move a reinvention.

"Germany is a graveyard," she'd mutter. "Everyone here is asleep."

She'd get up to do something, only to return to the living room a few minutes later.

"I am not just a housewife," she'd spit under her breath. "I'm meant for more."

I'd sit at the coffee table, legs swinging above the floor, imagining how impressed the kids at school would be if they found out I was moving to America. Hollywood was shiny. Even in Germany, it glowed like a promise on TV.

"One day," she'd say, staring into the distance. "I will marry a rich millionaire. I will marry Michael Jackson and then your father will see."

And somehow, in the silence that followed, it didn't feel like just a fantasy this time.

Mother didn't raise her voice to get us to do something. She didn't need to.

She crouched behind the TV, fingers calmly unplugging the cords, one by one, as the screen dimmed and died. My brothers and I watched in silence, the static in the room louder than any protest we could make.

"This stuff," she said, untangling the wires. "It's just a distraction."

She didn't look at us when she spoke.

"I was your age when everything changed. Seventeen. One mistake. I had Dima, and suddenly the world stops looking at you like you matter." She looped the cords into a neat bundle, placing them in a plastic grocery bag.

"No one cares about an old woman with kids and stretch marks," she said, almost to herself. "That dream I had is over."

She met our eyes with a quiet finality. "But I gave that all up for you."

She stood, brushed her hands off on her pants.

"I couldn't make it but you will."

Over the months, my brothers let their hair grow down to their chins, chasing the look of aging rockstars they saw on old album covers. They played their guitars with wild determination. Their fingers flew across the frets like they were born knowing where to go. Slava, always the one to push harder, would tilt his head back and reach for the high notes, straining with everything he had.

"I can't sing, Mom. I'm just not a singer," he muttered, frustration creeping into his voice.

Mother's response came without hesitation, her voice as firm as steel. "Yes, you are. You just need more practice. Think positive." Her determination was almost palpable, a force of nature that wrapped around us, compelling us to keep going.

Slava didn't argue, but his jaw tightened in that way it always did when he was caught between doubt and determination. There's a picture of him as a baby, clutching a tiny toy guitar before he could walk. Mother had placed it in his hands, convinced that music was his destiny before he had a chance to choose for himself. In a way, she shaped us all like a potter molding clay.

But the truth was, music wasn't forced on us. Dima, the eldest, had been the first to unlock its magic, his hands effortlessly gliding across keyboards and drum pads, conjuring melodies from thin air. His beats had a hypnotic quality, drawing us in and setting the tempo for the rest of us to follow. I'd join in the only ways I knew how, shaking maracas or blowing into a harmonica. We didn't need a reason to play; we played because we wanted to. Until Mother turned it into a prophecy, that is.

The prophecy came to her during a séance. She said the message was clear: if we followed her every instruction without question, we'd be on a path to unimaginable riches and success. It wasn't just a dream any more: it was destiny.

Music wasn't our only outlet. When we weren't rehearsing, we transformed into filmmakers, our stories brought to life through an ancient VHS camera Father had bought. Andy was the director, obsessing over every angle and lighting detail, his vision already sharp. Slava, ever the performer, dove into each role, sending us into fits of laughter.

When Slava and Andy finally began performing at local shows, Mother sat in the audience with an air of quiet authority. Her gaze never wavered, her posture rigid, her presence commanding. She didn't cheer or clap wildly like the other parents; she simply watched. When strangers approached her afterward to praise her sons, she would respond with a clipped "thank you," her tone devoid of surprise. She already knew what they were capable of.

It wasn't always easy, living under the weight of her expectations. But there was a strange kind of magic in our chaos. The music, the homemade movies, the bursts of creativity; it was the glue that held us together.

During that time, Mother began to look through me more than at me.

I talked back. Dragged my feet when she told me to make use of my time.

My toys vanished, one by one, confiscated like contraband. I spent most days tucked away in corners, reading or learning new languages on my own; this seemed to frustrate her more than outright defiance. It wasn't going to lead to fame.

"You're too young to be serious," she told me once. "Too unfocused to be shaped into anything."

My brothers had instruments and stage presence. I had dreams of becoming a librarian or a cashier. I liked handling money, organizing things, pretending to ring up snacks and toys from my bedroom shelves. I'd sell them back to my brothers using play cash, carefully counting change and scribbling receipts on scrap paper.

"Remember," she said one evening, "Oma had a bad relationship with her mother. That's why she's like she is. You don't want to end up the same. You need to have a good relationship with me. Be a good girl. Listen. Or you'll turn out evil, too."

Not long after, I found a single coarse, black hair sprouting from my cheek. I stared at it in the mirror, horrified, as if it confirmed something monstrous growing inside me.

When I showed Mother, she barely glanced at it.

"That's what happens when you have a nasty personality," she said.

Her words stung worse than pulling out the hair, sank deeper than skin, somewhere into the place where I was still forming.

I didn't want to be like this. Didn't want to become the ordinary she hated so much.

Now it was my turn to shine.

I stood at the edge of the living room, a microphone trembling in my grip. Mother's eyes locked on mine. My heart pounded in my ears.

"Go on," Andy urged, his voice gentle as he played the chords of 'Every Breath You Take'.

I opened my mouth and my first note came out thin and shaky. I froze, cheeks burning, waiting for laughter or groans.

"We've got ourselves a singer!" Andy shouted, his blue eyes bright with pride. His grin stretched wide across his face, and for a second, it felt like he saw something in me no one else ever had. He had that rare kind of kindness—the kind that made you believe in yourself simply because he did.

I laughed, breathless, the fear lifting from my chest like steam.

When the next verse came around, I sang louder. Off-key, imperfect, but unafraid.

And when I caught Mother's faint nod and the curve of a soft smile, something warm bloomed in my chest.

Our jam sessions rarely went unnoticed. The old man downstairs, infamous for his broom-thumping protests, never failed to make his presence known. A thud from below was our signal to turn down the volume, but it never stopped us for long. Sometimes he'd storm up to our door, dark, angry eyes glaring, a cigarette dangling from his lips as he muttered curses under his breath. Other times, the pounding reverberated through the heating pipes, a distant but persistent reminder of his fury. He was always there, lurking in the hallway like a storm cloud, his broom in hand, his face lined with resentment.

"This is the devil showing up in people," Mother said to us. "It's trying to steer us off our divine path. That's how you know you're chosen by God: because the world will try to stop you." She smiled and lifted her finger. "You are special. They'll never understand you. They'll never be on your side."

She watered the seed of our dreams daily with praise and whispered promises, soft enough to sound like love. And it grew slowly, twisting and climbing. Wrapping tightly around everything we were until we couldn't get away.

6

THE MADWOMAN

Mother summoned us at midnight for her makeshift circle of fire in our dining area. The only light in our apartment came from the burning white candles on the floor in front of us.

The hallway behind me stretched into darkness, the kind that presses against your back. I shifted uneasily and whispered, "Andy, switch with me."

He smirked but stepped aside, letting me slide into the spot with my back against the wall. Then he glanced over his shoulder, his light blue eyes narrowing as he stared into the shadows.

I don't know if it was just our imagination, but things had fallen in other rooms the past few weeks, objects toppling for no reason. Andy and I always paused. Always stared at each other and then nervously laughing it off. Maybe we were just more on edge than usual, already creeped out, already listening too hard. Or maybe it was just the bass from the music upstairs, rattling through the walls, making things shift ever so slightly.

But it always made me think of Kop Kop; my childhood creation, the darkness lurking, patient, waiting for what was to come. I told myself it wasn't real.

Still, I kept my back to the wall. Mother signaled for us to hold hands.

"But we have school in the morning," Andy groaned.

"Be serious," Mother snapped. "This isn't a game. We're calling in positive energy from the Sweet One."

Slava nodded solemnly. "Yes. Listen to Mother." He always did.

The Sweet One was a figure she claimed came to her in a vision: tall, cloaked in white, glowing faintly at the edges. She'd sketched him days before: a faceless man with a soft aura and outstretched hands. He was our spirit guide now. Our personal god.

Mother began to hum a happy melody she had made up. "All together now," she cut in sharply, and we began to walk in a slow circle. The candlelight washed over our faces in shades of gold and orange, catching in our hair, flickering in our eyes.

Mother's eyes burned with purpose, her grip tightening around our hands until her knuckles blanched. After one hour of the same rhythm, I stifled a yawn, blinking through the haze of candlelight.

Andy glanced at me, just a flicker, but it was enough. The corners of our mouths twitched, laughter bubbling just beneath the surface as Mother's voice rose, louder and sharper. She saw it. Her head snapped toward us, eyes blazing.

We fell back in line without a word.

The next day at school was a blur. The voice of Edward, a classmate who had only two brain cells and a scar on his forehead, pierced the noise of the hallway: "You might not stink like a corpse any more, but you still look like one!" His taunt lingered as he passed by, smirking. I pushed through the crowded corridor until I reached my classroom. Behind my desk sat Sabina with another curly-haired girl.

"That's her," Sabina mouthed, jerking her thumb in my direction as I approached. My heart sank; even Sabina was making a spectacle of me. The girl with curly hair leaned forward, her eyes curious.

"So, is it true? You're moving to America?"

"Well, not ye—" I started, casting a disappointed look at Sabina. This was supposed to be a secret.

"Because your mom is marrying Michael Jackson?" the curly-haired girl said with disbelief.

"Yeah," I replied, feeling their heavy skepticism pressing down on me. I needed to prove myself somehow.

"You're joking!" scoffed the girl, her laughter ringing loudly.

"She is! I saw it in the newspaper this morning," Sabina cut in, stretching out her legs nonchalantly. There was no newspaper.

I felt the heat rising to my cheeks and I turned away to prepare the study material on my desk. "But I'll show them." I thought. "I will become famous."

During class, I was asked to write a story, and for once I lost myself in it, forgetting everything around me. I poured myself into the tale, my fountain pen moving almost on its own as the words spilled out. When I finished, I caught a glimpse of my teacher Mrs. Whirl's sharp, hooked nose in the corner of my eye. She was standing behind me with her short brown bob, reading over my shoulder with her eyes squinted. I was terrified of her; she never missed a chance to call me incompetent in front of the class. In my mind she wasn't just a teacher, she was something monstrous. When she moved down the aisles between our desks, her tall body seemed to contort, her limbs shifting as if she were transforming into a spider, crawling toward me with a fury that felt personal. Her eyes, dark and cold, drilled into me as if to warn me against ever dreaming I might be good at something.

A few weeks after my eighth birthday in January of 2004, the halfway point report cards arrived. By the time we got back from school, the dining table had transformed. The tablecloth smoothed to perfection, flickering candles in place of the usual overhead light, and a parade of our favorite cakes Mother baked lined up like rewards for surviving the semester. We passed our report cards around like sacred scrolls. Slava went first in reading his out .

"Social, very loved by the class, good understanding of human nature," Slava read aloud as we all nodded in agreement.

Andy's card was next.

"Always helpful, tries very hard even when missing the mark; kind." Mother reached over to ruffle his hair. He grinned.

Then mine.

THE MADWOMAN

"Awfully quiet, keeps to herself, but intelligent and has a talent in writing worth cultivating."

My family cheered.

I just stared at the paper.

It wasn't just that I finally had something to be proud of. It was that Mrs. Whirl wrote it. It meant something.

When I tell you how fast Mother jumped on the idea of cultivating my talent, it could give you whiplash. One moment, I was handing in a short story at school; the next, I was writing a children's poetry book.

The deal was simple: if I wrote a few poems a day, I earned thirty minutes outside.

Mother tirelessly compiled my pages. Over the course of months, into spring, she brought the book to life. She illustrated every poem herself, her hands always smudged with ink and watercolor. Each night, she worked late under the soft glow of a desk lamp, long shadows stretching across the table as she painted.

We were working toward the end of the book when the neighbor sisters from upstairs tossed pebbles at my window, their giggles rising up from the courtyard, an invitation to come outside and play. I looked out longingly, the sunlight catching dust in the air, the freedom just beyond the glass. But Mother's stern gaze always pulled my eyes back to the page in front of me. Sometimes, I scribbled nonsense; just enough to earn my thirty minutes of freedom. When I finally stepped outside, the air was thick with the scent of fresh grass, and the wind moved gently across my skin, like a quiet reward. From our window, Mother would toss down little bags of candy from her hidden stash, her way of offering a distant kindness. She had always found ways to care for others, but lately, it was as though she could only do it from the sidelines. I'd often find myself looking at old photos, snapshots of a different woman, smiling at picnics, riding her bike with the wind in her hair. But now, those days seemed far away. She rarely left the house except to shop or attend my brother's guitar concerts. My school events, no matter how much I hoped, never made the cut.

The two sisters and I played in the field in front of our home, far from any streets or passing cars. Every ten minutes, Mother's face would appear in the window, her watchful eyes scanning the scene. We ran through the damp laundry hanging on drying racks, our laughter filling the air as we chased each other. Suddenly, something whizzed past my head, striking the ground with a dull thud. We stopped, breathless, and inspected it; a rotten, shriveled apple.

We looked up and there she was: the madwoman from the third floor, grinning down at us with a wild gleam in her eye. Her disheveled hair peeked from beneath a peculiar black wig, and as usual she was trailing a bunch of mismatched checkered rolling carts behind her. No one could ever escape her path quickly enough; she seemed to appear at the worst times. The entire complex reeked of mothballs and the lingering stench of decaying meat, a smell that clung to the walls.

When I told Mother about it, her eyes narrowed, lips thinning into a sharp line. She blamed my bad energy for attracting the apple, then quickly concluded that the sisters' jealousy had cast a shadow over me, drawing misfortune my way.

Maybe she was right. The sisters often whispered behind my back. Later that evening, as the sky burned orange with the setting sun, the familiar clink of pebbles hit my window. I looked outside and saw them below in golden light.

"Come play!" they called, their voices bright, almost pleading.

Mother appeared beside me, shaking her head. Her presence was firm and unyielding.

Outside, children chased each other across the front yard, their laughter echoing between the apartment buildings.

I pressed my forehead against the cool glass, watching my breath cloud the pane.

But that was the price of wanting a different life.

"Look at Dima and his friends. Look at all that wasted talent. Look at how they poison him with drugs and alcohol," Mother would say, her voice sharp whenever she caught my eyes trailing after children laughing in the fields we passed. She was right, of course. They weren't the ones heading to a publishing office in the cobbled corners of old-town Regensburg. We were.

THE MADWOMAN

It was the only publishing house in town.

Mister Henkel, the man behind the desk, looked like he belonged to the dust jackets he shelved; his wisps of hair floated like cotton candy in a breeze, barely clinging to the sides of his polished scalp. Glasses low on his nose. Frown etched deep like he was born with it.

The office smelled of old pages and burnt coffee.

He barely glanced at the poetry pages. Mother's carefully inked illustrations were passed over with a flick of the eye. His fingers tapped the desk, fast and impatient, as if our dreams were just another chore in his already long day.

Mother's hands trembled slightly as she spoke, her voice laced with nervousness. "I did the illustrations," she said, her broken German revealing her timidity. Mr. Henkel leafed through the contents, his face impassive, his eyes scanning the pages. After what felt like an eternity, he looked up, his expression unchanging.

"It's not the type of work we publish," he stated flatly, handing the folder back without another word. His dismissal suffocated the small spark of hope that had brought us there.

A few months after, when we passed by the publishing company on our way to the old city, we saw that the sign on the door, once welcoming, had been replaced with a notice of closure. "Divine retribution," Mother muttered, more to herself than to me, her eyes distant and weary. She believed it was punishment for the publisher's failure to recognize my potential, which made me feel a vindictive joy.

Mother's voice turned gentle as she swept a loose strand of hair from my forehead. "We'll try again somewhere else, Nanya. We'll find a way."

There was still that glimmer of fight in her eyes. Yet even as she said it her gaze drifted past me, back to the shine of my brother's future and the forgotten pages were sealed away in some dusty box no one ever opened.

Early the next morning, the phone rang, sharp and jarring against the hush of dawn. Mother answered, the receiver pressed to her ear, her face stiffening with every word.

It was Oma. Her voice came through the line thick with panic.

"Your husband . . . he's in the hospital . . . a severe accident."

Mother didn't speak. She just stood there, holding the phone like it was a call from a telemarketer.

Oma's voice quivered, pleading,

"Don't you have any compassion for him? He was your husband for twenty-two years . . . the father of your children."

We hadn't seen him in a long while. Not since the day Mother told him to leave. He'd been living across the street with Oma and Dima, close enough that I could see the warm, amber glow of their kitchen lamp from my bedroom window. Every night, the same dim light flickered behind the curtains. Sometimes, I'd catch a glimpse of movement: silhouettes drifting past like quiet ghosts. But no one spoke of him. Not out loud. Not even in whispers. Even if we wanted to, Mother's stifling cries at night had us reconsidering.

According to Oma, that morning had begun like any other. He'd left before sunrise, the soft hum of his old moped fading into the gray light. I remember watching his figure disappear down the street. But that day was different. It wasn't just another morning—it was the day my parents were due in court to finalize the divorce.

They said fatigue had overtaken him in the early hours. He'd fallen asleep on the moped and crashed into a concrete wall.

At the hospital, they told him the damage was severe. A fracture so bad he would never walk again. Oma fought to have him transferred to a better hospital in Berlin, hours away by train. He would remain there for months.

Mother hung up the phone with a cold, deliberate click. Her eyes were unreadable, lips pressed into a hard line as she dried her hands on a dishtowel.

"No," she said simply.

No emotion. No hesitation. Just that one word, heavy as a slammed door. In her eyes, this was justice. The universe correcting its course. His pain wasn't a tragedy. It was consequence. Karma.

We were not to visit him.

And so, on the very day their marriage was meant to end, he faced the darkest moment of his life—aside from what was still to come—completely alone.

7

THE BEGGARS

Bills began to stack on our coffee table, taller with each day, a paper tower we could no longer pretend not to see. The envelopes sat unopened, their windows flashing numbers we couldn't afford.

Without Father around to work or scheme, and no relatives who liked us enough to lend a hand, the options ran dry.

Mother had already borrowed from everyone she could — even Oma. Neighbors, out of pity or politeness, slipped her fifty euros once so we could go to McDonald's together, the grease and salt tasting like a holiday. Most of them never looked at us again after we didn't pay them back.

Mother only shrugged. "That's their fault for giving it to us," she'd say, her voice flat, her face unreadable. No guilt. No shame. Just another lesson in survival disguised as indifference.

Even our piggy banks weren't safe. She cracked them open, spilling years of birthdays and scraped-knee savings onto the kitchen table. The coins clattered across the surface like loose teeth.

Her hands — raw, red, cracked from scrubbing with cheap chemicals — could no longer handle steady work. But her shopping never slowed. People would see her returning from the shops, arms wrapped around glossy bags of clothes and alligator-skinned boots.

"Wow, how do you afford all that?" neighbors asked, envy stitched into their voices.

Mother smiled, shrugged, as though the answer were simple. They didn't see the pile of unopened letters waiting at home.

When Slava finally sat her down, desperate to untangle the finances, she waved him off. "You have to look rich. Feel rich. That's how you attract the life you want. If you want extraordinary, you have to look like you're meant for it. Charisma and attention, that's how people rise. We'll pay it off later."

And in her way, she always made sense.

Slava came up with an idea for damage control: street busking. I could join him after school, my young face drawing sympathy. Mother sold it to me as an adventure. "We have to do what nobody else is doing, to be where nobody else is at," she said, her words planting themselves deep in me.

Andy, with his electric guitar but no amplifier, was excused. "Oh, thank God," he muttered, his cheeks flushing pink at the thought of performing in the open.

The sun slid low as Slava and I wound our way to Regensburg's old city. The cathedral loomed above us, its spires jagged against a sky of fading amber. The cobblestones glowed in the golden hour light, voices spilling from café terraces while commuters hurried past with their shopping bags.

We stopped at the square, choosing a spot beneath a towering statue. Slava opened his guitar case and strummed a soft melody that echoed off the stone. I shook my maracas, the rattling sound skipping into the spaces between footsteps.

The music floated through the air, weaving itself into the square. The older generation frowned and hurried past; the younger smiled, tossing change that clinked against velvet lining.

As we packed up, my eyes locked on a cart glowing with color. Spun sugar, candied nuts, clouds of pink cotton candy turning in the dusk. Before I could say anything, Slava tossed me a coin, the silver flashing in the light.

"Catch!" he grinned.

I caught it in my palms warm from his hand.

"Go get yourself something."

I hesitated, shy, afraid of walking up alone. But Slava only crossed his arms, waiting. He always waited; when I cried, when I screamed, when I swore I couldn't. He never flinched. He'd just stand there, steady and quiet, until I returned with the prize in my hands.

That night it was cotton candy. We split it, our laughter dissolving into the sweetness.

On our way home, a voice called out. A boy from Slava's school, his eyes wide with gratitude.

"My dad... he's better because of your mom."

Slava blinked, caught off guard.

"He thought she was crazy, telling him to drink urine. But he was desperate. He tried it." The boy's voice dropped, reverent. "It worked. He's eating again, getting stronger. My dad says he owes his life to her. We all do."

We walked in silence after that, the weight of his words pressing into us. If we ever doubted her, here was proof: Mother knew what she was doing.

That night, bills fluttered like autumn leaves as Mother licked her fingertips and counted our tips. She stacked the notes neatly, her eyes flashing with satisfaction. Sixty-two euros. I counted them myself, again and again, hardly believing it.

For weeks afterward, we returned. Our guitar and maracas became as familiar to the square as the cathedral bells.

Until one evening, German police stepped into our circle. Their shadows stretched long across the cobblestones. Their boots struck the ground with authority, their clipped voices informing us we needed permits to play. My heart pounded as I dropped my eyes to the pavement, afraid to meet their cold stares.

It took days of waiting, signatures, confused clerks who didn't know where to file us. But finally we walked away with papers in hand, thin slips of freedom that let us keep going.

One crisp autumn afternoon, the sky melted into rust and gold as I walked home from school. My pockets bulged with crinkled leaves I'd collected, their veins pressed like maps against my palms. The air smelled of foliage and cigarette smoke from teenagers lounging on benches. I just got home when a heavy knock behind me shook the hallway. Dima. His presence always arrived before he did. He stood there broad and tense, gold chains clinking against his chest, his skin an unnatural orange from tanning beds. His wifebeater clung to muscles swollen from steroids, making his frame look inflated, almost cartoonish.

"My friends say they've seen us begging in the streets," he spat, his voice low with humiliation. "It's disgraceful."

Mother's eyes flashed, her jaw set. "You always bring negativity."

"Why can't you be normal?" His fists tightened at his sides.

"Normal?" she hissed. "You think it's normal to drink, to do drugs, to waste your life? At least we're doing something."

Dima's face twisted. "I'd rather do that than live with this crazy family."

Mother laughed, bitter and sharp. "Then why are you here?"

Finally, Dima turned on his heel and left, the door closing with a resounding thud that seemed to echo long after he was gone, leaving behind the faint, acrid scent of cigarette smoke hanging in the air.

We went on with our day, using door frames as goalposts to play soccer inside the apartment. We laughed, leaning into each other as we kicked the soft, half-deflated ball across the floor. Our bare feet thudded against the ground, the frames on the wall trembling with each pass. Mother called out from the other room, warning us not to let them fall.

Later, Andy and I stretched out on the carpet, still breathless from running. I showed him CPR the way my teacher had taught me, counting out the beats as my palms pressed against his chest.

When we finally grew tired, the apartment quieted around us. The ball sat deflated in the corner, the air still warm with the echo of our voices. We curled into our beds, unaware of how quickly the night could turn.

Slava's scream pierced the night, jolting Mother awake. She burst into our room, shoving Slava's dark silhouette away from the bed. "Call 112!" she shouted, her voice trembling.

Slava sprinted to the landline, his fingers shaking as he dialed. Andy lay pale, his eyes half open, catching the dim silver light from the window. Mother picked up his shoulders, shaking him desperately, his head lolling side to side like a broken doll. Gurgling sounds filled the room, each one more horrifying than the last.

She pried his mouth open, but his lips were stiff. Blue.

"Grab a spoon!" she cried. I was already moving before I could even think.

Slava was on the phone, explaining in a voice that barely seemed his own. Unresponsive. Dying.

Mother forced the spoon into his mouth, pulling his tongue forward. Yellow mucus spilled down his cheeks, into his hair, a sickly, sticky mess. He shook violently, the mattress squealing under the force of his convulsions.

"You can do it, Andy. You need to make it. My son. Hear me. Andy, please." Mother pleads.

Agonal breathing.

"God, please don't take my son away from me."

The shaking subsided slowly, his body going limp.

"God, do you hear me?" Mother screams, pleading.

His eyes were blank, staring into nothingness.

Mother started chest compressions, her hands moving frantically. "Breathe!"

Slava pulled me into the dining room, his grip firm but gentle. Sirens grew louder, the wail echoing through the night.

The intercom buzzed, allowing paramedics into the complex.

"Are you okay?" a voice asked, but it felt distant, unreal.

Red coats blurred into the room.

I trembled and sat down, my body numb.

They lifted Andy onto a stretcher, placing an oxygen mask over his face.

"Are you coming?" The paramedic looked at Mother, but it was Slava who went with Andy, since he could communicate fluently in German, unlike Mother.

"Stay here," Slava whispered, his voice breaking.

The door closed. The vehicle engine started, then faded into the distance.

Mother sat beside me, her shirt soaked with fluids and tears.

We were quiet for what seemed hours before the call came for us to come to the hospital for a visit.

The world felt fragile, as if a single stone could shatter it into shards. Dawn pressed low and pale, the sky a washed-out white that seemed to strip the colors from everything it touched. The bare trees stood skeletal and unyielding, their branches etched against the morning haze. I could see the cold in my fingertips, in the sting of my breath, in the way Mother tugged my scarf tighter around my neck without looking at me.

Engines hummed past, muffled and distant. I matched my steps to Mother's across the endless stretch of gray pavement.

"It's your fault."

The words cut sharp.

"What?" My eyes snapped to her face. Her brows were furrowed, her gaze fixed straight ahead, unblinking.

"The CPR you did on him last night. You shouldn't have done that."

The ground tilted beneath me. Nausea surged, hot and heavy in my stomach.

"You brought that energy to him," she snapped. "You're always picking on him."

"I didn't mean to…" My chest tightened, each breath snagging on itself. What were the odds? That the one night I practiced CPR, Andy would need it hours later? The thought crashed into me like a wave, cold and merciless.

I almost killed my brother.

The hospital smelled of antiseptic and adhesive bandages, the sterile tang clinging to the air. Fluorescent lights buzzed overhead, flickering faintly as we followed a nurse down the corridor.

Andy sat propped up in bed, a hospital gown slipping off one shoulder, his fork dragging through pale mashed potatoes and limp greens. His face was drained of color, but his eyes were alert. The steady beep of the heart monitor filled the silence, each pulse reminding me he was still here.

Slava slumped in a chair by the window, his hair tangled, shadows sunk deep beneath his eyes.

"Hey," Andy said awkwardly, like a boy caught in mischief. He shifted, wincing as pain rippled through his arm.

"How are you feeling?" Mother leaned in, her relief spilling out as she hugged him, setting a bar of nougat chocolate on the table like an offering.

"Sore." He pressed his tricep, face tightening. "Everything hurts."

"Do you remember what happened?"

Andy's brow furrowed. "Not really. Just… a hazy memory of you yelling at me. That's it."

Mother's gaze sharpened. "What happened?"

"Seizure," Slava answered, his voice rough with fatigue. "The doctors found a mass in his brain. They think that's the cause, but it's not life-threatening enough for surgery."

Mother's eyes searched his face as if he might hold a hidden answer. "Where does that come from?"

"They don't know. Could be heatstroke, maybe stress. Too many factors." Slava's shoulders sagged.

Andy reached for her hand, his grip weak but steady. She turned toward me, her voice firm. "Tanja, apologize to your brother."

The air seemed to thicken. My legs moved stiffly toward his bed, my guilt pressing down like lead.

"I'm sorry," I whispered. "For not treating you right."

Andy studied me for a moment, his lips pale but curving faintly. "Okay."

"I promise to be nice from now on."

"It's okay." His voice was quiet, but there was forgiveness in it.

The monitor beeped on, his lips slowly regaining color. Relief flickered through me, fragile and uncertain.

But the question burned:

What if I caused this? What if the darkness that follows us everywhere... has always been me?

8

THE SKY

Mother stood in the center of the living room, arms lifted, the frame pressed against the wall as dust motes drifted in the afternoon light. She stepped back, tilting her head, one eye narrowed as if the whole world depended on this exact angle. The painting caught the light first: two lovers intertwined, their bodies bending together like branches grown from the same trunk. They clung to one another as if their lives depended on it. Her long brown hair spilled across his chest like liquid silk; his dark hair brushed his chin as their mouths hovered just shy of meeting.

Behind them, a storm of color swirled. Crimson and rose, curling like smoke, blooming outward in waves of hunger and need. It was the kind of love that looked eternal.

And yet, Mother had sworn herself against love entirely.

To her, love wasn't tender like the painting. It was a rot that sank deep and hollowed you out. She told my brothers it would poison their dreams until nothing was left. Even as children, she tried to protect them from it, to bind them away from its reach.

I remember Slava at fifteen, his hands swallowed in heavy wool mittens, tape wrapped tight around his wrists so they couldn't slip off. The sound

63

of the tape ripping in the kitchen still echoes in my mind. She said it was to stop him from touching himself in his sleep. Said if he didn't, it could twist into something darker. A rapist.

The questions didn't stop when we got older.

"Do you touch yourself?"

The words were soft, but the disappointment already lived in her voice, curling at the edges. And when the answers came, she dropped the blade: dirty. Weak. Undisciplined.

In her eyes, my brothers were always boys, standing at the cliff edge of ruin, and she alone had to drag them back.

If their eyes lingered too long on a girl, she snapped them back with shame dressed as wisdom, her voice ringing sharp in the room. I remember Andy's fourteenth birthday. For the first time, girls were allowed to join. I was five, yet I noticed the way Andy looked at Karina with his eyes soft, almost glowing with something unspoken, something just beginning to grow. Mother noticed too. And she cut it short before it could bloom.

Even now, Andy still says her name sometimes, and his voice carries that same weight of resentment.

Movies weren't safe either. She let us watch, but only until the music shifted, until fabric loosened, until mouths found skin. Then click — the sound of the remote like a gavel cracking through the room.

"Too mature," she said. "Not in this house."

Desire, touch, longing, all of it forbidden.

And yet here she was, standing before a canvas drenched in it.

I frowned, imitating the disapproval she had drilled into us. But when I asked about the contradiction, she barely turned her head.

"This is different," she said. "This is art."

And that was the end of it.

She pivoted, leaving me in silence, my question dissolving into the air. On the wall, the painted lovers stayed locked in their embrace, untouchable by her rules.

I carried my confusion to Slava, who sat hunched over the glow of his boxy computer, its fan wheezing like an old man's breath. His fingers clicked across the keyboard as I asked him the questions no one else dared to.

"Even Mother can't deal with you," he chuckled, nudging me with his elbow. He said I read too much, saw too much. There was pride in his voice, but sometimes, when his laughter trailed off, I wondered if he meant it as a warning.

I tried to understand her contradictions. I wondered about Father. If she hadn't met him, hadn't fallen into love, hadn't surrendered her dreams... would she have become the artist she once imagined? Is that why she hated love and desire?

I pictured her painting wild visions into existence, barefoot in a candlelit studio, her hair undone, her laughter echoing through some distant European city.

But love came like a tide, and she let it pull her under.

She resented him for it. She resented us too. She spoke of sacrifice, of years wasted, of how the universe owed her another chance. So when Slava's draft letter arrived, she didn't just see danger. She saw an opening. A crack in the wall wide enough to slip through to finally live the life she wants.

She had been waiting for a sign. Now she said it had come from God himself.

Slava died the moment that letter arrived.

Mother rechristened him "Glap Stewart," a name whispered to her during a séance, rolling like a prophecy across the table. His rich artist name. Slava was a child of scraps, building parachutes out of umbrellas, dismantling televisions just to see what sparked inside. But Glap was meant for more. Glap would rise above the small, hungry boy. Glap was her invention, a persona who undoubtedly will be famous, untouched by the adult world.

But a name wasn't enough. She gave him a voice too like Michael Jackson's, soft and airy.

She adored Jackson. To her, his voice was innocence suspended in glass, forever untouched. She said if we never grew up or had sex, maybe we could live forever.

Adulthood, she warned, killed magic. It crushed wonder with its questions, its doubts, its responsibilities, its hungers.

THE SKY

So she built her own Neverland, and we lived inside it.

Slava — no, Glap — became the star-in-the-making. Whenever we slipped and used his old name, she corrected us sharply, her voice like a whip.

Mother pressed her fingertips into the draft notice as if she could push the words out of existence. The army, with its rules and its silence, felt like a death sentence for that boy.

Then she looked up, her eyes steady, her voice rolling low like thunder.

"We'll go to America," she said. "We'll run."

That winter was our last together in Germany.

The tree glowed gold in the corner, its branches heavy with fragile, hand-painted ornaments that caught the light like tiny glass planets. The air smelled of pine sap, candle wax, and something sweet cooling on the oven.

I cried over the gifts I didn't get, to my brothers' laughter. They pointed to the mountain of boxes already stacked around me, my small body dwarfed by abundance. Past midnight, we bundled into boots and scarves and trudged to the hill near our home. Teenagers tipped buckets of water down its curve, letting the night air freeze it to glass. Our sleds flew faster with each run, the wind slicing against our cheeks until our laughter cracked open the sky.

The air was razor-cold, our voices echoing like bells. Snow crunched under our boots, sharp and sugary, each step a sound I can still hear. And then, between breaths, I looked up.

The sky was burning orange.

For a heartbeat, the world stopped. Just that hill. That night. That sky on fire. And the sound of us, still together.

The days blurred forward: New Year's Eve, my ninth birthday, and then, the morning after, Glap was gone.

He had to leave when the Holidays ended before the military noticed. He would go first, find us a place, prepare a landing. There was no time for the ceremony. No long goodbyes. Only the quiet understanding that things were changing fast. He packed light: a few hundred dollars in his pocket, a guitar slung across his back.

He jumped into the taxi and didn't look back. Maybe he couldn't because he wasn't only leaving us; he was leaving Slava behind too. The engine roared, and the taillights bled red into the dawn until they vanished. Silence pressed in.

The home grew hollow. Only me, Mother, Andy, and our Siamese cat, Sima, remained.

The ghosts that frightened me most weren't the ones that knocked in the night.

That haunted me were the toothbrush slots left empty. The remote untouched on the table. The moment I set too many plates at the dinner table.

9

THE SUMMER

It didn't take long for the military to realize that Glap had evaded his draft. Loud, insistent knocks pounded on our door. We huddled in the dimly lit hallway, hearts racing, hoping they would leave us in peace. But the military's threats to break down our door forced Mother to open it reluctantly.

"Where's Slava Ross?" they demanded, their voices stern and authoritative, faces shadowed by the hallway light.

"We don't know," we insisted, our voices trembling with fear, our eyes wide.

They barged into our home. They searched everywhere, their heavy boots echoing against the floors. They moved methodically, checking under beds, in closets, even behind curtains. Outside, a police car sat waiting daily in front of our apartment, a constant reminder of the relentless pursuit. Our neighbors peeked through their curtains, whispers spreading through the building. And then, finally, they left.

Two weeks later, Glap called. His voice trembled beneath the static.

He was panicked.

He spoke of nights spent at LAX, sleepless and fluorescent, where time didn't seem to dissolve under the artificial glow. The airport never darkened.

Never hushed. Announcements echoed endlessly through the cavernous terminals: Flight delayed . . . Final boarding call . . . unattended baggage . . . a constant murmur that blurred into the clatter of luggage wheels and hurried footsteps.

He couldn't sleep. Not really.

The benches were cold and narrow, their metal armrests designed to keep people from lying down. He'd get into arguments with homeless men, all of them fighting over a few feet of unforgiving space.

He had arrived in America with just $300 in his pocket and a guitar strapped to his back.

Now he survived on a single jar of peanut butter, scooping out slow, measured spoonfuls like they were gold. His hygiene, he confessed with quiet shame, came from public bathroom sinks, hurried scrubs beneath flickering lights, the smell of bleach and strangers thick in the air. There was no privacy, no warmth, no peace. Just cold water and pure chaos he was thrown into.

But still, he stayed.

Mother, ever the optimist, encouraged him to keep faith and suggested he try his luck in Beverly Hills. She urged him to knock on doors, convinced someone would recognize his potential and offer assistance. "Just believe in your dream, Glap," she said, her voice filled with unwavering conviction. "America is the land of opportunities."

Despite his initial reluctance, Glap boarded a long, rattling bus bound for possibility since things truly couldn't get worse. The journey stretched through gray hours and sun-bleached freeways, the landscape shifting from dust to concrete, palm trees flickering past like mirages. He'd nod off, only to jolt awake miles too late, his stop long gone behind him.

Then came the journey back, tracing unfamiliar streets with a crumpled tourist map he'd picked up for free at the airport, its glossy folds already softening at the edges from sweat and handling. He'd ask strangers for help, pointing at the map, his fingers tracing streets that twisted and looped. But he didn't understand much.

Their replies came too fast, too layered, the words falling over each other like rushing water. He'd nod anyway, pretending to follow, even when all he caught were fragments of words of a language he didn't understand. Still, he thanked them. Still, he walked on.

Beverly Hills towered over him in clean lines and locked gates, glittering just beyond reach. With chapped lips and aching feet, he rang doorbell after doorbell, that guitar pressed tightly to his back like armor.

Polite refusals met him at first. Curiosity. Confusion.

Then came the sharper rejections, doors closed mid-sentence, narrowed eyes peering out from behind curtains.

People recoiled as if his dreams were contagious.

He wandered aimlessly at times, the city's sprawl disorienting, its roads folding in on themselves. Some days, the sun beat down like punishment.

Other days, the weight of not knowing where to go next was worse than the heat.

On more than one occasion, residents called the police.

He'd be stopped, questioned, sized up by men in uniform who didn't see a boy with a dream, only a soliciting homeless man.

After months of hardship, Glap finally landed an under-the-table job at a Russian butcher's shop in West Hollywood. The scent of raw meat and sawdust clung to his clothes, settled into his hair, a heavy, metallic fog that followed him home, wherever home happened to be that week. The work was rough, the hours long. He borrowed money from the owner once, out of desperation. He never paid it back.

The owner made sure he remembered: sharp words muttered in Russian when they crossed paths, reminders tossed like scraps. But nothing ever came of it. Glap was always moving, slipping just out of reach.

He hopped from one place to the next, the floor of a kind stranger's apartment, a battered couch in a friend-of-a-friend's living room, the backseat of a car once or twice.

On sidewalks and street corners, under flickering neon signs, his guitar case lay open like a hungry mouth. The music he played wasn't polished, but it was honest. Sometimes it earned him enough for a hot meal. Sometimes just a few coins and a nod.

And once in a while, when he could, whenever he starved himself enough, he sent me a box.

A small cardboard package filled with American candy in wrappers so bright they looked like toys. Gumdrops, bubblegum, peanut butter cups, treasures I'd never seen before, glowing like magic in my hands. A sweet, stubborn reminder that no matter how far he was, he hadn't forgotten us. Hadn't forgotten me.

In the spring, he sent us a photo of dinner chairs adorned with drawings of our faces taped to them, a poignant reminder of his longing for home. Though his message conveyed his intense desire to return, it also raised concerns about his well-being. Moved by his plight, Mother decided to travel to L.A. to help him for the summer and lead the way, as he was days away from giving up. But he couldn't return to Germany. It would mean jail time.

The summer of 2005 was a child's dream.

Mother had gone to the U.S., and suddenly, the rules went with her. My hair was unkempt, unbleached, a tangled mess that danced in the wind. I hadn't showered in weeks, hadn't brushed my teeth or done laundry, but of course, I was only nine.

I ran through the bushes with a stick in my hand, which to me was no stick, it was a sword, forged in the fires of imagination and I was on a quest of my own making.

I hardly spent time at home. It was too quiet, too hollow. Andy was somewhere in the apartment, but mostly I saw only the back of his head, his body hunched in front of the computer, his mind swallowed whole by pixelated worlds and fantasy realms.

Sometimes, he remembered I needed to eat. He'd toss a frozen pizza in the oven, and when he gave it to me, the middle was still icy. I'd poke at the cold center with a fork, then slip out the door, my stomach half-full, my heart tugging elsewhere.

I escaped to Oma's. To Dima. To Father.

It filled something in me that had begun to feel missing, a space too large for silence, too tender to name. When Mother did call briefly, she'd remind Andy to keep an eye on me. He'd groan and then chase me through the park in half-hearted bursts of duty. I'd race ahead on my bike, pedaling like my life depended on it, his voice trailing behind me, shouting about bad influences and Mother's rules.

To keep the peace and earn myself some freedom, I learned to bribe him. Oma had slipped me some money, and I used it wisely: burgers, chocolate, anything that would soften his resolve. A few snacks could buy me an entire afternoon. Father was out of the hospital by then, moving slowly, carefully, a metal implant drilled into his knee like a hinge on a stubborn door. He hobbled on crutches, each step cautious, uneven. Yet, there was something lighter in him. Something softer, like a shadow had finally passed.

Maybe it was Oma's relentless love. Or maybe it was just the simple fact that he had survived. And I was still here, still wanting my father.

Grandma's home was a sanctuary. The air always smelled of freshly baked bread, and her garden was a wonderland of blooming flowers and hidden nooks. Everyone welcomed me. Despite being confined to crutches and a leg cast, Father, worried about us, made every effort to visit and check on me and Andy. He often woke us around 2 pm, finding us still asleep on the pull-out couch in the living room, the one place we felt safest. He often traveled miles on foot, his determination evident in every step, just to bring me what I needed, even if it was something as simple as an ice cream cone.

One day, during one of Mother's rare check-ins, Andy casually mentioned Father's visits. Her anger came fast, sharp and unforgiving. Still, later that evening I pinky promised Father I'd keep seeing him in secret. The coldness that Mother and Slava felt for him was missing in the warmth and tenderness of my heart. I could see that even Andy needed him.

Father indulged my every whim that summer. Maybe because he knew it was our last summer together. He bought me roller skates with pink laces, and a pair of little plastic heels, the kind meant for dress-up, but I wore them like they were real.

I'd skate in circles at the park, my arms flailing, terrified at my own clumsiness.

His crutches clanked rhythmically against the pavement as he hobbled beside me, his face lit with pride and something softer, something like hope.

We didn't talk much during those visits. We didn't have to.

One afternoon, we sat side by side on a sun-warmed bench, sharing some French fries.

Then, gently, he turned to me.

"If it came down to it," he signed, "would you want to stay in Germany with me?"

I shook my head without hesitation.

Too swept up in the promise of somewhere else, in Mother's stories, in the glittering vision of America she had built in my mind. A place where everything would be better. Bigger. Brighter. Where I would finally belong.

Father's face fell just slightly—a flicker of something wounded passing through his eyes—but he nodded, slowly, like he already knew.

He looked out toward the trees. Then turned back to me and signed with a soft smile:

"Just remember, no matter where you are, I'm always here for you."

Even if I couldn't fully understand what it meant yet, even if I didn't stay.

Somewhere inside me, I tucked his words away like a charm. Something to carry across oceans.

Mother called with the news that she wasn't coming back. Her voice crackled through the phone, each word chipping away at my hope. "I'm staying in America. Permanently." Tears welled up in my eyes, streaming down my face uncontrollably.

"I want you to stay in school there," she insisted. I could almost see her tired expression, the one she wore whenever she called me a bad girl. Her tone implied more than just a need for me to stay; it felt like she was tired of me, tired of my questions and my presence.

She made it clear how much easier it would be to leave me with Father, that we already preferred him over her anyway. If I stayed, Andy would stay too, and she wouldn't have to deal with the headache of packing up the apartment and selling everything. Father could move back in, take over, and tidy up the loose ends. It was a clean solution for her.

But for me, it wasn't so simple. The thought of being left behind, of our family splintering even further, gnawed at me.

I pleaded with her, my voice cracking with desperation. Finally, she relented. "Fine, I'll come back and take you with me."

Alesia, my cousin, arrived shortly after, taking in the disarray of our home. "Wow, this place is a disaster," she muttered, rolling up her sleeves. We tackled the piles of garbage together. Later, as she tried to comb through my hair, she let out a sigh. "Oh my goodness," she exclaimed, the brush snagging on a particularly stubborn tangle.

"What's wrong?" I asked, wincing at the tugs on my scalp.

"Your hair is a giant knot," she replied, frustration evident in her voice. She worked diligently, but after several futile attempts, she pulled out the scissors with a resigned look. As she carefully snipped away the tangles, her tone softened. "You know, you could stay here if you wanted to. We all love you and don't want to see you go."

I looked at her, my eyes wide with sadness and determination. "I know," I whispered, my voice barely audible. "But I'm going to be famous there." In my mind, the streets of America glittered with opportunities, a place where dreams come true after hard work and suffering.

Alesia sighed, her breath warm against my damp hair. "Why can't you do that here?" she asked.

"Because," I replied, lifting my hand as if to emphasize the point, "Mother said if I stayed here, I would turn out like the rest of you."

10

THE GOODBYE

Mother returned just before the school year began in September. I lasted barely a month in fourth grade. She came back from America different and sharper, like she'd seen the future and wasn't about to let it slip away again.

Three months gone, and now everything had urgency. She pulled me out of school without hesitation. The principal tried to protest, but her mind was sealed.

"The curriculum will only crush her spirit," Mother said, her voice steady and certain, as if I were some rare prodigy being smothered by the dull machinery of the ordinary. I didn't argue. I just sat quietly, watching the walls of my classroom blur into memory.

For the first time in my life, I was the talk of the neighborhood.

Tanja is really leaving. She's going to America. Her mother is going to marry Michael Jackson and become famous. She wasn't lying!

I could almost hear their voices in the schoolyard, the swirl of fascination and disbelief echoing in the spaces I'd just left behind. For a moment, I was someone with a story too big to stay. And that was enough.

Even our kitchen changed.

Almost overnight, we became vegans. Not because of health or ethics but because a lot of celebrities were vegan, and that meant we had to be too. If fame had a diet, we would follow it. But this was before veganism became trendy. There were no easy substitutions, no almond milk lattes or dairy-free ice cream waiting on supermarket shelves.

I stood in the doorway, helpless, as Mother tossed our food into the trash one item at a time: salami, Milchschnitte, yogurts, the creamy cheeses I loved. Each one landed with a soft, final thud.

Then she stormed into my bedroom like a gust of wind, her eyes gleaming.

She and Glap had read a book about Joe Jackson, the man who carved stars out of his children—including Michael Jackson—with discipline and control. That was the missing link, she said. We had the talent. What we needed was pressure. She would be the force behind our greatness. She pinched the sides of my hips, sharp and sudden. I flinched.

"These extra pounds from all those summer burgers have to go if you want to be a model."

Mother called on Dima to take my head shots. I stood in the middle of the dining room in a tight pink outfit, lip gloss sticky on my mouth, heels pinching like punishment. I balanced on my toes like a wind-up doll. Dima's camera clicked and clicked, a relentless metronome keeping time with Mother's hunger for success. She sent these out to agencies that we didn't hear back from. She moved through the apartment like someone already gone, folding clothes with precision, wrapping plates in newspaper, listing our things in the classifieds like shedding a second skin. Now strangers walked through our home, scrutinizing and picking apart the place we had loved so deeply. They complained about the scratches and dings, scars from where we played too rough and loved too much. Some even pocketed small items, like a half-empty ink pen or a chipped teacup, leaving nothing of our past. They bargained over the pieces of wood that made up our furniture, carelessly tossing them into their cars. The dining table, once the center of our family meals, was now just another item to be haggled over. The walls, stripped bare of their colorful drawings and photographs, resembled skeletal remains. The only thing Father took with him was the coffee table: no family photos, no drawings, no videos. He didn't want to be reminded.

FAME OR DEAD

When the divorce proceedings between my parents reached their final stages, it was decided that Mother would have custody of us. It was clear we wanted to be with her, and Father didn't want to stand in the way of any opportunity that might come our way.

Besides, he knew he couldn't win in a German court.

He could hardly read in German, was deaf, walked with difficulty after the accident, and was, now, unemployed. He stood barely any chance against her, not on paper, not in court.

Mother made her boldest move yet. She asked Father for an advance on my child support, a significant sum. Fifteen thousand dollars. A loan he agreed to, repaid slowly over time, so the move could go smoothly for us. Almost overnight, our lives transformed. Cashmere blankets were in shopping bags Mother brought home. Gold jewelry shimmered on Mother's wrists and neck, catching the light with every gesture. New clothes filled our luggage, the kind with tags still attached. She used part of the money that was left to purchase plane tickets to Los Angeles. It was official. The dream had a departure date. Somehow, she even convinced Dima to come, not easily, not without protest, but she was relentless.

She painted vivid scenes of what could be: "Imagine it, Dima. You could become a famous videographer, discovered on the vibrant streets of L.A."

Dima hesitated but Oma took Mother's side. "The family must stick together," she said to Dima, like she had said to me many times before, like it was a rule written in blood. And if things didn't work out, Mother added breezily, he could always come back. It was the kind of logic hope feeds on. Even Andy changed. Something in him lit up, a warmth that had been buried resurfaced in bursts of excitement. He spoke fast, eyes shining as he dreamed aloud: of becoming a guitarist like Stevie Ray Vaughan, Eddie Van Halen: a star.

Father stood in the doorway, watching Andy as the wail of his guitar echoed through the apartment, vibrating through the walls. He had been allowed to visit during our final week in Germany, as Mother wrapped up the last of the paperwork and made arrangements about the apartment. He moved quietly during those visits, just watching it all absolve.

Andy, lost in his music, looked up from the guitar and met Father's look. "I'll make it, Dad," he said, with eyes so big I knew he truly believed he would. "I'll buy you a one-million-dollar house. This will be worth it." Father didn't speak. The muscles in his face struggled to contract properly when he tried to smile. It was a smile that accepted, or tried to fool itself, that at least after all this pain, he would see us off well and wealthy. That, somehow, a million dollars would make it all worth it.

When the big day arrived, I hardly slept. Mother was still packing and rearranging suitcases as my alarm buzzed at 4 am, the quiet of the early morning broken by the rustle of clothes, the zip of luggage, and the urgency in her movements. A taxi took us to the Munich airport in under an hour, Father riding with us but silent for most of the drive.

At the polished airport, he walked alongside us, his eyes fixed on Mother's face, as if willing her to look back and see not the arguments or the distance but the seventeen-year-old boy she had once fallen in love with in Kazakhstan. There was a quiet desperation in his gaze, a longing to remind her of the dreams they once shared.

But she never looked back. Her grip on my hand tightened instead, and she steered us forward, steady and sure, toward the security checkpoint.

Father, still limping, struggled to keep pace with us through the maze of travelers. The airport buzzed around us, the low rumble of luggage wheels, the sharp staccato of heels against tile, the endless loop of overhead announcements, but his presence began to blur in the periphery, shrinking with every step we took.

When we reached security, the air seemed to still. Tension wrapped around us like fog. Mother's expression hardened as she turned to him for a final goodbye, her jaw tight.

Father stepped forward slowly and placed a delicate necklace around my neck, its silver pendant etched with the symbol of Capricorn, my zodiac sign. The chain was cool against my skin, grounding in a way that made everything else blur for a moment.

"Something to remember me by," he signed, his fingers moving with such softness they almost trembled. His eyes met mine, full of love and sorrow, wide with everything he couldn't say aloud.

"You're so little," he signed, the words shaped by regret. "You're growing up . . . and I won't see any of it."

Then, with a bittersweet smile, he leaned in and pressed his nose to mine, a quiet farewell that felt sacred.

"Someday," he signed, "when you come back and knock on my door, and I don't recognize you any more . . . I'll remember you by these two birthmarks."

His fingers brushed the mark on my cheek, then the one on my left shoulder.

"Just show them to me," he signed, "and I will know who you are."

Father gathered us kids for one last hug, his embrace tight and lingering. He slipped a piece of paper into my pocket, a lifeline for when I needed him most. "Oma's number when you need me," he signed. The final hug came, charged with a sense of desperation. Letting go felt impossible. My fingers slowly uncurling from the fabric of his jacket felt like releasing a rope that kept me from falling. The world around me blurred, the female voice on the intercom, the sea of luggage and travelers, all fading into the background. As we moved forward, I glanced back one last time. My father was wiping tears from his eyes. He grew smaller and smaller until he disappeared into the crowd, a moment that would replay in my mind for the rest of my life.

II

THE AMERICAN DREAM

11

THE LAX

As we passed through security at Munich Airport, the scanner let out a sharp, jarring beep, loud enough to snap me out of the fog I was in. One of Mother's bags had been flagged. A security officer, tall and stone faced, stepped forward with a crispness that made my stomach tighten. His Bavarian accent cut through the low hum of the terminal.

He unzipped the suitcase with mechanical precision, rifling through layers of carefully packed clothing until his hand emerged holding a long, cold glint of metal. A needle-like object that looked far too sharp, far too strange.

"What is this?" he demanded, eyes narrowing.

Mother leaned toward Andy, her face tight, voice barely above a whisper. She spoke in Russian this time—meant only for us.

Andy swallowed, standing straighter, but his voice wavered as he translated into German:

"It's . . . it's an art tool."

The officer stared at him, unmoved. For a moment, none of us breathed. The people behind us shifted, the line stalled. Overhead, a flight announcement echoed meaninglessly into the silence between us and the uniformed man.

"This can be considered a weapon," The officer said. Without another word, he tossed the needle into the bin behind him. The zipper hissed closed, and the bag was waved through.

Dima, a few steps back, let out a low, incredulous "Jesus Christ" under his breath, shaking his head in disbelief.

Mother's lips parted to protest, but Andy quickly stepped in, placing a gentle hand on her arm. She straightened her shoulders and continued walking, her head held high, eyes fixed forward as if nothing had happened.

As we moved through the airport, Dima rolled his eyes. "Of course Mother would try to bring a murder weapon on a plane," he said. Andy's chuckle was tense, his gaze flicking nervously to Mother.

"Don't call it a murder weapon," she snapped, her voice sharp.

Curiosity gnawed at me. "Mother, what is it really for?" I asked, bracing for her secretive nature. She sighed, her expression softening slightly. "It's a spiritual tool," she confessed.

We knew better than to press further; her explanations often led us down winding paths with no clear answers. We had to trust her, even if we didn't fully understand.

The flight itself was roughly ten hours long. Dima sat beside me, his face flushed a deep red, gripping the arms of his seat as if sheer willpower might keep the plane from plummeting. I tried not to laugh. On my other side, Andy had settled in, earbuds in place, already deep into a world of anime on the tiny screen in front of him, completely unfazed. Our beloved cat Sima rested inside her carrier on the ground in between his legs.

Ahead of us, Mother was already in a discussion with the flight attendant. They had forgotten her vegan meal. It wasn't the flight attendant's fault, of course, but that didn't stop the commotion.

LAX was like stepping into another world. Overhead, announcements echoed in a monotone, directing people to places I couldn't pronounce. The sheer size of it all was staggering, the ceilings high, surrounded by people of all color. I clung to Mother's side as she nervously clutched her bag. None of us really knew English. Andy's was the strongest among us, though even his was shaky at best. I could get by with the English I'd picked up from books at home, enough to understand, enough to pretend, but speaking it was another story. Mother and Dima knew no English at all and watching them try to communicate made me feel embarrassed.

I wanted to be excited—this was America, after all. But standing there, the chaos of it all was dizzying: the bright lights, the constant movement, the smell of coffee and fried food mingling in the air. For the first time, it hit me just how far we had come. There was no going back now.

When we approached border control, the security officers, clad in their dark uniforms, greeted us with stern faces, scrutinizing our passports under the fluorescent lights. "How long are you planning to stay?" one officer asked, his gaze boring into Andy.

"Three months, for travel." Andy's voice trembling slightly. One by one, we placed our fingers on the scanner. The machine beeped reassuringly for each of us until it was Mother's turn. Her thumb stubbornly refused to register, the screen flashing red. The officer frowned, gesturing for her to press harder. Andy relayed the instructions, but Mother's next attempt was too soft. The officer sighed irritably. "Mom, you have to press harder," Andy urged, a flush of frustration creeping up his neck and into his cheeks.

"I am," Mother retorted, wiping her thumb against her pants and trying again, her movements growing more frantic, but we could tell she was not pressing down.

The security officer clicked his tongue in annoyance, stepping forward to demonstrate. His fingers pressed down firmly on Mother's thumb. She recoiled instantly, gasping in shock. "Don't touch me," she snapped in German. The officer might not have understood the words, but it was clear from her body language what she meant.

The officer stepped back, his expression detached as he muttered into his handheld transceiver. The device crackled with static, adding to the tension. Dima, standing a few feet away, clenched his fists. "Here we go. They're going to send us back home," he muttered.

Mother's eyes blazed with defiance. "He shouldn't have touched me," she declared. The security officer's expression was unreadable as he communicated with someone on his transceiver. The minutes felt like hours, the uncertainty weighing heavily on us.

Dima couldn't hold back any longer. "Why couldn't you just press the goddamn finger on the scanner?" he hissed. Andy, overwhelmed, buried his face in his hands, his fingers pressing into his temples. A gesture that would become all too familiar in the months to come.

"Excuse us." A stern voice sliced through the crowd, causing heads to turn and people to make way. I knew they were coming for us before I even saw them. Four officers, larger and more intimidating than before, approached us with purpose. The one leading the group, with a bald head that seemed to gleam under the lights, reminded me of a serpent.

"Please come with us," he instructed, his voice devoid of any warmth as he gestured towards a pair of doors at the far end of the customs lobby. We followed them obediently into a private room, where they instructed us to sit in uncomfortable metal chairs. Mother, attentive to my comfort, handed me her sweater as a cushion against the cold surface to keep me from getting an inflammation in my bladder.

The officer scanned each of us before speaking. "Who here speaks English?" he inquired, his gaze lingering on us expectantly. Andy, his eyes darting between us like a trapped animal seeking escape, raised his hand. The officer consulted his file and then motioned for Andy to follow him through another door. I stole a glance inside and saw a smaller room with a table and several more officers.

As we waited, exhaustion from the flight washed over me, but the artificial lighting made it impossible to relax. I tried to curl up against Mother for comfort, but she remained stiff and distant, her focus elsewhere. When I looked up at her, her eyes were closed, her face set in concentration. I knew she must be praying.

My leg started to fall asleep, so I sat up again, unable to find any comfort. Even Dima, usually the most vocal among us, remained silent, his expression strained.

Finally, after what felt like an eternity of waiting, the door creaked open, and Andy emerged from the interrogation. Mother leaned in close, searching for answers.

"What did they want?" she whispered, her voice filled with concern.

"They're worried," Andy said. "They think we won't leave the country." We had visas, of course, but they were temporary; visitors only, with strict limits on how long we could stay. I didn't know the exact rules, but I could tell from the tension in the air that the officers weren't convinced we intended to follow them. And I don't blame them. The defiance they saw within Mother earlier spoke to the truth of the situation—we truly weren't planning to leave this country once we entered.

A knot formed in my stomach as I absorbed the implications. If we failed to convince the authorities, they would thrust us back into our old life. But now it would be a broken, shattered version of what it once was. We wouldn't even have an apartment to go home to.

Andy turned to Mother, urgency in his voice. "Give me the rest of the money, we need to show them we have funds." There wasn't much left. Out of the fifteen thousand dollars Father had loaned us, only a few thousand remained by now.

"I knew this was a mistake." Dima grumbled.

"Stay positive." Mother said and looked ahead.

A gentle poke jolted me awake, the fluorescent light causing me to squint against its painful glare. The dim back room of the airport felt surreal, and Germany felt like a distant dream. "We can go now," Mother's voice came, pulling me back to reality.

"Go where?" I muttered, rubbing the sleep from my eyes. The clock on the wall showed that eight hours had slipped by unnoticed, a blur of restless waiting and uneasy sleep.

"To Glap," came the reply. A spark of excitement ignited within me. The authorities had let us enter.

Despite the ache in my neck and the stiffness in my limbs, anticipation fluttered in my chest. Images of palm trees swaying gently in the breeze and luxurious villas with sunlit terraces I'd seen on television danced through my mind. With renewed determination, we followed the exit signs, my eyes scanning the unfamiliar language written on them.

The air felt heavier, saturated with the pungent scent of car fumes and the constant hum of bustling strangers. As I scanned the crowd, a wave of unfamiliarity washed over me. The diverse faces and the melodic cadence of their languages painted a picture starkly different from anything I'd known. A pang of doubt struck me: had we landed in the wrong place?

"Mother!" A familiar voice sliced through the cacophony. There he was, emerging from the throng. Glap's wheat-blond locks cascaded over his shoulders and he moved with a languid sway that made him look like a slender, drugged-out rock star from the 1970s, freshly stepped off a record cover. His face lit up with a wide grin as he spotted us, waving frantically. Relief washed over me. It had been nearly eleven months since I'd last seen him. He pushed through the crowd with long, determined strides, his eyes wild with a desperation I had never seen before. He'd been in America for three months already and that changed everything. His status had shifted, sliding him into the shadowy category of an illegal immigrant. He lived in constant limbo, every decision tinged with the fear of discovery. Leaving wasn't an option; if he stepped foot out of the country, the door would slam shut behind him, never to open again. And if he returned to Germany, he'd get charged for evading the draft. The pressure to make it, to turn this risk into a triumph, clung to him, and I could almost see it settling over his shoulders like smoke, trailing him from room to room.

"You made it!" he exclaimed, his voice brimming with joy.

I couldn't help but smile, the fatigue of the long journey melting away. He turned to me next, pulling me into a hug. "I missed you," he said, squeezing me tightly.

"Brother!" Dima's booming voice echoed as he embraced Glap. We moved through the bustling crowd, Andy recounting our ordeal with the authorities, how we had to prove that we had enough money for our vacation to be able to stay, his words punctuated by Sima's restless meows from her carrier.

Glap glanced at a nearby airport bench. I followed his gaze to see a disheveled homeless man slouched there, his once-yellow puffer jacket now grimy, his jeans torn and stained. A cluttered shopping cart overflowing with garbage and old magazines stood nearby. The man's anguished yells were lost in the empty air. The sight made me wonder if this was the fate of those who failed to find their place in the city of dreams. I gulped.

"It all worked out in the end," Glap said, relief evident as he took Mother's luggage from her.

A sleek black limousine awaited us. "Is that for us, Glap?" Mother's voice was high-pitched with surprise. The corner of his mouth curled with self-satisfaction. He wanted to give us the full Hollywood experience with the little money he had and, knowing him, he probably saved every penny to make this happen. An Armenian man in a tuxedo, who seemed familiar with Glap, stepped out of the driver's seat and opened the door for us. The limousine smelled of sweet leather with a hint of tobacco. Neon lights changed colors on the ceiling in time with the soft music playing in the background.

As I stepped inside, I ran my fingers over the plush leather seats, marveling at the opulence. I rolled down the window, imagining my school friends' faces back home, a smug grin spreading across my face. The city lights blurred past and I realized it was truly happening.

The limousine slid through the city's veins, gliding past glittering storefronts and bright billboards. Scaffolds and cranes stretched overhead, their metal limbs clawing upward, trying to keep pace with the city's endless hunger. The scent of Los Angeles seeped through the air vents, a heady mix of street food, car exhaust, and something unnameable, yet distinctly urban. There was an undeniable allure here. It was nothing like quiet, medieval Regensburg, rooted in preservation. Los Angeles is all about reinvention.

This was where "the industry" lived and breathed. Where lives could shift overnight with the right glance, the right meeting, the right moment.And above it all, the Hollywood sign hovered on the hillside, just like you see in the movies.

Like a flame luring in every moth from miles away.

The driver let out a gruff laugh, thick with a heavy Armenian accent.

"Welcome to Hollywood."

12

THE GREEK

The limousine halted in front of a building with a red-brick exterior, cloaked in the flickering glow of yellow streetlights. Tall pines swayed gently above us, their shadows stretching long across the cracked sidewalk. The terracotta roof tiles were barely discernible in the dark, but the white trim around the arched doorway seemed to glow. Down the street, we could see Paramount Studios, just visible from where we stood in the middle of the road.

The front door creaked open.

A figure stood in the threshold. The hallway light behind him blazed so brightly it erased his face, casting him as a black silhouette, motionless, watching.

The brightness poured down the entryway steps, catching the iron railing and the chipped pink paint as we climbed the stairs, our suitcases dragging behind us.

The man in the doorway introduced himself as the landlord: a Greek man with eyes like polished obsidian and a tight-lipped smile that never quite reached them. Apparently, Mother had told Slava it had to be a Greek man. And the apartment had to be number three. That's what the spirits showed her through a vision, she said.

When he finally turned and swung open the door to our apartment—number three—a hush fell over us.

I don't know what I had expected. Something grander. Something more . . . American. Maybe a house of our own. Maybe this man would turn out to be our butler. But instead, there was silence. The kind that fills empty rooms with your own hope falling flat.

The $1200 studio was small, with light green walls and a brown carpet that had clearly seen better days. At its center sat a vintage orange leather couch, slightly sunken. A cabinet with glass display shelves stood waiting for Mother's treasures: her golden jewelry and delicate porcelain figurines, each piece carefully cushioned in layers of clothing during the flight over. A single closet struggled to contain our meager collection of clothes, while air mattresses claimed most of the floor space, turning the studio into a patchwork of temporary comfort. The bathroom was small, with a stand-up shower that felt unfamiliar. I had only ever taken baths in Germany.

The kitchen, tucked behind an open doorway, was outfitted with pastel-yellow cabinets, their paint chipped at the edges, and a dated gas stove that ticked softly before igniting with a quiet roar. Every now and then a cockroach would poke its head out from the crevices, sending our cat Sima into a frenzy. Her tail would whip in frantic bursts, body coiled, but she was still smart enough to stay off the counters.

Mister Greek didn't allow pets.

So whenever he visited, we stashed Sima in her carrier or slipped her into the little coat closet, where she waited patiently in the dark, as if she understood the stakes, still and silent, her blue eyes glowing like jewels in the darkness.

In the nights that followed, as I sat curled on the edge of an air mattress, the weight of everything began to settle in. The shimmer of the dream, of America, of a new life, was beginning to rot at the edges, revealing the quiet horror underneath. There was no room of my own. No door to close. Just five people and a cat crammed into a studio apartment, each breath overlapping the next. The feeling I used to get in the dark, that creeping, familiar weight, had never left but now it felt different. Like the darkness itself was laughing at me, mocking how far we'd come only to land here. My heart pounded so hard it felt like it might break my ribs from the inside.

Andy noticed.

"Something's wrong with my heart." I said, grasping my chest.

"You're okay." Andy tried to calm me down.

"We should talk to Mister Greek." My voice was thin. "He's a doctor. He can help."

Andy hesitated, unsure. Then, with a quiet sigh, he nodded.

"Let's ask him," he said. "Can't hurt, right?"

Ten minutes later, Mister Greek stood in our living room, his expression calm, almost amused. "What's the problem, huh? You think something's wrong with your heart?"

I nodded, clutching my shirt where my chest ached.

He waved a hand dismissively, a smirk playing at his lips. "It's nothing. Stress. Breathe slower, drink tea before bed. You'll see, it will go away." He said this with an air of practiced authority. Then he chuckled, as if struck by a sudden brilliance. "If anything, I'll do surgery on it and fix you myself."

I glanced at Andy, whose expression mirrored my own unease.

But something about this man's confidence felt hollow, like he was playing a role. The longer I stared at him, the more his stories unraveled in my mind. Heart surgeon or not, I wasn't sure I wanted to take his advice.

Mister Greek invited me to his apartment, which was only two doors down, for a cup of tea.

Despite his bed being as soft and comfortable as a billowing cloud, my body remained stiff on it. Beside me, Missus Greek, her hair long and black, was tucked in and watched the bulky television that sat in the middle of a tall wooden cabinet across from us. Mister Greek, in his striped pajamas with a silk collar, held a tray of tea cups.

"I'm a self-made millionaire," he boasted. "Came here with nothing, just like you." His words were wet and slick, making me want to step back in case he spat. Greek wasn't their real surname, but I never actually knew their name. He slithered under the covers with the inflexibility of the elderly. My eyes were glued to the screen, but I wasn't aware of the show, sandwiched between these strangers who had invited me to their apartment just five minutes ago. I always accepted his invitation out of politeness. Mister Greek and his wife were the only people we knew in this city. Mother always said it was smart to keep people like them close: landlords, business owners, the kind of people who could help us. "They own the apartment complex," she'd whisper, her eyes alight with hope. "They must be rich. Maybe they can help us."

From time to time, Mister Greek addressed me, his heavy accent making his words difficult to understand. Grandma Greek (his mother) peeked into the room, her fluffy maroon head smiling eerily at me. Elderly women often took a liking to me, leaving lipstick kisses that carried the scent of rotting gums. I mustered a strained smile, hoping she wouldn't come any closer. Mother and Glap soon entered the room to escort me back to our apartment. With a continuous smile, Mother beckoned, "Come, Tanja," though I could sense her discomfort, not wanting to offend our landlords.

"We have always wanted kids," Missus Greek said, glancing at me fondly. "She is so beautiful. Wish we could keep her longer."

Glap bid a polite goodnight, and as we made our way back to the apartment, Mother whispered to me excitedly, "Maybe they can adopt you."

"I don't want to be adopted," I replied firmly. The thought of being in a new country with an unfamiliar family was a nightmare.

"We have to do what we can right now. They're millionaires," Mother insisted in a hushed voice, trusting the séance that led us here. "You'll be better off this way, and you can help us eventually."

The hallway lacked windows and emitted a musty odor of wet mold and fresh paint. In the dim lighting, I often glanced behind me nervously. Muffled, angry voices emanated from the stairs leading to the second floor. They belonged to a woman in her thirties, often clad in a salmon-colored nightgown with her hair styled in a black beehive. Once I observed her dragging a little boy by his arms out of her apartment as I ascended the stairs to the rooftop. The boy cried and whimpered, but Dima and I pretended not to notice, abiding by the motto: what happens in the family stays in the family.

Sometimes, Slava, Andi, and I would band together like rebellious warriors during our free time, stealing Dima's cigarettes and hiding them in the strangest places; behind couch cushions, under the laundry basket, inside empty cereal boxes. It was a game, until it wasn't. Dima would explode in a rage. We'd scatter like cockroaches through the apartment complex, shrieking as he charged after us, bare feet slapping against tile, his booming voice echoing off the walls. We'd dive behind parked cars or under stairwells, stifling giggles and gulps of air. When he caught us, it was no longer a game. We'd end up wrestling on the floor, three siblings squirming under the weight of one burly man, who smelled of tobacco and cheap cologne.

When we weren't being rascals, Andi, Slava, and I were brushing each other's hair and giving each other kisses every morning. Mother insisted we show constant affection. We were soft with each other, maybe too soft, because that's what she wanted, children who clung. Dima would lurk nearby, arms crossed, his mouth twisted in quiet disgust. He'd mutter under his breath about us being hippies and recoil. Mother would shoot him a look and say, "You see? That's what happens when you grow up too negative. He doesn't know how to accept love."

"No," he'd snap, waving us off. "You guys are just weird."

To get out of this situation and find footing in this new land, Dima marched straight to Paramount Studios, his shoulders squared with determination. He had no appointment, no resume, and only a handful of broken English phrases in his arsenal. Mother had made everything sound so easy, like you could just show up and God would provide everything for you.

But slowly, we were beginning to learn that wasn't true. There was going to be a struggle—a grinding, relentless struggle we hadn't anticipated.

When Dima came back that evening, his face was flushed.

"They didn't even look at me," he said, throwing his hands up. "I tried to explain—tried to say I can work hard—but they just laughed. Like I was some kind of joke."

It's only been a few weeks but we were running out of money, and the weight of it pressed into every corner of our lives. We needed to move, to create, to find any crack in the pavement we could slip through and earn something, anything, before it all ran dry. A week ago, Mother handed me our last twenty-dollar bill a quiet gesture made after noticing I hadn't touched the pile of forgotten toys in the corner for weeks. I walked to the store with it crumpled in my fist, but as I stood in the toy aisle, something shifted. I returned the doll I'd been clutching and instead chose a dance DVD, determined to bring something more useful to the table. If I couldn't play instruments like my brothers, maybe I could dance. Maybe I could earn something too. Meanwhile, we hustled. On the glittering sidewalks of Hollywood Boulevard, my brothers strummed their guitars while Glap's voice rose and fell through the din of tourists and traffic. But the energy was off, like they were singing into a void. The crowd drifted. The tip bucket stayed mostly empty.

Back home, I practiced. The dance DVD became my obsession. I studied the fluid moves, the sharp turns, the rhythm that felt like something I could finally control. One afternoon, seeing how tired my brothers were, I offered to take their place, just for a while.

My hands trembled as I stepped forward. My heart pounded so hard I thought it might drown out the music. But as the beat filled the air and my body began to move, something clicked. The world around me faded. And when the music ended and I finally looked up, a small crowd had gathered, clapping, cheering. The bucket at my feet jingled with coins.

We became obsessed with getting better. Back at home, we dissected music videos, rewinding and pausing to catch every move. That's when I discovered my signature: a Matrix-style back bend that never failed to draw gasps.

It was Glap who had the idea, that he and Andy should join me as backup dancers. Andy protested, of course, his pride prickling at the thought. But after a few nudges, some teasing, and a sibling rivalry he couldn't resist, he gave in.

Soon, the three of us became a team, an odd, charming trio. Glap's lanky limbs flailed with joyful abandon, Andy's dorky moves somehow working in our favor, and me in the center, doing my best to hold it all together with what I hoped was grace. People stopped. People laughed. The tips grew heavier. My tenth birthday came and we didn't dare lose momentum by taking a day off.

But not every day was golden. When the rain came, Hollywood emptied.

FAME OR DEAD

The boulevard transformed into a ghost town, lights flickering on wet pavement, puddles swallowing the stars on the Walk of Fame.

We had thrown garbage bags over our gear and now stood our ground, hair soaked, skin chilled, feet slipping on the slick concrete. Performing the normal routine I nearly fell, my body sliding out from under me mid-dance. I wanted to cry. I wanted to go home. But we kept going.

And then: kindness.

He came out of nowhere, a man with cascading dreadlocks and a girl clinging to his arm. He slowed as he passed, watching us, his eyes catching on our soaked figures and trembling hands. Without a word, he turned back, reached into his pocket, and dropped something into the tip bucket.

When we dared to look inside, we froze.

Two crisp, rain-dampened hundred-dollar bills lay among the loose change and crumpled singles. It felt like maybe God was watching and every now and then, when we needed it most, He answered.

So did Dima when we needed him.

"Mayday, mayday!" Andy's voice erupted into the walkie-talkie, frantic and sharp.

"Dima on the line," came the cool reply.

"We're almost at the bus stop. Start walking," Andy instructed.

"On my way," Dima responded as if this was some kind of serious mission.

The crackle of the walkie-talkie sliced through the rhythmic hum of the Metro bus as it jolted down rain-slicked streets, our bodies swaying with every turn on the ride home from another long day of street busking. Glap gripped the cart, steadying our tangled mess of cables and gear as the bus lurched forward, just in time to accidentally slam a car battery into a woman's ankle. He apologized profusely while she yelped in pain.

Ever since my brothers narrowly escaped an attempted mugging near Hollywood and Vine when they went to perform in front of a bar late into the night, everything had changed. Glap and Andy kept their heads down now, scanning the sidewalks for danger, while Dima, having slipped into the role of protector, flanked them like hired security. His black beanie was pulled low, his heavy jacket adding to his bulk, though the recent diet of fried chicken certainly helped too. He was never going to eat the vegan food we ate.

"Sexy ladies!" someone shouted. A group of homeless men leered from a corner, mistaking Glap and Andy, with their long hair and tight jeans, for girls. But Dima's glare was enough to choke the comment off before it could fully land. They went quiet. People usually did around him.

When we got back and the apartment finally fell quiet, sleep refused to come. I tossed and turned on the lumpy blow-up mattress, the plastic cool against my skin, its waffle-patterned indentations pressing into my back. Mother, roused from her slumber by my restless movements, admonished me to cease my fidgeting. I missed my own bed.

As the hours dragged on, the cacophony of my brothers' snores filled the air, their rhythm disjointed and chaotic. Heaviness pulled at my limbs, and I finally managed to fall asleep. My dream twisted into a nightmare, morphing from exhilarating flights through the sky to descending slowly into a fog. As the sand of the beach below became visible, I saw something else standing there: a dark entity awaiting me, patiently. It had no face. Stricken with a silent scream of horror, I fought the descent like it was a rope pulling me down, clawing at the air for anything to pull me up, but the faceless creature greeted me with open arms.

The front door burst open with a jolt, crashing the stillness of the morning. In stepped Mister Greek, his frame filling the doorway like a storm cloud. "What's for breakfast?" he boomed with a grin, striding in as if the apartment were his own. He made his way to the stove, lifting lids and poking around the pots and pans.

Then, as if on cue, he sank into the orange leather couch with a satisfied sigh, oblivious to Sima perched on the windowsill just behind him. Her blue eyes tracked him warily, tail twitching in slow arcs, coming dangerously close to brushing the back of his head. A small gust from the window stirred the air, and Mister Greek scratched the side of his neck, blinking like he'd felt something but couldn't place it.

"How's everything?" he asked, voice easy, eyes roaming the room without really seeing us. Glap, still groggy and disoriented, sat upright, trying to pull himself together in the chaos of waking up.

"Good," he managed, his voice uneven, polite but strained.

"Ah, good," Mister Greek replied, crossing his legs and flashing an array of golden rings on his fingers. "Got rid of the cockroaches?"

Glap took a tense sip of air. "No."

"Damn pests," Mister Greek muttered, chewing on a piece of skin around his pinky. "Can't seem to get rid of them. Called the exterminator ages ago, but those critters just won't stay away. Reminds me of those filthy cats in Greece, spreading disease everywhere. Disgusting creatures," he added with a disdainful shake of his head. "Heard roaches could survive an atomic bomb. If it were up to me, I'd eradicate them all."

Before exiting the room, he turned back abruptly. "By any chance, do you guys need a car?"

Glap raised an eyebrow in surprise. "Actually, we do."

"I knew it!" Mister Greek exclaimed knowingly. "Relying on the bus system in a city like L.A. is a nightmare."

With a mischievous grin, he beckoned, "Come with me."

Next door, in the bustling public parking lot, vehicles of all kinds clustered together, from the modest cars of nearby employees to the glamorous trailers of the film production studio across the street. Among them stood a weathered, boxy car, its once vibrant colors faded into a dull blend of gray and metallic blue. The paint was chipped and peeling, revealing patches of rust underneath. Mister Greek led us to it, fumbling in his pants until he produced a solitary key.

"Here you go," he announced, handing the key to Glap with a grin. "It's yours if you fix it." We gasped in disbelief.

Glap's hand shook as he reached out to take the key, his voice catching in his throat. "Really?"

Mister Greek nodded, satisfaction playing on his lips. "Take a look inside."

Glap opened the door, and the distinct scent of warm vinyl and exhaust fumes wafted out. The seats were ripped with the insides wh. Dust coated the dashboard, and a few cobwebs hung in the corners. Glap ran his fingers over the steering wheel, his eyes wide with wonder. "I hope you know how to drive manual," Mister Greek said casually.

"Oh, that's no problem," Glap replied, trying to sound confident despite never having driven a car before.

"It does need some work," Mister Greek continued. "The bolts need replacing, and the belt is a bit loose."

"Thank you so much," Glap murmured, staring at the key in his palm as if it were a golden ticket.

"Pay me later when you have the money," Mister Gargoyle said with a wink before heading back toward the house.

"See? Rich people help people," Mother exclaimed gleefully, her eyes sparkling with satisfaction.

"He's still an ass," Dima grumbled, inspecting the car's back tire. "Walking in on us like that." He glanced at Glap. "You should've said something."

"Say what?" Glap countered, his voice still tinged with disbelief.

"I don't know, how about 'this is illegal'? Not to mention he almost saw Sima."

"We should just tell him about her," Mother said.

"No," Glap protested, opening the back door to inspect it. An empty soda can rolled out from the side pocket. "We'll get kicked out."

"If we don't tell him now, he'll find out eventually. If he hears it from us, he's more likely to be understanding," Mother reasoned.

We exchanged uncertain glances. "Well, she does have a point," Andy conceded. "He'll find Sima eventually."

"Not to mention, he just gave us a car. That's the least we can do," Mother insisted.

"But you have to tell him he can't just walk in on us like that any more. Be a man about it," Dima added firmly.

"Okay," Glap agreed reluctantly, scratching his head. "For Sima."

On that chilly, starless night, the desolate streets took on light. What felt cramped and bustling during the day now stretched out vastly before us.

The distant sounds of laughter mingled with the flickering light of a makeshift fire set by a group of homeless people in an alleyway. I glanced briefly at the trash bag ablaze, quickly averting my eyes for fear of drawing attention to myself.

"Dead body," Mother whispered, wrinkling her nose at the putrid stench that hung heavy in the air. "It smells like a dead body."

I wondered how she knew that. Mother returned to the apartment.

Meanwhile, Glap surveyed the deserted street, seeing a perfect opportunity to test out our new car. Andy dashed up, clutching a manual in his hand. "I found it!" he exclaimed. Neither of them possessed a driver's license or any experience behind the wheel, but they pored over the manual diligently, seeking guidance from Dima, who remained aloof from their antics.

"We need the car for transporting our equipment," Glap insisted, recalling the struggles of lugging guitars and speakers on crowded buses to street-busking locations in Hollywood.

"Are you sure about this, Glap?" Andy said, scanning the manual once more. "If we get caught, we're screwed. No license, no registration, no insurance."

"It'll be fine," Glap reassured himself, inserting the key into the ignition. After a few attempts, the car sputtered to life, emitting a low rumble.

"You ready?" he asked nervously, a hint of laughter in his voice.

But as he attempted to shift gears and press the gas, the car stalled. "Um, I think there's a pedal for shifting gears somewhere near your foot," Andy offered tentatively.

Glap glanced down uncertainly. "Which one is the brake?"

"Maybe we shouldn't do this," Andy suggested, the weight of the situation suddenly bearing down on them.

But Glap, determined, took a deep breath. "No, we need this," he said, his voice steadier. He tried again, and the engine roared to life. The car jerked forward, and for a brief while, a grin spread across Glap's face. "Here we go," he said.

After a few tense tries, the car lurched out of the parking lot at a snail's pace, navigating onto the main road with caution. A passing car honked impatiently, its driver shooting them a glare that spoke volumes. As they ventured further, the car picked up speed, only to emit a strange grinding noise before coming to an abrupt halt. "Oh, shit," Glap cursed, attempting to restart the engine to no avail.

"Start the car!" Andy's voice cracked with panic, his eyes darting around the darkened street. Glap's fingers fumbled with the key, his breaths shallow. The wail of a siren pierced the air, and the rearview mirror lit up with the flashing red and blue lights of a police cruiser. The cruiser's ominous glow cast long shadows inside the car.

"Oh, shit," Glap muttered, his knuckles turning white as he gripped the steering wheel. "What do I say? What do I say?"

"I don't know! It was your idea!" Andy's voice was strained, his nerves fraying.

The cruiser loomed closer, the tension in the car making our hearts pound.

Suddenly, the screech of tires and a sickening crunch shattered the moment. A silver car lost control at the nearby intersection, colliding with a lamppost.

The police cruiser diverted its attention to the accident. "Let's go!" Glap commanded, seizing the fleeting opportunity. They hastily pushed the car back into the safety of the parking lot, which luckily wasn't too far away.

Breathless and bewildered, they sank back into the car, adrenaline coursing through their veins. "God almighty," Andy murmured, his voice barely above a whisper. The sheer improbability of the distraction felt like the work of a madman's play, an uncanny coincidence that had spared them.

After discovering we'd broken the car, Mister Greek demanded six hundred dollars for repairs. "But you said it was a gift," Glap countered, confused.

Mister Greek's expression hardened. "I said if you fixed it, but now you just made it worse."

Mother had made a grave error in displaying our jewelry in that glass cabinet, unwittingly providing Mister Greek with a roadmap to our most prized possessions. Slowly, he began to collect our valuables. He took the one thing I had left from Father: the Capricorn necklace. It didn't help that when Mister Greek trespassed into our apartment next, he caught sight of Sima. She cowered in the dark closet. The unannounced entrances of Mister Greek must have spooked her more than usual. Out of anger, he unplugged our refrigerator every few days.

Mother was furious. She grabbed the refrigerator plug and shoved it back into the socket, her movements jerky and fierce. Mother poked her head inside to check on our food. "That's it!" she fumed, slamming the door shut. "That was the last time."

With rent looming and our finances stretched thin, we couldn't afford to let our food spoil. We'd burned through fifteen thousand dollars quickly. Kashmir blankets, musical equipment, and now rotten produce were all we had left.

Mother's retaliation came swiftly, and it was so whimsical and outrageous that it left us in stitches. In our dire situation, her antics brought much-needed laughter. She came home carrying a package of diapers, her eyes twinkling with a mischievous light. Without a word, she beckoned me over. I stood by, puzzled, as she carefully unpacked a diaper and spread it open on the counter. My confusion deepened when she reached for the peanut butter jar in the pantry, unscrewed the lid, and smeared the creamy spread all over the diaper, mimicking a messy disaster. Her laughter, low and almost maniacal, bubbled up as she pressed the peanut butter-covered diaper onto Mister Greek's apartment door with a final, triumphant slap.

An hour later, an explosive knocking shattered the stillness. "Open the door!" Mister Greek's voice roared, vibrating with rage. Keys jangled and scratched against our lock, desperate to find their way in.

"Wait for it," Glap whispered, his eyes gleaming with anticipation. The doorknob turned, but the door held fast.

"What the fuck!" Mister Greek's furious curse echoed down the hall as he pushed against the unyielding door.

"It worked!" Glap exclaimed, his voice bursting with triumph, a grin spread across his face. He had changed the locks earlier that morning.

"Here we go again," Dima sighed, slipping his headphones on to drown out the impending chaos.

"Open the goddamn door! I know it was you!" Mister Greek's voice was sharp with anger.

"What?" Glap called back, his voice dripping with mock innocence.

"The—the diaper! What is wrong with you people?"

"What diaper?" we replied, struggling to contain our laughter.

"The one on my door!"

"There are a lot of crazy people in this building, Mister Greek, and it's certainly not us," Glap retorted, a smirk playing on his lips.

THE GREEK

The warfare dragged on for weeks. We didn't use the front door any more. Mister Greek and his mother lurked like shadows in the hallway, always circling, always sniffing around for rent. So we climbed in through the window.

Mother used to whisper that the grandmother brought bad luck. We laughed it off, but lately it was harder to dismiss. Every time we crossed paths with her, something went wrong. Our tips dried up. Our performances fell flat.

But tonight was different.

We crawled through the window, breathless and soaked, the rain still clinging to our clothes. And then the stillness hit.

Sima lay in the middle of the floor.

Motionless.

Andy dropped to his knees, gathering her gently into his arms. Her body was limp, lifeless. The warmth had already left her. Her final breath had slipped away, and Andy's arms were the last thing she'd known.

I couldn't move. Couldn't cry. I stood there, stomach twisting, while Andy's sobs shattered the silence, soaking her fur with tears.

Glap stood frozen, his voice low and jagged.

"It was my fault. I killed her."

A month earlier, he'd sprayed her with flea spray, a cheap brand that reeked of synthetic citrus. We didn't know that citrus was toxic to cats when sprayed directly on their fur. It was meant for surrounding furniture and carpets. Even after we called the poison control center, they assured us she'd be fine. After that, she'd slowed. We don't know what exactly killed her. But the refrigerator was unplugged once again.

"Whoa, it's like a horror movie in here," Dima groaned, his voice echoing through the room like a nervous joke that landed too hard.

His suitcase lay open on the floor, clothes spilling out. He'd had enough.

His ninety-day visa was nearly up, and so was mine, but Dima wanted out. Back to Germany. Back to some version of stability, whatever that meant. Mother and I had hidden his return ticket, hoping that if we stalled long enough he might change his mind. That he might stay. That the dream might still hold.

But when he found out, the panic was instant. Raw. He turned on us like a wounded animal. "You trapped me," he said, eyes wide with disbelief, betrayal in every syllable. He promised to make our lives a living hell.

In the end, we gave in. Watching him fall apart was worse than watching him walk away.

"Are you coming?" he asked me, one last time, standing in the doorway. There was a flicker of hope in his voice. And something else: desperation. Not for himself, but for me. Because he knew what the future of my life would look like if I stayed.

I shook my head.

"No. I want to stay with Mother."

His shoulders sank. He didn't argue. He just nodded, turned, and disappeared.

The door closed behind him with a soft finality. The silence that followed was the kind of emptiness that never ended.

"Not everyone can endure the hardship it takes to become rich," Mother said. "That's why most people are poor."

Each corner was a reminder of the absence of our Sima and Dima. It was time to leave it behind once more.

13

THE KIDNAPPER

Six months passed. The scent of unfamiliar homes clung to our clothes as we carouseled from one temporary abode to the next, unable to keep up with the rising tide of expenses. A cramped motel in the heart of Los Angeles cost us around $75 a night and that was just for a roof. Then came the taxis, expensive but necessary, since the buses barely reached the stretch where we were staying, and more often than not the bus drivers wouldn't let us on with all our equipment.

We carried a full-sized speaker now. Instruments. A piano. The weight of our hope.

I had started learning the keys, fingers fumbling over songs I half knew, half felt. Even Mother played the maracas. We'd quit dancing altogether, no more street routines or comedic skits. That wasn't going to get us discovered. We were a family band now. That was the new dream. The serious one.

But even then, there were days when we hardly made enough to break even. The money slipped away like sand through a sieve: motel, food, guitar strings that snapped from the cold or the heat. And when one of us got sick, there was no time to rest since we'd fall so far behind. We'd show up with snot running down our faces, eyes half closed, dragging ourselves through songs. Sometimes strangers would walk up from behind and yank the cord out of Slava's guitar mid-performance, convinced he was faking it or pretending to play along to a backing track. The music would snap off with a sickening jolt, followed by a sharp, high-pitched screech of feedback that cut through the crowd.

All eyes would turn.

Slava would freeze.

The person would stammer apologies, their face flushing red under the weight of our silence and the crowd's boos. And it didn't happen just once. It happened multiple times.

That's how you know we were good—really good.

(And by good, I mean my brothers. Truly. I was just there as the cuteness factor.)

I engaged in conversations with strangers, taxi drivers, passersby, always holding out hope that someone, somewhere, might be willing to lend us a hand. With each exchange, my English skills sharpened, growing closer to fluency day by day. I wasn't afraid to ask Do you have a place we could stay? Do you know someone who does? Sometimes it was the clerk at the El Capitan Theater opening their space to us. Sometimes it was a stranger, moved by something in our music.

With my big blue eyes and pigtails, people had a hard time looking away.

No one put me up to it. I came up with it on my own. Because I knew if I didn't do it, none of us would. And we would've ended up sleeping on the streets, next to the crackheads. And nothing scared me more than that.

So I made it my mission. I scanned faces the way others scanned the ground for loose change.

Whenever I caught Angel watching us perform, I ran toward him without hesitation. I'd strike up conversation the way children do, with open curiosity and no fear, always on the lookout for the next kind stranger who might save us. Tall and Spanish, he stood out against the usual blur of tourists and street performers. He wore high-top Converse, the white rubber scuffed and gray from city dust. His black hair parted cleanly down the middle framed a handsome, stubbled face. Even in the constant noise of the Hollywood and the centre of Highland, he exuded a calm friendliness that made it hard not to look back. I often spotted him chatting up wide-eyed Japanese tourists outside the pastry shop on the first level, his charm magnetic.

"Maybe he's rich," Mother mused, swooning, her voice glazed with admiration. But his shoes, she said, were too dirty.

Soon enough, he approached me with two small gifts, wrapped in red and gold paper. I tore them open and found two dolls tucked inside. Without thinking, I threw my arms around him. He laughed and lifted me off my feet, swinging me like I was weightless.

Days passed but he visited often.

Twilight had begun to fall over Hollywood Boulevard, softening the neon glow of signs and draining the noise from the streets. Most of the tourists had gone, and shopkeepers were dragging metal gates shut behind them.

That's when Angel appeared again.

He ruffled my hair, knocking my hat sideways. "I have a birthday present for you," he said, grinning. There was something glimmering behind his glasses, something playful, something unreadable.

"Really?" I asked, excited. "What is it?"

"It's a surprise," he said.

"Where is it?"

"At my place. Just around the corner."

Without hesitation, I grabbed his arm. "Okay. Let's go!"

We walked through the now quiet shopping center, the lights above flickering and reflecting off the polished floors in colored shards. But halfway through, something inside me tensed. A slow tightening, low in my belly. I glanced back at my family, still distracted with packing up the equipment, still unaware.

"I should tell my mom," I said.

Angel waved it off with a smile. "It'll just take a minute."

He moved faster.

We slipped out of the mall, into side streets lined with graffiti-tagged walls and the acrid smell of urine. I hesitated outside a run-down apartment building as Angel pulled out his keys and motioned me inside. The hallway was dim, lit by a single buzzing bulb.

He left the door to his apartment slightly ajar. "Wait here," he said.

I stood in the hall, alone. My heartbeat drowned out the silence. Through the crack, I could see him pacing inside. Something in me screamed run.

Eventually he returned, his smile forced, lips tight. "I couldn't find it," he said.

"Okay," I whispered.

I turned, walked fast but didn't run. I could feel him behind me, his silence heavier than words.

"What a bummer," he muttered. "Maybe next time."

We descended the stairs and stepped back onto Hollywood Boulevard and into a line of five police cruisers parked just outside. The red and blue lights spun silently, painting the pavement with flickering color.

Andy stood talking to a cop, his face pale, his hands animated.

The moment Glap saw me, he broke into a run. I ran too, straight into Glap's arms.

"Where were you?" he snapped, gripping me tight.

"With Angel," I said softly.

Glap turned on him, voice sharp, fists clenched. "You can't just take her like that."

"It was a misunderstanding," Angel said, lifting his hands. "I just wanted to give her a present."

Glap didn't reply. His eyes said everything.

"It won't happen again," Angel promised, backing away.

Andy crouched beside me. "You can't ever go off with someone like that," he said.

"He wasn't a stranger," I mumbled.

"If it's not one of us," Glap cut in, "it's a stranger."

I nodded. "Okay."

Angel disappeared. I never received my present.

Tonight, we had nowhere to go. Finally we managed to negotiate a cheaper rate at the nearest motel. Its faded blue sign flickered against the night sky, buzzing dimly over the stained concrete of Whitley Avenue. We checked in, dragging ourselves through the door. The room greeted us with garish neon-orange walls and bedspreads covered in hideous patterns that made your skin crawl just looking at them. Still, we collapsed into the beds after another long, exhausting day of street busking, too tired to care.

At first, it was like a distant tone, like someone trying to yell at me underwater. The words rose slowly, the volume building from a quiet fade to a sudden sharpness that cut through the haze. By the time I realized what was being said, I jolted awake.

"He's dead. He's dead!"

Glap's voice tore through the motel room.

A wave of dread surged through me, thick and paralyzing.

Glap leapt from his bed, panic written all over his face as he rushed to Andy's side.

Andy lay still.

Eyes wide.

Lips a chilling shade of blue. We were too late this time.

"No. No. No," Mother's voice trembled as she shook Andy's shoulders. Glap and I hovered nearby, paralyzed by fear. Mother's hands moved with fierce urgency as she performed CPR, her blows to Andy's chest and breaths into his mouth a rhythm of desperation. Her unbearable wails and anguish tore through the air with such force that I pressed my hands over my ears. Glap fumbled with his flip phone, his hands shaking as he dialed for an ambulance, his voice quivering as he explained the situation.

Andy's body convulsed, a harsh retching sound tearing from his lips. Then, a flicker. Life returned to his eyes.

Relief surged through us like a wave breaking. Mother dropped onto the bed, cradling him in her arms, her whispers of comfort tangled with her sobs. But something wasn't right. Andy's eyes darted wildly, unfocused. His body moved like it didn't belong to him. He suddenly pointed finger guns at Mother, making shooting sounds through his lips, then bolted toward the window in a burst of chaotic energy.

Glap lunged, grabbing him just in time and dragging him back.

The door burst open, and Mother hurried the paramedics into the chaos of our cluttered motel room. Their arrival felt like a cruel spotlight on the reality we'd been trying to survive. They scanned the room, their eyes catching on the disarray: boxes stacked in corners, open luggage spilling clothes, Andy lying disheveled and pale across the bed.

Suspicion settled over the room. They scanned the surfaces, no doubt searching for signs of drug paraphernalia, a fair assumption to make in a place like Hollywood. Glap tried to explain that we didn't do drugs and it wasn't an overdose, but his words slid off their hardened expressions. They moved with clinical efficiency, preparing to transport Andy.

I sat on the edge of the bed, hands clenched in my lap. One of the paramedics turned to me, his voice unexpectedly soft.

"Are you okay?"

I nodded, though I could feel my body trembling.

He glanced again at my face. "Shouldn't you be in school?"

I shook my head. I didn't go to school any more.

The paramedic stared at me for a little while, his expression unreadable, before returning to Andy. Outside, the ambulance lights painted the motel front in dizzying colors- red, blue, white—a kaleidoscope that flickered through the thin curtains as they wheeled my brother away.

Later that night, the hospital released him. The doctor confirmed it had been another seizure, then handed us a bill we couldn't afford and never paid.

We were in such shock we didn't perform that day. We did switch motel rooms, hoping to outrun the darkness that had settled over us. The new room felt a little cleaner, the air lighter and the sheets unstained by Andy's saliva. I lay awake, listening intently to Andy's breathing. Whenever his breath would catch, my whole body would tense until he finally exhaled and turned over. My heart pounded against my ribs, a quiet, relentless alarm that had been echoing since I was four whenever I felt the darkness come too close. I felt it here, lurking in the corners of the room, feeding off our turmoil. It felt like I was waiting for something. For the inevitable.

14

THE FLEE

One evening, as the sun dipped below the horizon of Orange Drive, Mother sat on her luggage in the fading light, eyes locked on a distant hostel down the block. Around her were towers of cardboard boxes: fragments of our old life in Germany stacked awkwardly on the curb. Christmas ornaments, my childhood toys, porcelain figurines from the living room. My brothers grumbled about dragging them everywhere, but we couldn't bring ourselves to let them go. And with every move they broke. Glass cracked. Paint chipped. It was as if the longer we lived in transition, the more our past disintegrated, piece by piece.

I didn't think about Germany much any more. It felt far away, like something I had only imagined. But sometimes, in the quiet moments, Father would cross my mind.

He didn't love you enough to keep you, Mother once said.

And maybe she was right.

I idly kicked a pebble along the ground. Being homeless once again didn't kill my spirit since Mother reminded us that struggle is necessary for anything great, and also temporary. All famous people went through struggle.

Andy perched on the curb, back turned to us, shoulders slumped in silence. Whenever we found ourselves without a home to return to, he would disappear inward, locking his thoughts and emotions behind that hollow, unblinking stare. He didn't speak. He barely moved. Minutes dragged like hours. Then Glap returned, his face drawn tight with frustration and quiet defeat.

"Too expensive," he muttered. "That hostel was our last option."

He hovered for a moment, as if searching for something else to say, then sank down onto one of our suitcases. The weight of it all settled between us.

And maybe that's what gave us away.

"Hey!" The call had come from a Black woman with a nice smile watching from the balcony across the street. Her arms were wrapped around herself against the evening chill. "Do you need a place to stay?" Glap didn't hesitate, accepting her offer gratefully. We followed her inside an orange building, our footsteps echoing in the hallway.

Her name was Edwidge and her two lively children filled the apartment with constant chaos, their high-pitched screeches traveling through the air like pterodactyls in flight. They ran wild from room to room, leaving a trail of toys and noise in their wake. Edwidge's exasperated yelling echoed through the apartment so often that Mother began calling her "the bad witch."

After two months, the air in Edwidge's apartment had shifted. The greetings at the door became shorter. She no longer lingered in the doorway to talk, no longer asked how our day went. She walked heavier now, keys jangling, shoes still on, grocery bags thudding on the counter with more force than necessary. The cupboard doors opened louder. Closed harder.

Hints arrived in the form of silences. In how she'd glance at the dishes left in the sink, how her eyes lingered on the electricity bill on the table just a little too long.

At first, she had said it lightly. "When things get better, maybe a little help with rent?"

But Mother stiffened at the mention. Her face pinched, her lips pressed tight. "She knew what this was," she muttered later. "No one invited us here out of the goodness of their heart. They always want something."

After that, every comment Edwidge made became an accusation in Mother's eyes.

"She wants us out," she said one night. "They all do. They pretend to help, only to turn around and try to make money off of you."

Eventually, Edwidge did ask us to leave. We nodded. Apologized. Promised we'd find somewhere else. And then we didn't.

The door locks never changed. She worked double shifts, leaving her kids home alone. Came home too tired to argue.

So we stayed. Ate quietly. Moved softly. Lived like ghosts in the corners of her home, pretending we were invisible.

There was no reason we couldn't contribute. The summer of 2007 was like riding a high. It felt like God had finally looked down and, just before we gave up, reached out a hand. During our performance one day, a woman stepped through the crowd and handed us a card. It was Jimmy Kimmel's assistant. His studio and stage were right behind us on Hollywood.

"We'd love to have you on the show," she said, the corner of her mouth curled in a tight smile. The offer was three hundred dollars. A few hours of our lives, and a moment on real television. After we negotiated between ourselves, Glap called her back the next day. "We expect more from a television appearance," he said plainly. So she returned with a counter-offer: six hundred dollars. We accepted.

When the day came, we set up our instruments like always, tourists drifting around us, weekend traffic humming. We poured ourselves into the music—"Hotel California", "Sweet Child O' Mine", "Stairway to Heaven", "All Along the Watchtower", "Sweet Home Alabama"—our eyes flicking toward the crowd, scanning for cameras, waiting for something to happen.

Then, without warning, Jimmy Kimmel appeared. And behind him, a man in a full Elmo costume, one of the many Hollywood Boulevard street performers who made their living posing for tips with tourists.

They strode toward us like they had something to prove.

Jimmy walked right up and shut off our speakers.

"Please, for God's sake, go back to Germany," he groaned after asking where we were from, his voice thick with mock desperation.

Elmo dropped to his knees beside him, miming a dramatic prayer.

"You keep playing the same five songs over and over. We're going to kill ourselves. When is this going to stop?"

Jimmy's voice rang out, bouncing down the boulevard, and the crowd roared with laughter. Then he held out airplane tickets like a punchline.

And truthfully . . . he wasn't wrong. We did play the same five songs. After twelve-hour days in the sun, we didn't have the energy to rehearse new ones. When we tried, they didn't bring in money like the others. Those five songs worked. The other songs we knew we saved for the rare nights where we jammed for fun, once the crowd has long gone.

As the cameras rolled and laughter swelled from the crowd, as we felt like we were being discovered, it almost felt like success. But the laughter had an edge to it and it left a sting that settled deep in the chest. We weren't just musicians. We were immigrants who had left behind everything familiar, chasing something we didn't fully understand but believed in with everything we had. Music was the only language we knew how to properly speak here. The only thing we could offer. And now we had become a punchline on national television for it. Still, we didn't stop. We couldn't. The next day, we returned to our usual corner just outside Jimmy Kimmel's office, setting up our instruments like we always had, turning the volume knob on our equipment even louder.

We became aware of things we weren't aware of before. Such as the irritation in glances from shopkeepers who'd heard our songs too many times. We knew some people found us grating, repetitive, hard to tune out. But beneath all that, something else stirred. People were paying attention now.

It was evident as Mother and I trudged home along Sunset Boulevard, our arms heavy with groceries. A stranger stopped us mid-stride. "I saw you guys on TV with Jimmy Kimmel! That was hilarious!" he blurted, then vanished into the crowd before we could respond. Mother turned to me, her eyes lit with something like triumph.

"See? It's finally happening," she whispered. "We're becoming famous." And in some strange way, she was right. Back in Germany, Father had seen us on TV too. That brief clip on national television was the only proof he ever got that we were still alive. He never wrote to me. Dima wrote to us sometimes to update us through email. Just a few lines: Father had remarried. I had a stepmother now. He had moved on. Built a new life. Forgotten us just like Mother always said he would. But at least we were succeeding.

People pressed through the crowds to get to us, drawn in by the music, the spectacle, the rhythm of something raw and desperate blooming on the boulevard. Sometimes they'd lean in mid-song, waving a business card or scribbling their number on the back of a receipt. "We're having a party tonight," they'd say. "Can you come play?"

We'd nod, pack up fast, squeeze into a taxi with our gear stacked high and the windows rolled halfway down, the wind knotting our hair. A few hours of music beneath string lights or in echoing halls, then three hundred in cash slipped into Glap's palm and just like that, we were back on the street, instruments reassembled, voices hoarse, chasing crowds like shadows. We rotated our spots with the rhythm of the city. Outside the Highland Mall on Hollywood Boulevard during the day. In front of the Pantages Theater in the evening. By the glowing arches of the Hollywood Bowl, waiting for the tide of showgoers to spill into the street after midnight. At Universal CityWalk we even had a real spot. A scheduled performance. The sky would fade into a pale, bleeding blue like blackberry juice sinking into white cotton as we set up in the stillness of early morning. A mist hung in the air, brushing my cheeks while I watched the great spinning globe of Universal Studios turn slowly on its fountain pedestal. Even though I was excited, I felt my eyelids pulling shut, my limbs heavy and slow behind the keyboard. I began falling asleep mid-set, lulled by the cold air and the heater running near my legs. Someone must have said something to the office. They also realized I was there on school days. There was no argument, just a quiet dismissal and then we were gone from the schedule. Even without it, on Saturdays, we made as much as six hundred dollars in thirteen relentless hours. Fridays and Sundays, a little less—four hundred, maybe—but still enough to breathe easier.

We rode the fame wave as long as we could, but the higher we rose, the harder it pressed back. The police began to notice us; more than just a nuisance now, we were a target. Slava, the oldest, was arrested more than once for "blocking the sidewalk," a vague excuse that let them swoop in, seize our equipment, and strip us of our hard-earned cash. We'd lose entire weekends this way: thirteen-hour days gone in an instant. No music. No income. We'd have to wait until Monday to reclaim our instruments from some bleak impound office in downtown L.A., like beggars asking for our own bones back. And pay all the fines.

So we got smarter. Mother stopped performing the maracas altogether and took to the sidelines, sharp-eyed and still as a hawk. Every hour, Mother would swoop in like clockwork as she'd clear the tip jar, folding the crumpled bills into her purse before the LAPD could lay eyes on it. Sometimes passerbyers would stop and yell, accusing her of child labor while she stood off to the side.

But Mother would just smile, calm and unmoved.

It wasn't just the cops we had to outwit. Thieves lurked close, just outside the circle, pretending to be part of the crowd. Some watched our fingers dance over strings while theirs crept toward the bucket. They'd lunge for the bucket, snatch what they could, and vanish into the crowd. Even the other street performers came for blood. The sidewalk wasn't a stage. It was a battlefield. They'd roll up with their speakers blasting, planting themselves right beside us with fake smiles and louder amps. "Hey fam," they'd say, while elbowing us for turf. Some didn't bother with pretense. They'd just kick the bucket as they passed, coins scattering like frightened birds.

But we never moved.

Sometimes the chaos worked in our favor. Tourists caught the tension and that flicker of pity translated into tips. But the money never stayed safe for long—Mother's access to it all might've been worse than the cops or the thieves or the other performers. She spent it just the same.

To try to bolster our dwindling finances, I began to sing.

At first, it was barely noticeable. A microphone set discreetly by my keyboard, a few harmonies slipped in behind Glap's lead. But over time, I began to fill the silence between his verses, then stepped into them entirely. Eventually, he stopped singing altogether, his voice retreating as mine grew steady, more certain. Then came the moment I was handed my first true solo of a Christmas song. It happened without warning. Slava simply looked at me, counted down from three, and pressed the microphone into my hand. "You're up," he said, and turned away. My hands trembled. The cold wind needled my skin. I stood there frozen, shaking like the tiny Chihuahua Mother had recently bought with what was left of our Jimmy Kimmel money. She'd named her Shayla.

Now, as I stood ready to perform, Mother stood nearby, arms wrapped tightly around the trembling dog. She was radiant with pride, fussing over Shayla like she was a newborn, her coat pulled protectively around the small frame. My brothers had protested the purchase. It was impractical, given our situation.

"She wants it," Mother had said, nodding toward me. "And she's the breadwinner now. She gets a say." And it was true. I had wanted the dog, at least at first. I'd seen her on the street, a man selling her near the spot where we performed. All the children had gathered around, drawn to her oversized ears and tiny pink-hued body. I was no different. Chihuahuas were a symbol of Hollywood itself; of fame, of celebrities with sunglasses and small dogs tucked into handbags. It hadn't taken much to convince Mother.

But now, watching her cradle Shayla against her chest, always tending to her needs, doting on her, something tightened in my chest. I was jealous of the love she received. Mother didn't pretend otherwise; she admitted it easily, with a shrug or a laugh: she loved the dog more. So I sang. The pain had to go somewhere.

Shayla wasn't the only thing Mother indulged in; she had resumed her shopping trips. She'd return with her arms full of glossy bags, her face glowing with the kind of satisfaction only consumerism could offer. Andy was horrified but Mother waved him off. "You're complaining," she said, gesturing at his full plate, "but look at you, enjoying all the food we finally have."

And it was true, our meals had improved. No more spaghetti with ketchup or limp noodles drowned in vegan mayonnaise. Now we ate dishes that looked like something from a real kitchen, warm, colorful, sometimes even hearty. She'd bring them to us around lunchtime in plastic containers, still steaming. We'd sneak off with them into the mall, find a tucked-away bench somewhere between storefronts, and eat like kings in hiding. Those were the golden hours, when our backs weren't sore, our instruments were packed away, and laughter echoed between us in hushed bursts. We stayed sitting longer than we should have. Stretched our break just a bit more each time. Until Mother's voice found us again, sharp with frustration. But for those brief moments, under the fluorescent lights and surrounded by strangers, we felt like kids again. Not performers. Not survivors. Just kids.

And I needed to feel like one. Like a kid. So I begged Mother to take me to Disneyland for my birthday. "It'll make us happy. And happy people attract happy situations," I told her, parroting her own gospel back to her, hoping it would work.

I didn't care about the rides. I just wanted to be around kids my age. To laugh until I cried. To eat an ice cream cone in the sun without guilt gnawing at the edges. I wanted what I saw in flashes; those children at the birthday parties I performed at, sticky with frosting and free in a way I wasn't. Sometimes they'd ask me to join them, tug at my hand or call me over to the bounce house. But Mother would shoot me a look before they could finish their sentence. I wasn't there to play. I was there to work.

Mother hesitated when I asked about Disneyland. Her jaw tensed, but her eyes softened. After a moment, she nodded. "All right," she said. "After all the hustle. We'll reward ourselves."

Andy was livid. "This is our only shot at getting an apartment," he snapped. "We finally have a few thousand saved and you're blowing it."

"We will earn it back," Mother shot back. "Besides, it's three against one." Glap was already next to her, silent but aligned with what Mother wanted.

Andy deflated, anger giving way to resignation.

We took a taxi all the way to Anaheim, counting folded bills with dirty fingernails. To cut corners, we shared two tickets between four of us, slipping them back through the gates like seasoned thieves. We snuck Shayla into the hotel beneath someone's oversized hoodie, holding our breath through every hallway. For three days, reality loosened its grip.

For once, I felt like a girl who had just turned eleven.

But even then, watching the other kids, their faces flushed with sugar and sunshine, I felt something sharper underneath the joy. I didn't belong to them. I felt older. Even with the mouse ears and churro dust on my fingertips, I knew I was never going to be one of them.

Still, for a moment, I let myself pretend. We all did. We let ourselves believe that maybe this marked a shift. That maybe the worst was behind us. That we were inching toward something easier.

The streets began to quiet after my birthday week; the holidays were over. The tourism of Hollywood Boulevard faded into the hiss of wind and the shuffle of hurried footsteps. My eyes stung from the icy gusts that whipped past my scarf, turning my cheeks raw and red. People moved faster now, heads down, hands buried in their pockets, ignoring the sound of our music. The tip jar sat there like an open mouth, barely fed. The money ran out.

We stayed at Edwidge's longer than we'd stayed anywhere. Her own bills started to pile up. Then one morning, taped crookedly to the doorframe, the thing we'd been silently bracing for: eviction notices.

And so, the cycle began again.

Stay. Flee. Repeat.

15

THE CHEESE

The Scientology Celebrity Centre stood just a mile from where we performed, rising like a storybook castle in the middle of Hollywood. At night, it glowed with an eerie sort of majesty. Gothic windows lit from within, casting warm amber shadows across its perfectly manicured lawn. It looked like it didn't belong in this city. As we walked there, streets around it reeked of urine and exhaust, littered with crumpled flyers and lost souls. Maybe that's what made it so magnetic. It looked like an escape hatch from the world we were trapped in.

A sign out front told us exactly what it was: Celebrity Centre.

Inside, the place felt even more surreal. The floors reflected everything like water. Dark wooden hallways flickered with torchlight. Portraits of famous people I didn't recognize loomed from the walls, their smiles frozen in glossy perfection.

Katherine was the first Scientologist I met. She set up her booth just a few feet away from our usual performance spot, a table draped in a bright red cloth. She was blonde and magnetic, with an easy confidence and a warmth that felt practiced but effective. She told us she lived in a beautiful building—for free. I realized they might pull us from the sidewalk and plant us somewhere permanent.

Katherine offered me a "free stress test", which is conducted using a device called an electropsychometer, which is used during a process they call auditing. She placed two metal cylinders in my hands and turned on the machine. Its needle jumped erratically, like it was panicking for me.

At first, the questions were soft.

"What's your name?"

"How old are you?"

But they turned hard.

"Do you feel like no one understands you?"

"Are you afraid of failing?"

"Do you think your family holds you back?"

I didn't know what felt stranger—the way the questions cut straight through me, or the way Katherine seemed to take comfort in watching it all unfold.

"You've been carrying a lot of emotional charge," she said, her voice syrupy. "But don't worry, we can help you strengthen your mind. Guide you toward success. Toward who you're really meant to be."

Soon we found ourselves back at the Celebrity Centre, this time for an acting class they invited us to. Even though none of us acted, we went anyway. We just wanted to show face, to prove we were serious. We handed over fifty dollars from our meager savings without hesitation. There were maybe twenty of us in the office that was cloaked in dark wood from floor to ceiling. Shelves heavy with thick Scientology books lined up, awards arranged next to them. The instructor, who was supposed to be someone prominent, promised connections, auditions, transformation.

But slowly, the charm began to fray. The invitations turned into expectations. The courses multiplied. So did the promises. And then came the price tags. Thousands for sauna treatments, stacks of cash for mysterious supplements labeled "Purification" that we were told to take without question.

The free housing? It was never really free.

During what would become our final visit, Glap accidentally knocked over one of the prestigious L. Ron Hubbard awards with his elbow. It crashed to the floor, a loud, crystalline shatter that silenced the room. Everyone turned. A Scientologist stepped forward, calm and composed, but his eyes betrayed him.

"It's all right," he said smoothly.

But it wasn't. Not really.

The moment landed like a crack in the dream, and something in us shifted. It broke the trance. Embarrassed, we didn't return.

And when they realized how homeless we actually were, despite how carefully we dressed, how well we carried ourselves, they stopped trying to reel us back in. No more street encounters. No more pressure. We weren't worth the investment any more.

All summer like unwitting mice lured by the scent of cheese, we slipped too easily into the traps others set for us. Red Beard, some self-proclaimed talent agent with a scruffy orange beard and a glossy business card was one of them. Sometimes these agents led to real gigs, but most of the time they wanted compensation. A cut. Control. And that was always a no from Mother. She wanted help, sure but not if it meant splitting the earnings.

Red Beard said he didn't want anything. Just wanted to "help." He offered to submit Glap and Andy's photos to modeling agencies, no strings attached. I was eleven. I stood straighter than usual that day, hoping maybe he'd look at me too. But his smile, full of yellow, corn-kernel teeth was aimed only at my brothers. A few days later, Glap and Andy met him at a motel off the boulevard. They came back quiet, carrying an envelope filled with glossy 4x6 prints, images of them in underwear, posing awkwardly on a cherry-colored bedspread, hands placed over their crotches like props.

"Never again," Andy muttered, his face tight as he tossed the envelope onto the table.

Mother leaned over my shoulder, flipping through the photos. Her voice stayed flat. "Why'd you take them if you didn't feel comfortable?"

"I didn't know," Glap snapped, grabbing the envelope back. "I thought he was legit. He said it was normal. Told me to grab my junk and look sexy, models do it all the time."

He paused, then added quietly, "Yeah. I think we got fooled."

During that time, we received housing from a taxi driver we knew—a kind man named Harvinder from India, who always gave us rides for less than most. He understood struggle. He was waiting for his wife to join him in the States, both of them suspended in the slow, aching drift of the green card process. Immigrants looked out for other immigrants.

Sensing the weight we carried, he convinced his brother—a real estate investor—to let us stay in one of his vacant houses. The place was a hollowed-out shell tucked deep in the valley, forty-five minutes from Hollywood by car. Harvin would drive us back and forth in his taxi for forty dollars. No electricity. No running water. The walls were yellowed with age, the floors layered in dust, our voices echoing off every empty corner. But it was a roof.

Our first night there, we huddled around the soft flicker of a single candle. We laughed at the absurdity of it all, how life kept twisting, how we somehow kept landing upright.

At night, my brothers and I would climb onto the roof, chasing the only breeze the place seemed to offer. We lay on our backs in the open dark, the stars blinking overhead. The cool air felt like mercy after the oven of the day.

We told stories. We cracked jokes. For a while, we forgot how little we had.

Still, I carried a dream tucked deep in my chest. A house like this perched high in the hills, where you could see all of Los Angeles spilling out below like a sea of stars. A house like the ones that belonged to the people we performed for at their private parties.

That dream kept me going. Through the exhaustion. Through the invisible grind of trying to be seen in a world that barely looked.

But when they did look, when they stopped, when they watched, when they clapped and smiled and their eyes caught mine, that was when I felt it. Someone finally seeing the person I was underneath it all, not the desperation, the chaos, not the suitcases by my feet, but me.

Winter had just begun to peel the warmth off the boulevard when Vincent Gallo stopped to watch us perform. He didn't move much, just stood there in the cold: tall, lean, tousled curls catching the glow of the Pantages Theater like a halo gone crooked. Just by the way he lingered, you knew he was someone.

Afterward, he walked up to my brothers, and they lit up like machines hitting the jackpot. His number scribbled on a scrap of paper felt like a door. Another breadcrumb. And we followed. It was because of him we left the house in the valley, the one with no water. He knew someone at the Highland Gardens Hotel and talked them into letting us stay, pay in fragments, when we could.

The Highland Gardens was a fever dream. A time capsule wrapped in cracked tile and swaying palms, caught between glamour and decay. The lobby still carried the bones of elegance, mirrored walls and velvet chairs. Past the desk, the hotel opened into courtyard rooms tucked around a pool. Women in sunglasses flipped through worn magazines on lounge chairs. Kids shrieked as they cannonballed into shallow water. Fathers played slow games of ping pong under a shaded awning near the humming vending machines.

Some people had moved in decades ago and never left. Weekly rates became lifetimes. The place had ghosts. Artists, junkies, dreamers who'd come for the weekend and never left. Janis Joplin died there. Vincent was an actor, director, provocateur. He was known for being offensive, but that's maybe why we liked him. Some people didn't like us much either. He brought us guitars, coats, little luxuries wrapped in soft plastic bags. Took us to dinner, ordered steak before we could protest about being vegan.

"How could you not eat steak?" he'd say incredulously.

Mother leaned in and whispered, sharp as a pin:

"Eat it. Don't upset him."

He reminded her of my father. Same dark hair, same light blue eyes. She hung the things he gave us on the wall like in a shrine. I recognized the way she looked at him, because I looked at him just the same. When he asked me to sing "Moon River" with him in San Francisco—me in a wedding dress, barefoot, eleven—I said yes. He laughed at the idea, said the crowd would hate it. That was the point. He liked being hated. There was something in us he saw: something raw, something already broken, maybe even something honest. Whatever it was, he kept coming back.

But not forever.

The bills returned, as they always did. Desperation made the decision for us. We listed the vintage guitar he'd gifted us and watched it disappear into the hands of a stranger in exchange for a quick deposit.

The fallout came in a single message. Vincent's name lit up the screen.

You promised you'd keep it.

No anger. No explanation. Just that.

A sentence that landed like a slammed door.

After that, he vanished.

And as much as I hated watching people take advantage of those reaching for a hand, I knew we were the hand. Gripping. Tugging. Clinging to whoever reached back.

Sometimes, we didn't just hold on. We climbed. Over arms. Over backs. Stepping on shoulders, stepping on heads, just to get a little higher.

We became Hollywood.

16

THE SOULS

Henry, the Highland Gardens hotel employee with yellow-toned blonde hair and a dark mustache, flashed us a grin every time we dragged ourselves through the lobby after a long night of street busking. He always found a reason to linger, striking up new conversations that stretched longer than we could afford to entertain. At first, he was curious about what brought us here to L.A. Then, he'd ask, "What about your mother? Why isn't she working?" I met his eyes, steady but tired.

"Mother doesn't speak English so nobody would hire her," I said. At least that's what Mother would tell me.

Our hotel room was like a one-bedroom apartment, timeless, furnished with worn, brown-clothed sofas and a television. A round glass table to the right with black padded chairs in the kitchen. Small hallway leading to a bathroom and a bedroom with two queen beds and a cabinet. It smelled stale and looked seedy. The place had a quiet mood, like when you first enter a room where two people are discussing private matters and stop talking to preserve their secrets. But it was home.

Andy's ear was pressed against the wall.

"What are you doing?" I pressed my ear against the wall too.

THE SOULS

The muffled and distant sound of a woman moaning and the bed squeaking was traveling through the wall. "Ew, go to sleep you pervert. I'm going to tell Mother."

"Okay, okay." Andy went to sleep.

We hung around the pool on Mondays, our new day off after too many fevers and sore throats made it clear we couldn't keep pushing without breaking. Our bodies had drawn the line for us. Even then, we never swam. We didn't own swimsuits and none of us really trusted the water. Still, we lingered by the edge. I'd settle into one of the faded lounge chairs with a secondhand novel cracked open in my lap, reading until the words turned to fog.

Andy stumbled upon a camera by the pool, left behind by a Japanese couple who'd been lounging there earlier in the afternoon. It sat unattended on a sun-bleached lounge chair, almost begging to be claimed. Without hesitation, we pocketed it.

We used it to shoot our CD cover, just the same five songs we'd been performing on the street, rough and unpolished, recorded with a laptop and a single cheap mic. We posed with our instruments and even though I was only twelve now, I had high heels on that Mother bought me.

In the dim hotel room, I snapped pictures of myself with the camera. Each click took something from me before I even knew it.

I applied the makeup carefully, the way I'd seen women do in the magazines scattered by the pool. I pressed my arms together to fake cleavage, tilted my chin just right. Some were almost nude. My child's face became something older in the lens. I uploaded the photos onto our cheap laptop and watched the comments roll in.

Beautiful.

Sexy.

Where do you live?

I even thought I'd found connection on these social media pages, a group of friends my age on the page, young girls posting their own photos. But the excitement quickly faded when I called one of the girls only to find out it was a grown man. Men alone in dark rooms, the flickering blue light of their monitors reflected in their glasses. Their fingers hovered over my image, clicking, scrolling, pausing. Leaning closer, their breath catching as they lingered on the curve of my shoulder, the tilt of my hips. In reality, I was being carved out by the unseen eyes.

When Andy saw the pictures, he lost it.

"What the hell were you thinking?" he barked.

I shrugged. "It's for my modeling career," I said, flatly, like it was obvious.

Mother didn't say anything. She had stopped arguing with me a long time ago. She sat at the kitchen table, quietly painting, her eyes following me.

Glap tried, once. Said something about me being too young. But even he gave up.

I was no longer a child to be raised. The roles had reversed. I was the breadwinner now. The one who made the money. And they, the boys, the adults, were listening to me.

When we were done, we slipped the camera back to Henry at the front desk. He raised an eyebrow but didn't ask questions. He never did. One night, we came home late and found the courtyard in chaos. The pool at the Highland Gardens had been overrun by punk kids, loud and wild, flinging themselves off balconies into the water like it was a dare. Music blared from a tinny Bluetooth speaker, punk rock, all static and thrashing guitars, the kind that made your chest vibrate.

Their laughter echoed off the walls, bouncing between the balconies and the broken tiles like ghosts of a party that never ended. Henry stood near the front desk, helpless and small, watching the scene unfold like a man watching a house burn down from inside.

That morning, we left for work early, still yawning from the restless night of loud music that had made sleep impossible. The pool water had turned cloudy and a few guests were already swimming. By evening, blue and red lights flickered against the pale walls of the hotel. The scene unfolded slowly, like something out of a fever dream: a body bag being wheeled across the concrete, its shape unnervingly human, the zipper glinting in the fading sunlight. Police officers surrounded the pool, their movements deliberate, their expressions hard as they taped off the area with yellow ribbons that fluttered faintly in the breeze. I didn't hear anything, no screams, no sobbing, just the low hum of police radios. I heard that it had been a sixteen-year-old boy they'd pulled from the pool, his limbs stiff, his body stuck in a sitting position. His wallet and phone were gone. I couldn't stop thinking about it; how many teenagers had been at the party, the noise, the chaos, and yet not a single person noticed him disappearing beneath the surface, sinking to the bottom. The thought made my stomach turn. Mother, sensing my unease, told me to go inside the hotel room. She didn't want this bad energy clinging to us for the rest of the week.

The morning after, a man knocked on our door. He was middle-aged, with tired eyes and a weary expression. "I'm his uncle," he said, voice trembling. "Do you know what happened? Did you see anything?" But all I could think of was the body bag. The hotel had claimed another soul. We had to get out before we were next.

17

THE LOVE

For a long time, I hated L.A. The sprawling highways, the noise, the way the city seemed to be slowly choking on its own pollution. But something shifted the day we drove through the valley in a BMW owned by an older man named Joel and his son Joey, heading to a pool party with people we'd never met. It was sometime in May, warm enough to roll the windows down, the scent of sunburnt grass drifting in as we wound our way through the hills. They stretched out endlessly, covered in a patchwork of golden grasses and deep green shrubs, like the folds of a vast, rumpled quilt draped across the earth. The sunset cast a spotlight of gold and pink across the sky, the colors spilling out, marinating our minds, pulling us into its fever dream. I'd dream of this often for years to come.

We met Joel and Joey on Hollywood Boulevard, and a few days later, they picked us up from the hotel in the BMW. Joel talked the whole drive, gripping the steering wheel with one hand and the past with the other. Stories spilled from him like old tape, Bon Jovi, backstage passes, nights that bled into mornings. His voice rasped like it had been sanded down by years of smoke and shouting over amps, but he spoke like he still mattered.

People seemed to shrink in his presence, not because of who he was, but because of the myth he'd built around himself. He walked like someone who had headlined arenas, even if the truth was far less glamorous. He was a retired rockstar who had a glimpse of fame that didn't last.

"You've got real talent," he said to Glap, who was sitting in the passenger seat, clapping a hand on his shoulder. "Could use a guitarist like you. You too, Andy." He looked in the rear view mirror at him. His eyes never landed on me. But the eyes of the boy in the backseat did. Joey sat beside me, quiet, blond hair falling into his eyes as he kept brushing it away. His knees knocked into mine when the car hit a pothole and he'd move them away quickly.

I kept my pink sunglasses on, stared straight ahead. But I saw him. I felt every curious glance, every twitch of his hands, every breath held too long.

He'd been in the crowd the night before, I remembered because for the first time in a long while, I felt nervous to sing. Now, in the hush between Joel's stories, the boy turned to look at me. And in that flicker of a moment, something settled in my chest. Maybe this was why we'd come here to Los Angeles. Maybe this was what made it all worth it.

"Can we stop by a store? We don't actually have swimsuits," Glap asked.

Joel blinked, as if that hadn't occurred to him. "Oh. Of course," he said.

At Walmart, my brothers scattered toward the men's section. I wandered through rows of swimsuits. I settled on an orange bikini, the kind printed with oversized flowers.

As I turned to head toward the cart, I sensed Joey nearby, just a few paces behind, pretending not to follow. We passed the underwear aisle, and a bright orange thong caught my eye. I didn't hesitate. I added it to the pile. I wanted to seem mature, not like an ordinary child. Joel's voice came from behind me. "You sure you want that?" His eyebrow lifted, looking over at Mother. "Aren't you a little too young for that?"

"It's okay," she said. Joel gave a short shrug and didn't argue. At the checkout, he paid without another word.

Later, in the hills of Chatsworth, we passed a gated community tucked into the hillside, and for a moment, I thought that's where we were headed. But just past it, he turned right into a sprawling apartment complex, sun-bleached and humming with old air conditioners.

He pulled up in front of the pool house, the kind shared by too many tenants, and cut the engine. We changed in the public restrooms, the tile cold underfoot, the mirrors warped at the edges. Outside, Mother arranged snacks on a table near the jacuzzi, careful with the placement. I watched her from a distance and, for a second, I saw the version of her I remembered from Germany. Joel and Joey were already splashing in the pool, their laughter echoing off the stucco walls. "How deep is it?" I asked, dipping my toe into the icy water.

"It's shallow here. Gets deeper at the other end," Joel said, turning toward me. He did a double take, and then leaned in too close.

"That bikini looks sexy on you."

Before I could react or process, Andy's voice broke the air.

"Tanja can't swim," he blurted, flinging his shirt toward a plastic chair. It missed and nearly landed in the food. Mother snapped at him, irritated, and I laughed under my breath at his clumsiness.

"I can teach her. Let's go," Joel said, gesturing toward the water.

I hesitated. Then nodded.

In the pool, he kept his voice low and steady, telling me to lie flat on my stomach, keep my head up, relax. I tried. But the moment the water touched my face, panic shot through my chest. I flailed, coughing, arms slapping against the surface.

Joel's hand rested on my back. A gentle pat, a hush in his voice.

"There, there. Let's try again."

The second time, I eased into the water more slowly, letting Joel guide me with a steady hand. He showed me how to paddle, how to move my arms in rhythm with my legs, but all I could focus on were his hands around my hips, the press of his torso brushing against my ribs. Discomfort crept in like a slow leak, but I swallowed it down, tried to stay inside the motion, the learning.

"Maybe start with snorkels—Joey , grab those snorkels," Joel called out. Joey , still crunching chips by the table, wiped his hands on his shorts and tossed them over.

"Here," Joel said, pressing them into my hands. "Use these to get used to the water. Forget your head for now, just float."

THE LOVE

I slipped them on and let myself drift.

And then, like light cracking into an old reel, a memory rolled in: five-year-old me, squealing in delight as my father strapped me into the child seat behind his bike. Wind whipped through my hair as we sped toward the local pool, him surprising me with a swim on a hot day after work.

When I finally surfaced, the sky had shifted, soft streaks of pink and light blue bleeding across the horizon as the sun faded. Mother and Joel were crouched by the pavement, drawing with crayons like children, their heads bent close together. My brothers tossed a ball near the pool's edge. As the air began to cool, I slid into the warmth of the jacuzzi.

Footsteps echoed from the restroom and I looked over to see Joey walking towards me. He dropped into the water across from me, the tide his entrance created lapping gently against the tiles. A smirk played at the corners of his mouth. We held each other's gaze awkwardly.

"So," he said, "you want to be a singer?"

I nodded. "Yes. And you?"

I waited for something wild. Something artistic. A spark that matched my own.

"I'm focused on school." He said. I'm taking a year off after high school, then getting my degree." The words dripped with a tone that bordered on self-righteous. I was taken aback that a boy like him would want to go to school. I just nodded, but didn't add anything further.

The moment we returned to the Highland Gardens Hotel, a knock rattled through the room.

I tiptoed to the door and peered through the peephole. There he was: the Highland Gardens manager, arms crossed.

"Your payment's overdue," he said flatly when I made Andy crack the door open. "If it's not settled by morning, you'll have to leave."

He didn't wait for a response. He just turned and walked away.

We owed over $800.

I opened the laptop. My fingers hovered over the keys for a moment before I started typing. I told myself I was reaching out to Joel for help, maybe he knew someone, somewhere, who could put us up for a few days. But that wasn't the whole truth. Not really.

I wanted to stay with them, mostly to be near Joey .

When I drafted the email to Joel, I paused before attaching the photo. It was just my face. I'd chosen it carefully: parted lips, hair tucked behind one ear, the soft bathroom light catching the slope of my cheekbone.

I was at that age now where I'd started realizing things, how people gazed at me. How I was finally being noticed. How it could open doors.

My reflection in the dark screen watching me do it.

I hit send, then shut the laptop.

Joel replied quickly. He called me beautiful. He'd be by in the morning. Said he'd take us in. Relief poured through the room like air rushing into a windowless space. We leapt into action, throwing our things into bags, collecting scattered shoes and half-folded clothes.

I couldn't wait to see Joey again.

18

THE SMILE

Joel's two-bedroom apartment in the scorched hills of Chatsworth became our new home in the summer of 2008. Joel claimed one room, Joey the other, and the rest of us spilled into the living room. Faded tapestries of Bob Marley clung to the walls, their edges fluttering with the lazy sigh of wind that slipped through cracked windows. The L-shaped couch became our bed. Mother stretched herself across the horizontal cushion, I curled up along the vertical like a cat, and my brothers claimed the floor next to all our boxes.

Meanwhile, Shayla kept a cautious distance from the cat—whose name was stupid—a grey skittish creature with jittery paws and wild yellow eyes. It hissed and swiped every time she inched too close. Across the room, Tony, one of Joel's oddball Puerto Rican friends, had taken up permanent residence in the battered old chair, lounging like he paid rent there. His thick black curls spilled over his shoulders in a tangled mess, and his camo cap, always cocked to the side, looked like it'd been through more than he had. He swore up and down he'd served in the army, though no one could ever confirm that, and his eyes kept flitting around the room like he was seeing ghosts the rest of us couldn't see. Tony was always breaking into a high-pitched, cartoonish voice when he got excited. Like someone yanked a character out of a TV show and dropped him in our living room. "¡Oye, chica! Come here!" he hollered, waving me over with a crooked grin. "Let me show ya this move I learned in the service. Real slick self-defense trick, watch closely!"

I hesitated but walked over, curious despite myself. His wild eyes gleamed as he demonstrated a clumsy, exaggerated kick, but his aim was all over the place. Instead of hitting air, his boot slammed into my pubic bone with full force. Pain shot through me as I yelped, doubling over. "I didn't mean it!" Tony squawked, hands flapping like panicked birds. "I thought you'd move! You gotta be quick, girl, quick!" His voice reached an absurdly high pitch as he apologized.

Our new home sat miles away from our usual busking spots. The taxi fares were bleeding us slow—a hundred dollars just to make the round trip to Hollywood. After the 2008 recession, the money had thinned out like the crowds. The momentum was fading and we weren't pulling in nearly what we used to. On weekdays, we stayed put in Chatsworth, our heads bent over crumpled bills and notepads, running the math over and over. The cost to go was more than we could make. And so, we waited. We weren't sure for what, we had no plan, but maybe we were hoping something with Joel would come out of it.

With the extra time, I started going to Joey's baseball games. I once tried to sit through one, but the sun and the slow crawl of the sport lulled me right to sleep. Afterward, Joel took us to grab groceries and juice for us from a nearby grocery store. He moved through the aisles, slipping bottles into the bottom rack of the cart and breezing through checkout without ringing them up. Later that day, I was sprawled out in front of the PlayStation 2, a gift from Tony, who, despite all his chaos had his own odd way of showing care. The console was his offering because he knew how much I loved the old Tomb Raider games, something Father had once introduced me to back when things were different.

As Lara Croft scaled cliff faces on the screen, a young boy appeared in the entry doorway.

"No way!" he gasped, staring at me like I wasn't real.

"See? I told you." Joey appeared next to him, his smile smug. I shot him a puzzled look.

It wasn't until later that I found out Joey had told his school friend I was his girlfriend.

Joey plopped down next to me, spreading his math homework across the coffee table with a grunt. "I'm stuck on this one," he muttered, nudging the notebook toward me. Sometimes we'd work on the problems together. I still had it in me to solve equations for him.

But there was always an edge to Joey , a current of tension just under the surface, like still water hiding a rip. Even in the quiet moments, I could feel it; the way his jaw tightened when something didn't click right away, the way his leg bounced restlessly, like he was trying to shake something off, hold something in. It was the same edge I'd seen when his temper snapped out of nowhere, like that time he grabbed a knife and chased my brothers and me around the living room, laughing manically like it was all a game. It was terrifying. When we were outside climbing the cherry trees, we'd pop the fruit straight from the branches in our mouths, maggots and all. In those moments, away from his dad, Joey would open up. He told me stories about his playboy mother, lost to addiction, using him like currency for drugs on a trail of unstable homes. Joey and I understood each other in ways that didn't need words.

Just as we began climbing down the tree, Joel's voice cut through the air—he must've just gotten home from work at Aerospace. "Get in the car!"

We jogged toward the parking lot, dust kicking up around our feet, and again, his voice came, more impatient this time. "Let's go!" He unlocked the car with a flick of the wrist, the keys jangling in the hand inked with a rosary.

"Where are we going?" Joey asked, tugging open the back door.

"To the dentist."

"To do what?"

"What do you think, smart ass? To take Tanja to get her teeth cleaned." Joel gave him a look. Joey instinctively turned to me, his eyes drifting to my mouth. I caught the glance and quickly pressed my lips together, heat creeping into my face. The cavities on both my canine teeth were hard to miss. Blackened stumps where bright, white teeth were supposed to be. I hated that feeling of being exposed, of having my flaws seen up close, but at the same time, a strange warmth settled over me. I liked the idea of being taken care of, of someone noticing and wanting to fix what was broken, even if it was just my teeth.

After the dentist, when my teeth were finally cavity-free from all the polishing they did, Joel called me over to his bathroom, the one that connected to his bedroom. "Come here," he said, holding out a new toothbrush with a dollop of toothpaste already waiting on it. He grabbed his own and did the same. "Watch me," he said, brushing his teeth with slow, deliberate strokes. He tilted his head slightly, opening his mouth just enough so I could see how he reached the back. "Now, your turn." I mimicked his movements.

"Good," he said with a smile as I rinsed my mouth. He picked me up without warning and twirled me in the air, my squeals echoing through the room. With a playful grin, he flopped back onto his bed, and I landed on top of him, giggling as he started tickling my ribs. The room smelled faintly of incense, and the golden lamplight bathed his face in a soft, warm glow. "You're so beautiful," he mumbled, his tone suddenly quieter, more serious. "Tanja—"

Just then, the door creaked open, and Glap walked in. He paused awkwardly, his eyes flicking between us before retreating without a word. Joel sat up abruptly, his playful mood evaporating as if someone had flipped a switch. "I'm hungry," he said, standing up quickly. "Let's see what there is to eat."

In the kitchen, Mother was stirring a big pot of our usual cheap dinner: spaghetti mixed with vegan mayonnaise, ketchup, and cheese. Lately, we'd started letting dairy slip into our diet here and there. We sat on the floor to eat since there was no dining table, cross-legged around mismatched bowls.

"It tastes good," Joey said, chewing with his mouth half full, "but in a weird way."

Mother laughed, and I think she was just happy to be feeding someone new.

Even though living with other people had its fun moments, weekends were rough.

The bass thundered through the thin walls of Joel's apartment as we stepped inside after a long Saturday of street busking, the vibrations of explosions and tense music rattling in my chest. "Hey, guys," Joel and Joey called from the couch, barely glancing up from the screen.

We quietly settled into whatever space was left, waiting for the film to end so we could finally sleep. Joel didn't care; he made it known that it was still his apartment and he wouldn't be accommodating it to our schedule. The volume stayed up, the explosions kept coming. We exchanged weary glances, but no one dared to complain.

Finally, at 2 am, the credits rolled and the screen faded to black. They disappeared into their rooms, and I plopped onto the couch, too tired to do anything but close my eyes.

On Sunday, it was Mother's forty-fourth birthday and we had planned to celebrate after our performances with pizza and a vegan cake. By 11 pm, we were packing up our equipment on the Hollywood sidewalk, the night air warm against our sweaty backs, amps buzzing faintly as they cooled.

Then came the sudden burst of red and blue.

Andy's soft "Oh no" barely rose above the hum of the engines as three cop cars pulled up behind us.

Officer Rose emerged from the lead car, his boots grinding the pavement with deliberate weight. His belly pressed against the buttons of his uniform. His beard was salt-and-pepper, neatly trimmed, and his dark eyes scanned the scene with an air of practiced authority. He looked like the kind of man who liked rules more than people.

"Didn't I warn you against playing here last time?" he barked.

"We're just finishing up," Glap said, crouched down, gently looping cables with a kind of calm to display we didn't want any trouble.

But Rose wasn't there to be calmed.

"It's nearly midnight. Where are your parents?" His eyes landed on me.

I pointed across the plaza toward Mother, perched quietly on a bench near the Highland Center, her arms crossed, watching us the way she always did.

"Right there."

Rose sneered. "You Germans never learn, do you? I can get you deported."

My jaw clenched, heat crawling up the back of my neck. This wasn't new. Just weeks earlier, another officer had cornered me, waving paperwork and spitting threats, claiming he could deport us for performing on the public sidewalk. I was so pissed at them messing with my livelihood, I snapped—told him if he tried, I'd take his baton and kill him with it. The words had flown out like sparks off a pavement. Glap stared at me, wide-eyed, as did the officer I was talking to. Glap knew the only reason I'd said it with such boldness was because he'd once told me kids don't get arrested. That officer backed off after scolding me and never bothered us again.

My defiance surged once again. "So why are the breakdancers allowed to perform but not us?" I snapped, pointing toward the group spinning nearby.

"They're not either," Officer Rose replied. "But we get complaints about your group."

Then, without missing a beat, he pointed straight at Glap. "Arrest him."

Two other officers moved like machinery. In a blink, Glap's arms were wrenched behind his back, the handcuffs snapping shut. I rushed to his side, grabbed his flip phone from his pocket and handed it to Mother, who had just walked up.

"Step away," Officer Rose commanded.

"No," I said, planting my feet. "I'm not leaving him."

"Move."

Something snapped inside me. "Isn't Rose a girl's name?" I shot at him. His hands were on me in an instant as he spun me around and slammed me against the cold metal of the police car. The cuffs bit into my wrists with a sting that sent panic surging through my chest. The crowd around us stirred, uneasy murmurs rising in volume.

"Release her! She's just a child!" someone shouted, their voice slicing through the tension. Out of the corner of my eye, I saw one of the breakdancers lift his phone, recording everything.

"Turn that off or I'll confiscate it," Rose barked, lunging toward him. Mother rushed over, her voice sharp with panic as she argued with him in German, pointing toward me locked in the back of the car. Her eyes were pleading, but Rose didn't flinch. Moments later, Andy was cuffed too.

The police began packing our equipment into their vehicles. I thrashed in the backseat, pounding my legs against the door with everything I had. "Let me out! Let me out!" I screamed, the metal vibrating under each kick. An officer swung the door open and growled, "Keep it up, and you'll regret it." I went still, my breath tight in my chest, and slumped back into the seat, defeated. Through the window, I watched Mother standing helpless as strangers yelled at the officers, their faces lit by the flashing red and blue.

Happy birthday, Mother. Your children are in jail.

Throughout the ride to the police station which was just a few miles away on Wilcox Avenue, I screamed in a high-pitched wail, doing everything I could to drive Officer Rose crazy. "Quiet down, you brat," he snapped.

When we finally arrived, he yanked the door open and dragged me inside. A cluster of officers looked up from their desks, then burst into loud laughter at the sight of him hauling in a pig-tailed child. They interrogated me for hours in a cold, windowless room. I didn't say a word. Not even when they tried to bribe me with snacks, bags of chips, a warm cookie, a soda slid across the table. I stared straight ahead, arms crossed, lips sealed. I stayed silent until they had no choice but to let me go.

There, in the fluorescent glow of the station lobby, I saw Mother, Joel, and Joey speaking with the receptionist. Mother used Glap's phone to call Joel and somehow managed to communicate her need for his help. She pulled me into her arms, wrapping me in a hug.

"Did they do anything to you?" she asked.

"No, nothing," I said.

Joel stood nearby, filling out the paperwork to post bail for Andy and Glap. I stepped back and held out my wrists, the bruises dark and blooming where the cuffs had dug in. "Look," I whispered. Joey grinned. "Wow, look at you badass," he said.

I turned to Joel, the question already forming. "What was my charge?"

"Minor out alone past curfew," he said, shaking his head.

"But Mother was there," I said, confused.

"They claimed she wasn't," Joel replied.

For days afterward, I made a point of showing off my wrist bruises to anyone who crossed my path. Neighbors, cashiers, even total strangers got a glimpse of the dark purple marks that curled around my skin like badges of honor. I'd tug up my sleeves with theatrical flair, presenting them as if they were proof of some heroic battle.

"They did this to me," I'd say, watching their faces closely.

But most people just blinked, unsure how to react. Their eyes flicked from the bruises to my face, their expressions caught somewhere between discomfort and confusion as I smiled.

We still tried to celebrate Mother's birthday the day after, laughing at the situation like we always did. After pizza, Joey and I huddled under a blanket on the floor. I leaned in closer, the air between us buzzing with nervous energy. My heart pounded in my chest.

"I have to tell you a secret," I whispered.

"What?" Joey smiled, but there was a flicker of uncertainty in his reddish-brown eyes, like he could feel something heavy coming.

The words caught in my throat, unable to break free. Instead, I slipped out from under the blanket, grabbed a piece of paper and a pen, and scurried back to our hidden world. My hand trembled as I scrawled my secret onto the paper, then tossed it to Joey like it was too hot to hold. As he unfolded the note, a rush of excitement overwhelmed me, and I screamed into a pillow, muffling the sound.

Joey smiled as he read, his eyes locking onto the words. I held my breath, waiting for him to say something for what seemed like forever. But before he could, our world shattered.

"What's going on here?" Joel yanked the blanket off us. He snatched the paper from Joey's hands, eyes scanning the confession where I'd poured out my feelings.

His face twisted.

"No way in hell!" he roared, his voice vibrating with fury. "A girl like you will never date a son like mine. He deserves better than a porn star street rat. I know what girls like you do to men." Something broke inside me.

"C'mon, Joey," he snapped, shoving his son toward the hallway. "Go clean your room or something." Joey hesitated, glancing back at me with pain in his eyes, but Joel's grip was too firm.

"No, no, no," Mother lifted her finger. "You cannot do this." She didn't just say it in German—she showed it. She reached out and gently patted Joey's head, a quiet gesture urging Joel to show love instead of control, to stop pushing his son around.

"Who are you to tell me how to raise my son?" Joel's rage spilled over. "Look at your own messed-up children."

When things cooled down, we all pretended none of it had happened. I avoided Joey 's eyes, and he avoided mine. I was in the bathroom, preparing for a bath, hoping for just a few minutes alone to cry. I had barely turned on the water when I heard Tony's uneven footsteps dragging down the hallway, heavy and clumsy after a night out.

Without warning, the bathroom door jolted.

"Hey, let me in!" he slurred, followed by a sharp, maniacal laugh.

My heart leapt. Panic surged through me like lightning. I threw my weight against the door as I pushed hard to keep it shut. His body slammed into the other side with drunken force. The door groaned under the pressure. "Tony, stop!" I screamed, voice cracking with fear. But he didn't stop. "Mother!" I yelled, but nobody came to help me. Then, suddenly, the pressure eased. His footsteps stumbled away, his laughter echoing faintly before dissolving into silence. I slammed the lock into place, my breath coming in short, shallow gasps. My hands shook uncontrollably as I backed away from the door.

Joel also seemed to take a certain pleasure in tormenting me, dropping cruel comments like daggers. "Joey's got a new girlfriend at school," he'd say casually.

Every time he said it, it felt intentional, like he wanted to twist the knife and remind me that whatever fragile hope I had with Joey was crushed beneath his heel.

To escape the tension inside the apartment, Glap, Andy and I spent countless hours writing songs in the garage of Joel's apartment. The space, cluttered with old tools and half-collapsed boxes, became our creative haven. But even there, Joel couldn't help himself. He'd barge in uninvited, offering unsolicited opinions about how my vocals should sound, interrupting our flow and grinding the creative energy to a halt. One day, he even handed us a contract, proposing to become our manager. The terms were laughably one-sided, demanding I give up all rights to my songs. We declined immediately. The trust between us, already threadbare, began to unravel for good. After Joel realized he wasn't gaining anything by having us, things had taken a turn for the worse.

My brothers were at the pool and Mother was out on the balcony, lost in her painting. Her brush moved with ease, gliding across the canvas as she brought to life a pair of long, elegant legs in high heels. But the more I stared at it, the more it felt like it wasn't hers. It didn't feel like something she made for herself. It felt like an offering for Joel. Something she hoped would please him, something that might buy us more time here.

I walked into the living room, uneasy, as I always felt around him lately. Then I saw it—Joel hunched over our laptop, the one I had left on the desk the day before.

My stomach dropped. He was scrolling through my photo folder, his eyes gleaming with that unsettling, predatory look.

"What are you doing?" I yelled.

Joel didn't even flinch, still locked on the screen. "These pictures are hot," he said casually, like it was nothing. "Why don't we sell them somewhere, at least make some money?"

Panic rose in my chest. "Mother!" I called, trying to keep my voice steady.

She appeared in the balcony doorway, paintbrush tucked behind her ear, a streak of paint across her temple. Her eyes flicked from me to Joel, instantly alert.

"He's using my computer," I said in German, hoping Joel wouldn't understand.

"These pictures are hot," Joel repeated, completely unaware—or uncaring—of the discomfort thick in the room. I translated what he said, watching Mother's face harden yet she still carried her smile to appease him.

"No," she said.

Joel shrugged like it was no big deal, muttering under his breath as he moved aside, "Okay, missing out on big opportunities here."

Later that evening, when the only lights in the house came from the flickering TV and the reading lamp beside me, I was using the laptop in the living room. The usual hum of family life drifted through the apartment, voices, footsteps, the low murmur of the television. Without a word, he slid into the chair beside me. His hand warm and heavy landed on my bare thigh. Slowly, deliberately, his fingers began to creep upward.

"Stop touching me," I said, pushing his hand away.

"Ungrateful brat," he spat.

The room fell silent. Every pair of eyes turned toward us.

"You make me feel like a pervert!" he shouted, his voice thick with self-righteous rage. "How dare you speak to me like that after everything I've done for you?"

Then his eyes swept across the room. "You guys better be out by the time I return."

He stormed out, and Joey followed behind him like a shadow. The door slammed shut, echoing through the apartment like a final blow.

Mother stood across the room, her face unreadable, arms hanging limp at her sides. "Now we are homeless again," she muttered. "You shouldn't have reacted that way."

"But he was touching me." I wanted to scream.

Glap's voice broke through, uncertain. "Maybe he was just playing."

"Yeah, he's a horrible man," Andy said gently, trying to soften the blow. "It's okay. We'll find a different spot."

After a while of sitting there, staring into the darkness that stared back at me, I finally spoke.

"Okay." I smiled.

The same smile Mother smiled.

19

THE UNRAVELING

The rumble of an engine echoed down the street, cutting through the trees that were just beginning to turn copper. Tony rounded the corner in a beat-up U-Haul truck, Glap sitting beside him in the cab, his face barely visible behind the streaked windshield. The truck groaned to a stop, and without a word we sprang into action. Boxes, bags were hastily shoved into the trailer. There were only two seats in the front, reserved for Tony and Mother, while the rest of us were herded into the back. The door slammed shut with a deafening clang, leaving us in near complete darkness, save for thin slivers of light sneaking through the cracks. Mother had laid blankets and clothes on the cold, metal floor, trying to soften the harsh edges. We had no destination in mind but it didn't matter. We just needed to keep moving. Forward. Always forward.

Tony drove aimlessly, the hours blurring together. At some point, I must've drifted off, lulled by the truck's rhythmic bounce. But then, a sudden jolt snapped me awake. The trailer lurched violently to one side, the floor tilting at an impossible angle. Boxes and bags slid into us, and for a terrifying moment, I thought we were going to flip.

Then, just as suddenly, the trailer thudded back down. A screech echoed through the metal as the door rolled up, and the outside world spilled in with a rush of purplish dawn light.

"I always killed y'all!" Tony yelled, his voice unpleasant in the sudden quiet.

I blinked, momentarily blinded. The air, cool and crisp, rushed in, a sharp relief from the stifling heat we'd endured for hours.

"Wake up, fools!" He pounded on the truck wall. "We need a plan."

Bleary-eyed and stiff, we shuffled to the edge of the truck bed.

"What about a hotel?" Andy asked, his voice hoarse.

"That's not a long-term solution. Too expensive," Jimmy said dismissively. "Besides, I need to return the truck to U-Haul. We only rented it for a day."

"That's it! U-Haul!" Glap exclaimed, eyes lighting up. "Let's just rent a storage room."

"What?" Andy protested. "We can't sleep there. That's crazy."

"Why not? It's better than sleeping outside. Besides, it's only temporary until we save enough for an apartment," Glap reasoned.

"Okay," Mother agreed softly. "Let's try it."

"What about the cameras?" Andy asked, worry creasing his brow.

"Leave that to me," Glap smirked, a mischievous glint in his eye.

We found a storage facility close to the Pantages Theater, where we still performed. The building was large with windowless hallways. Our unit was dusty, medium-sized, and barely fit us and our belongings but it cost us less than sixty dollars a month.

Andy would leave the street busking show before the storage facility closed for the night, then unlock the door from the inside when we arrived late, after our performances, which were daily again now. The hardest part was avoiding the security cameras. We pressed ourselves against the walls, sliding through the hallway's back door. Every few days, we'd bathe in the public bathroom sink. We slept until six in the morning, then left the unit before the managers arrived. The exhaustion of sleeping five hours or less after performing was unbearable. The mile-long walk to find somewhere to sit felt like an eternity. When I finally collapsed on the bench at the Highland Center, I fell asleep within seconds. Mother's shoulder became my pillow until a security officer drove us away.

Henry, the blond employee with the dark mustache from the Highland Gardens Hotel was walking to work when he spotted us. "Where are you all staying these days?" Henry asked.

Glap explained our situation, how we were scraping by, and Henry paused, clearly thinking. After a long moment, he nodded. "I might be able to sneak you into a room tonight," he offered.

That evening, we carefully avoided the security cameras at the Highland Gardens Hotel and managed to stay in one of the rooms. The deal was simple: sleep on top of the covers, leave everything untouched for the next guest, and be out before the hotel staff arrived at 7 am. But sleeping in that bed was a small piece of heaven. I wished it could last forever.

Then Henry got fired. Apparently, we missed a camera and the manager of the hotel found out. Soon after, he asked if he could sleep in the storage unit with us. The request was strange, but considering how much he'd helped us, we agreed. "You don't want to stay at home?" Mother asked, and I translated. He shook his head, saying he preferred spending time with us. So, now there were five of us and a dog packed into the storage unit.

But Henry snored loudly, and it was already hard enough to sleep in that cold, metal box. We barely slept at all. Later, Henry confided that he was living in a homeless shelter, which made sense. It explained why he was so comfortable with our makeshift situation, probably more comfortable than where he was staying. Once we realized that, we didn't want to be associated with him any more and asked him to leave. Even though we didn't have a home, we weren't those kind of homeless people. We were homeless with a dream, with purpose.

I'm not sure how we got caught but the next morning, we were jolted awake by the sound of a man banging on the metal walls of the hallway. At first, we thought it was Henry being crazy but then we heard a man's voice. "You gotta get out," he shouted.

It was an employee. That was the end of that.

Standing at dawn, with nowhere to go, the sky heavy and grey, surrounded by others like me; lost, directionless, without a place to return to, and no hands left to reach for because every lifeline had already snapped. The weight of helplessness presses into the soul, an ache that's hard to name.

In Los Angeles, we were just . . . out there. I was leading the uphill climb with no summit, a journey that never promised rest, only more of the same, more of nothing. This moment marked the quiet end of everything we had.

On the bustling streets where we performed, a young Marilyn Monroe lookalike captured the attention of passersby. In her early twenties, her eyelashes fluttered like the delicate wings of a butterfly. Draped in the iconic white halter dress, she posed with effortless grace, her hand resting on her hip, embodying the timeless charm of the star. With a playful wave and a five-dollar bill held high like a flag, she beckoned tourists toward her for a photo, signaling her fee. Beside her stood Mina, another Marilyn, though older. Her thirties had added a sharpness to her smile, a wariness in her eyes as she kept her back to the freeloaders who tried to steal a photo without paying.

I had shared brief conversations with the younger Marilyn, Molly, over the past few months, but they always ended quickly. The words hung in the air, only to be cut short by Mother. "Time is money," she'd say.

When we spotted Molly again, basking in her spotlight of attention, I thought it harmless to ask for help. "Do you happen to have an extra room? We could really use one," I asked, the words slipping out before I could second-guess myself.

Molly hesitated, her green eyes flicking to Mina, her roommate, who smiled but the politeness in her smile barely concealed her reluctance. Molly's hand dipped into her satin purse, swollen with tips, and she pulled out a flip phone. "How about I take your number?" she suggested. "I'll let you know in a little while if we can help."

I handed her Glap's number, noticing how her gaze lingered on him for just a second too long. In that moment, a thought crossed my mind, would she want to be near him the way I wanted to be near Joey? And I was right. She did offer to let us stay.

Funny enough, the building Molly stayed in was the same orange building Edwidge had lived in. But this time, the two bedrooms belonged to Molly and Mina. Relegated to the living room, we made do with the couches and cushions.

Without her wig and makeup, Molly was even prettier: a frizzy-haired blonde girl with a surprisingly soft presence. She offered us something to drink as we settled in, ever gracious, and before long we were swapping stories about our nomadic existence. Tales that, by now, had become a strangely normal part of our lives. But for the people listening, they were still exciting, their mouths hanging open in disbelief as they heard about our unconventional existence, as if they couldn't quite grasp the reality of it. As I recounted our journey, Mina—a brunette with braided pigtails—tilted her head. "It's not something to be proud of," she said with a slight Dutch accent. "You talk about it like it's a badge of honor, but it's real hardship."

I was taken aback. For the first time, I saw our struggle through her eyes, no longer a triumph over adversity, but a wound I hadn't fully acknowledged.

Seeing Molly perform her street character over the next few weeks sparked something in me. Inspired, I decided to give it a try during the weekdays. Mina's sewing machine sat in the corner of the living room, its steady hum filling the quiet space as Mother worked late into the night with leftover fabric. The machine had seen better days, its chipped paint and squeaky pedal worn from countless unfinished projects, side gigs and dreams that never quite took off. Mother worked tirelessly, her fingers moving deftly over the fabric, the rhythm of the sewing machine steady and soothing. When she was done, Molly handed me an old blonde wig and a half-used tube of red lipstick. "Here," she said, stepping back to admire my costume. "Now you're Marilyn."

I joined Molly and Mina on Hollywood Boulevard. Shortly after I could feel the eyes on me, the heat rising in my body, but I kept my head high. When my dress fluttered upward from a subway vent, echoing that iconic scene, Mina's disapproval came fast and sharp.

"That's just wrong," she said. "You're a child, not a sex symbol."

"I think it's fine," Molly said, dismissing Mina's worries.

Mina didn't want to be seen with me. I could feel it in the way she pulled back, uneasy in my presence.

But I wasn't just a child.

I was something more. I was special.

Molly and I sat on the edge of the curb, counting the $200 we'd made after a long day of performing. When we got home, I handed it to Mother, watching Molly's face twist in unease. "Technically, that's your money," she muttered.

Slava and I only performed together on weekends now. The energy between us had hollowed out. We didn't want to do this any more. Andy had completely checked out. He disappeared behind the laptop most days, lost in his games, and for weeks, I had only seen the back of his head. His hair was messy, his focus unbroken. He didn't want to notice the real world any more. Mother was doing a similar thing through a different medium. She sat at the table, absorbed in her drawing and a world of her own making.

Then Mina's frustration boiled over like a pot left too long on the stove, her voice ringing through the small space. "Will you two do something for once?" she snapped, her eyes flashing toward Mother and Andy, whose idle hands had become a constant backdrop to our struggle. "Your little girl is out there working every day while you sit here. Who's the adult in this house?" She stormed off, the slam of her bedroom door echoing like a final punctuation to her words. Mother and Andy seemed to not hear her.

Meanwhile, Glap and Molly 's connection quietly blossomed in unseen spaces, like roots twisting beneath the soil, growing stronger with every passing day, unnoticed by the rest of us. They spent long nights together in her bedroom, their voices threading softly through the darkness, lingering until the first blush of dawn. At twenty-three, it was Glap's first romance, and he seemed to surrender to it, unaware of how the world around him was shifting. As their bond deepened, Mother began appearing in Molly's bedroom unannounced, her eyes narrowing at the way Molly's hand lingered on Glap's arm or how he leaned in just a little too close when she spoke. One afternoon, as Molly went to the kitchen, Mother spoke up.

"I know what you're doing," she said in German, her sharp smile belying the venom in her voice. It was sweet, yet dripping with contempt.

"What?" Molly asked, awkwardly laughing as she quickly retreated to her room.

"She's bewitching him," Mother said, her accusation casting Molly as the villain in the unraveling of her control. "You'll see. She'll tear us apart."

Fearful of the storm brewing just outside her door, Molly began locking herself in each night.

"You don't need to live in your mother's shadow," she told Glap, planting small seeds of defiance. She encouraged him to break free, to make choices that were his own. With each whispered word, and most importantly, hearing it from an outside perspective, those seeds took root in Glap's soul, slowly untangling him from the invisible chains that had bound him to Mother's grip. And in turn, it confirmed what I'd felt deep inside, that this wasn't how my life was supposed to go. It slowly untangled me from her too.

Mother was saying cruel things about them, words I tried desperately to block from my mind, until I could no longer keep quiet. "Don't talk about them that way," I snapped, my voice sharper than I intended.

Glap's smile widened, brighter than I'd ever seen it. It demanded something from me.

Mother glared at me, her eyes cold, muttering profanities in Russian under her breath, words I understood all too well. The sharpness of them wasn't just aimed at Molly, but at me too, for daring to take their side. Once again, I was the bad girl. The traitor.

Without another word, she rose from the table, her silence settling between us like a wall, and stopped speaking to me altogether.

Molly constantly made us realize how dysfunctional our family dynamic really was by her reactions. As she sat at our laptop one day, something inside her cracked open. Her calm demeanor shattered when she stumbled upon a folder, her hands trembling as she opened it. There, staring back at her, were photos—my photos. The color drained from her face, and before I knew it, she was on her feet, her voice shaking with disbelief. "Why do you have that?" she cried. Tears streamed down her face as she pulled up the images, one after another. "Delete it. All of it." Glap froze, confusion clouding his expression. Deep down, he knew something about it felt wrong, but he had convinced himself otherwise, numbed by the strangeness of our lives. Everything we did was unconventional, with boundaries blurred by Mother's strange rules. He had let himself believe this was okay too. And I could see it in his eyes—the shock that he wasn't his own person, he couldn't make his own choices or come to his own realizations. His mind, his very will, belonged to Mother.

But Molly wasn't having it. She was livid. "Don't you know we could all go to prison?" she screamed, her voice shaking. Glap stood there, helpless.

I stood there, silent, watching the scene unfold, and before I knew it, I started bawling too. I tried to hold my head up, to act like an adult, but the weight of it all felt too much for me to carry. I realized, in that moment, that I didn't understand the world at all.

Deep down, I longed for what Molly was demanding and that was the right to simply be a child.

We needed a reset. Molly offered to take us up northwest for Christmas, to the place where she had grown up. She told us about her guardian and uncle, Mark , who had raised her after her mother passed away from cancer. Molly, too, had lived an unconventional life—exposed to things far too early, something we had in common. Her father had been absent, and Mark , a friend of her mother's, had stepped in to raise her. We wanted Andy to come with us. We were a trio. "I'm not going," Andy said firmly, and Mother, standing beside him, nodded in silent approval. Then she turned to me, her finger pointing like a loaded weapon. "And neither are you." But Glap wasn't going to leave me behind.

I packed lightly, just the essentials, knowing I didn't have much—let alone winter clothes. Mother lingered in the kitchen, sensing something was off. We were in the living room when Glap told me to run. My heart leapt, and I bolted toward the front door. Glap turned right; I instinctively veered left. But the sound of Mother's footsteps echoed close behind me, her pace quickening. I raced into the dimly lit parking garage, breath ragged, panic clawing at my chest. My feet pounded against the cold concrete, and I sprinted up the stairs to the backyard of the complex. But when I reached the gate where I could see a car running, the gate itself wouldn't budge. I was trapped.

I spun around. And there she was. In her hand lifted high, something glinted, clenched so tight it seemed like an extension of her rage. Fear surged through me. I screamed. A piercing, desperate sound that seemed to rip through every inch of me.

Windows flicked open above me. "Hey, what's going on?" a neighbor called out. Mother froze, gathering herself in an instant. The fury melted away, leaving a cold, unsettling calm.

"Come back inside," she said, her voice eerily steady, as if nothing had happened but I could see the spit forming in the edge of her lips.

"No," I managed between sobs, my voice trembling but firm. "No, I won't." I looked at her—really looked—and saw not the mother I once knew, but the dark presence of a stranger.

Glap found me and led me out to Mark 's car. We were all shaken by what had just happened. Mother stood there, motionless, her eyes cold and unblinking as we drove away.

Whatever that scream had been, it left me raw and hollow, an emptiness that no time could fill. The world around me seemed muted, distant, like I was floating just outside of it. Something inside me had shifted, something irreversible, and I knew, in that moment, that I had been changed forever.

20

THE ESCAPE

We drove for sixteen hours straight, pushing northward as the world outside transformed. Snow fell thick and heavy, coating the landscape in a blanket of white. I had never seen anything like it before, this kind of snowstorm, one that turned the pine trees into towering, frozen ghosts. Mark , his big, broad frame filling the front seat, was the picture of rugged warmth in the midst of the storm. His bald head gleamed in the dim light, and his coarse, silver beard gave his face a soft, weathered look. He was chubby in a way that made him seem like someone you could lean on, both physically and emotionally.

Mark and I sat up front together and passed the time with music, filling the cabin with exaggerated opera voices that echoed through the air, our laughter blending with the steady hum of the tires crunching through the snow-packed roads.

But as the miles passed, the conversation took a darker turn. The topic of death came up, as it often did with me, something I found both fascinating and haunting.

Mark glanced over at me, his usual playful expression replaced with something more thoughtful. "You're an odd child."

165

But there was no judgment in his voice, just a quiet acknowledgment of the complex places my mind wandered. In his eyes, I wasn't just a kid lost in strange thoughts. I was something deeper, someone he understood, even if only a little, and I felt seen.

But in the backseat, there was a different kind of energy. Molly and Glap, wrapped up in each other, thought they were being discreet. They spooned beneath a shared blanket, their bodies pressed close together in a way that felt wrong in the confined space of the car. They thought their subtle movements were hidden, but nothing escaped my notice. The quiet intimacy they shared disturbed me, a closeness that felt out of place in a space where everything was too close, too exposed for someone like me.

Every time I saw Molly and Glap wrapped in each other's warmth, something inside me twisted. It wasn't just jealousy, it was deeper. It was the hatred I had unknowingly built, the way I had been conditioned to see intimacy as a threat, as something that eroded independence. And maybe I felt like I was losing Slava too. Instead, I stayed quiet, letting the bitterness coil tighter around my heart with each passing moment. I didn't know how to voice it, nor did I fully understand it.

When we arrived at Mark 's property shared with his brother Robert, the beauty of the place struck me immediately. It sprawled expansively, featuring a frozen lake that glittered faintly under the weak winter sun. The main house sat perched by the serene, ice-bound water and Robert's family lived in it. Mark 's own space was more modest; an apartment above the garage, set slightly apart from the main house. My brain struggled to comprehend how non-famous, non-wealthy people in America could live like this too.

Mia, Molly's sister, who looked like a near twin, same soft features and same bright green eyes, greeted me with a warm hug. The resemblance between them was uncanny, yet the subtle differences in their energy became clear. While Molly was rebellious, Mia was deeply rooted in family life. Mia gave me the haircut I had been craving, sharp, short, and fresh. With each snip of the scissors I felt lighter, and I knew it wasn't just the loss of my thick, weighted hair that had reached past my waist. When I looked in the mirror, it marked the beginning of something new.

FAME OR DEAD

Then Christmas came. It had been a long time since I'd seen a fully decorated tree in a home. I thought back to the twinkling lights reflecting off the ornaments, half of my father's face hidden behind the camera as he clicked away. I remembered my brothers setting up board games, their voices carrying through the house. The sweet scent of Mother's baking drifting through every corner. Here in Washington, I looked toward the window, watching the snow fall outside. In the reflection, Slava and I stood side by side, hands shoved into our sweatpants pockets, facing the tree without saying a word.

Our nervous systems softened in the ordinary. The need to become something, to be somewhere, faded. In the morning, we'd wake up and head to a local diner for pancakes, thick, warm stacks drenched in syrup and melting butter. Later, we'd wander through the snow, our breaths puffing in the cold as we passed fields dotted with slow-moving cows. Evenings unfolded in quiet contentment, spent watching movies while Molly lounged on the couch, a magazine in hand, her feet tucked beneath her like she had all the time in the world.

After two weeks, Mark drove us back to Los Angeles. As we stepped into Molly 's apartment, the contrast between the warmth I had felt with them and the cold reality of my home life hit me like a slap in the face. It didn't take long for Mother's sharpness to surface. She spotted my freshly cropped hair and immediately burst into laughter. "Ugly boy," she mocked, shattering the fragile confidence I had begun to rebuild.

Mina, sitting nearby, overheard the exchange. Understanding German because of her Dutch heritage, she instantly caught the cruelty in Mother's words. Her face flushed with anger, and without hesitation, she jumped to my defense. "You cannot talk to your own daughter that way." Mother's laughter died in her throat. Mina stood firm, her eyes blazing. She pointed toward the door. "Out!" she commanded, her gaze shifting to Andy, who had been quietly watching, frozen on the sidelines, saying nothing.

Mina rose to her feet, aggressively gathering Mother's boxes and shoving them into the apartment hallway. To my surprise, Mother and Andy vacated without much fuss. Finally, someone had stood up to Mother.

A few days later, a neighbor approached me. Her face was gentle, her smile warm but slightly hesitant. She told me she had taken Andy and Mother in, and I agreed to meet with her, though something about her tone hinted there was more behind her words than a simple check-in.

We sat at a small kitchen table in her apartment, Mother and Andy close together across from me, the soft hum of a vinyl record spinning in the background.

I glanced at Andy and saw how strong Mother's grip had become on him once she lost hold of Glap. The neighbor's voice was soft, but there was an urgency in it I couldn't ignore. She had heard a version of our story—the one that painted Mother as a victim of circumstance, a woman doing her best but caught in impossible situations, and me as nothing more than a runaway child.

Mother and Andy were planning to return to Germany, and she was lending money to help them get back, money that would never be repaid.

"You need to go with your mother," she said earnestly, her hands folded on the table, her eyes fixed on me with quiet insistence.

"No, I don't," I replied, my voice colder than I intended. "You don't understand."

"I understand children and their mothers," she insisted. In my mind, I saw Mother's fist raised above my head. "No. You have no idea," I snapped, my heart pounding as the anger flared. I stood up abruptly, the chair scraping sharply against the floor, before turning and walking away without another glance. I knew I could survive without her. In fact, her leaving would be one less mouth to feed, one less burden to carry.

A few days later, Slava received a call asking for me. "Hello?" I answered.

"This is the German embassy," came the response, delivered with the cold efficiency of bureaucracy. "By law, you are required to return to Germany with your mother."

Germany, once a place I called home, now felt like the embodiment of everything I had run from. Returning meant admitting defeat, swallowing everything I had fought for, and accepting that my life had been damaged for nothing.

I didn't want to face the ruins of the life I had once loved.

"I don't want to," I kept repeating, though I knew the caller wasn't listening.

When the call ended, I sat there, numb, staring at the empty space where the conversation had just been. Molly and Glap walked in, their light chatter fading the moment they saw my face. "You okay?" Molly asked softly.

I blurted out, "I don't want to leave."

"No," Glap said firmly, stepping closer. He crouched down in front of me, his eyes meeting mine with a quiet intensity. "You won't."

Together, we began to devise a plan, a way for me to stay in the U.S. legally. To do so, I would have to be removed from Mother's custody. It wouldn't be easy; laws never were, but it was a chance. We plunged headfirst into the bureaucratic maze of the foster care system, where paperwork piled high and meetings stretched endlessly, filled with stern faces and relentless questions.

They asked me the same questions, over and over. "Why don't you want to live with your mother?" "What has she done to you?" "How do you see your future in the U.S.?" "Do you trust Molly, even though she's only twenty-three?"

Each question felt like a needle, prodding at wounds I never had the time to process. I told them how she made me work, but in the same breath, I found myself defending her, saying she didn't have a choice; like I was trying to make sense of the pain, like I needed to convince myself it wasn't as bad as it felt. The caseworker nodded, her face serious. "It was never your responsibility to work," she corrected me, her voice firm but gentle.

There were things I held back—like the photos of me—buried somewhere deep inside because I couldn't bring myself to send her to prison, no matter how much I wanted to escape. But I did mention that I had only completed the third grade and hadn't been back to school since. I was supposed to be in seventh grade right now. Needless to say, I had a strong case.

Slava didn't apply to be my guardian. He knew that if he did I wouldn't be able to apply for my U.S. residency card. So, we kept pushing forward, clinging to the hope that somehow this would work, despite the uncertainty of what lay ahead.

Then more help began to arrive. It started small—a phone call here, a promise of support there. Soon, a group of women caseworkers appeared, their faces etched with quiet determination. They weren't just helping; they were building something, laying the foundation for my freedom.

Molly sat next to me, her hand resting lightly on my shoulder. Glap hovered nearby, his presence steady. The women explained what needed to happen next, outlining each step clearly. I needed my own room. I needed to go to school. The path forward was becoming real, and it felt both terrifying and hopeful all at once.

At a dimly lit vegan restaurant, the last place I'd see Mother before her departure to Germany, Mother, Glap and I shared a meal wrapped in a heavy silence. Mother realized she couldn't win this battle of taking me with her, that the paperwork was already in place for me to stay here. Andy didn't come. Each forkful we took felt deliberate, weighed down by the words we couldn't say. When the check arrived, it felt like a tangible sign that our time together was drawing to a close. Glap paid the bill with the money we had left over, then she stood and pulled my brother into a tight embrace.

"Goodbye, Glap," Mother said, her voice soft.

"It's Slava," he responded. With Mother leaving, and perhaps Molly's influence, he had returned to his original name. But I knew that this version of Slava would never be the same again. I stood and pulled Mother into a brief, tight embrace. She clung to me for a moment before pulling away, her figure receding into the bustling street outside, slowly swallowed up by the crowd. Then, she was gone.

After I blew out the candles on my thirteenth birthday, Molly's gaze lingered on the red lipstick I wore, the same one I had used for my Marilyn Monroe performance.

"That's not appropriate any more," she said one evening, plucking the lipstick from my hand before I could protest.

I stared at her as the tube disappeared into her pocket, my mouth tight, the defiance rising from somewhere deep inside. She closed in, drawing invisible lines where there had been none, and said, "You're still a kid."

And in that moment, I realized, now I was.

III

THE DREAM

21

THE CORPSE

I wish I could tell you that my life was better. That I wasn't counting down the days to my eighteenth birthday, the moment I could escape and start over elsewhere. But the truth is, the new beginning to my life started falling apart quickly even though Mother had only left two months earlier.

Every morning, I biked to school through the roughest parts of the graffitied neighborhood we now called home on the east side. The pavement was cracked, littered with remnants of city life, broken bottles, scraps of paper, and plastic bags. I pedaled fast, my legs burning, the chilly air biting at my face, the scent of exhaust and fast food hanging in the streets like a cloud. Cars slowed beside me, their drivers whistling or shouting crude comments, their eyes lingering. I pushed through it, turning the corner, finally locking my bike in front of Bancroft Middle School. There were no issues with my seventh-grade placement. Somehow, despite all the years I'd missed, I was still academically ahead.

My classmates quickly pegged me as different. My "otherness" became a frequent topic, and I often overheard snickers about my "too German" ways and accent in a mostly Hispanic school. Even one teacher made a snarky remark when she tried to hand me a pencil, and I refused, pulling my own from my bag. "You think you're better than us?" she asked, her voice laced with something I couldn't quite place. Confused, I shook my head.

Some students, brazen and unfocused, passed around "Superman pills" under their desks, their pupils a black hole, voices hushed. Their siblings, members of L.A. gangs, supplied them with the drugs to sell. The same kids, always looking for an excuse to assert their dominance, would corner me. But I had learned an unusual defense: smiling. Not just any smile, but the one I had seen Mother use; a cold, unsettling curl of the lips reserved for those she despised. When I mimicked that smile, the bullies paused, confusion and unease flickering over their faces before they turned away, leaving me in peace.

Despite the social minefield of school, it became my refuge. I made friends. The rhythm of classes, the predictability of assignments, and the encouragement of teachers who found my story and resilience fascinating, these were the things I clung to, holding on tightly, as they gave me something stable in a world that often felt anything but.

I tried to keep my head down, straight As tucked in my pocket, moving through the halls as quietly as I could. But I couldn't let go of the need for something more, something to feel in control of, something that was mine. That's when I turned to the gum. Bulk packs, cheap from wholesalers online. I slid the packs into my bag, fingers brushing against the smooth plastic, and began selling them in the corners of the school—between classes, under desks, quick exchanges in the hallways. The crumpled bills I collected in my pocket added up slowly.

It didn't take long before Slava and Molly noticed. At first, I thought they might ask, maybe even pretend to be curious. But instead, their eyes narrowed, and their voices turned sharp. They didn't ask what I was selling—they accused me outright of selling drugs.

"Teenagers lie and do horrible things," Molly said. She compared her teenage years to mine. The air thickened with their distrust, and I could feel my defenses rise. I tried to explain, to defend myself, but nothing I said could bridge the gap growing between us. I wasn't sure how we got here, but the walls were going up fast.

It extended into every corner of my life. They monitored everything. What I ate, what I brought home, what I tried to hide. Even the smallest indulgence didn't go unnoticed. The snacks I stashed under my bed never lasted long. A half-eaten granola bar here. A crumpled candy wrapper there. It was all confiscated. Every crumb of comfort turned into evidence.

Even my diary wasn't spared. It lay open on my desk like a brain cracked wide, lobotomized. Every private thought I had dissected and laid bare. Molly's finger jabbed at the page. "Hiding things from me again, aren't you? You liar."

The simple act of refusing a cigarette from a friend spiraled into yet another reason for Molly to clamp down harder. Instead of acknowledging that I'd handled the situation responsibly, she twisted it into a crime.

"I didn't even do anything!" I protested.

"But you withheld this from me. That's lying!"

"If I told you, I'd be in trouble anyway. So what's the point?" I shouted.

"I saved you from your mother. I'm giving you a green card. And this is how you repay me? You're ungrateful!" Her words hit the walls like glass shattering. "You're grounded from school for a week."

I just stared at her, stunned until I caught it. That flicker of satisfaction in her eyes. She didn't even try to hide it. She knew what school meant to me. Not just the lessons, but the space, the breath, the sliver of autonomy it gave me. And now she'd found the one way to make me unravel. The one place she could strike that would actually make me panic.

When I woke up early and realized I wasn't going to school, I noticed something new—Slava had added a piece of artwork to the living room wall. At first glance, it looked like a rough sketch. But as I stepped closer, I saw the arrows. The labels. A timeline, charting a slow descent. At the top was a girl with tangled hair and dark circles carved beneath her eyes. Her expression was blank, vacant. Beside her, in thick black marker:

Drugs → Pregnancy → Prostitution → Death.

Each word was aggressively underlined, like it was a prophecy.

And then it hit me—

It was supposed to be me.

Their warning, spelled out in permanent ink. A caricature of what they believed I'd become if I kept pushing back. I tried to talk to Slava about it, but he just deflected and told me to talk to Molly. Slava, who had once been my shield, now moved in sync with her like a soldier under orders. The softness in his eyes, the quiet, steady concern that once made me feel safe, was gone. Replaced with something distant and cold.

He barely spoke to me now. Molly had forbidden it.

She didn't need to explain why; I already knew. Our bond had always unsettled her, a closeness she couldn't control or understand. Still, every now and then, in the hallway, or when he lingered too long in a doorway, I'd catch it. A flicker of the old Slava. A moment's hesitation. Like something inside him wanted to reach back. Say something.

But it would pass. He'd look away, drop his eyes, and keep moving.

All week I lay on my bed, staring up at the ceiling. Posters of singers lined the walls. I could hear the hum of the refrigerator downstairs. The stress of being here was so constant, so corrosive, that I started breaking out in itchy pustules. My body couldn't hide it any more: even it wanted out. 1692 days until I am eighteen, I thought. And I'll be free.

Then I heard it. The familiar thump of equipment cases being dragged across the floor. I got up and looked over the loft wall. Molly and Slava were hauling out the gear we used to perform with. The speakers, the mic stand, even the little tip jar I'd decorated with stickers. Pieces of a life that used to be mine. I stood there watching, frozen, as they loaded everything into the trunk of Molly's old purple car like it belonged to them.

When I asked where they were going, they said, "Pantages Theater."

The same corner I used to sing on. "What songs are you playing?" I asked.

"Same ones we performed." Slava wouldn't meet my eyes.

He stared at the ground, fiddling with the cords on his guitar. When Molly went to grab something, he muttered to me, "I didn't want to do this with her. She can't really sing . . . but I need to support her." I didn't respond. I wondered if this had been Molly's plan all along . . . a way to worm her way into my space, my dreams.

At night, after their busking sets on the boulevard, the apartment transformed. The front door would swing open with force and, like clockwork, the drama would begin. From my spot in the loft—my so-called bedroom that overlooked the living room with only a half-wall for separation—I watched it all unfold. It felt like I was in a mezzanine of a play.

Slava stormed in first, his guitar case hitting the wall. Molly followed close behind, her heels clicking fast across the tile, already breathless with fury.

"Fine!" Slava snapped, throwing his hands up. "I'll go to China. I'll become a monk. Just to get away from this!"

He said it often enough for it to lose its punch, but tonight it landed differently. Maybe because he sounded like he meant it. Molly froze near the balcony door, her eyes wide and glassy. "You leave—" she said, her voice breaking, "and I'll do it. I'll jump!"

She yanked the door open, the night air rushing in. Her hair whipped across her face as she climbed over the railing, the wind tugging at her clothes.

From above, I watched Slava freeze. He stepped toward her slowly, hands raised in surrender. "Okay. Okay, I'm not going anywhere," he murmured.

Molly stepped back inside, her face wet with tears.

They retreated to their bedrooms. The lights were turned off, the air still cold, but the show was over for now. And the play, as always, reset for tomorrow.

And in a twisted way, it made sense why Slava stayed. The dysfunction. The control. The slow erosion of choice under the weight of a woman's will. It was familiar to him—comfortable, even. This was the life he knew how to survive.

This realization hit harder than I expected because I was back where I'd started. The same cage, just a different shape. A different kind of body.

Steam curled around me as I sank deeper into the bathtub. My wet fingers left smudges on my best friend Julie's phone while I waited for a text from Joey . My own phone was confiscated, leaving me desperate enough to beg Julie in the school hallway that morning during our eighth-grade classes. She hadn't hesitated, just slid her phone into my hand with a quick glance over her shoulder.

"You better not get caught," she whispered.

Julie was an Egyptian-Romanian immigrant with wild curls that framed her face like a lioness and gold eyes that missed nothing. She saw into me in a way no one else did—saw the grit behind the softness, the way I kept pushing through when it would've been easier to give up. And she stood by me. She had a soft spot for love stories, especially the tragic kind—the ones that burned too bright and ended too soon. She believed in fighting for them, no matter the cost. So when I asked her for her phone, she handed it over with no questions asked. She was no stranger to taking risks for me. After Molly read my diary a while back, she'd cornered Julie in the hall. She was the one that smoked.

"You know what smoking does to you?" Molly snapped.

As if failing to parent me wasn't enough, now she was trying to parent my friends too.

"Ten pages on why smoking kills. Tonight," she demanded. "Or I'll have a talk with your mom." Julie grumbled about psycho bitches all week, but she still filled every page.

The damp screen flickered and a soft vibration followed. I stared at Joey's reply, my chest tightening.

hi. <3

A smile cracked through the tension that had been sitting in my ribs all day. No matter what, we always found our way back to each other. I sank deeper into the bath, letting the water hug my shoulders. The rest of the world slipped away, and the screen's glow pulled me into his world. He sent dumb jokes, lyrics from songs we both loved, and I told him about the things I went through at home. We texted until the bathwater went cold.

In a rare moment of lenience, Molly let me hang out with Joey on a weekend.

I found out later that Joey had been smart about it: he'd texted her himself, politely asking if he could see me. Something about the gesture must've disarmed her, because instead of snapping back with a cold "no", she agreed.

I think, deep down, everyone rooted for us just a little.

She leaned against the car that afternoon, one hand outstretched, waiting for the crumpled bills I pulled from my allowance stash.

"Gas money," she said.

I handed it over without a word, not daring to test my luck.

At the mall, Julie walked beside me, practically buzzing with excitement to meet my crush. Joey had brought a friend, a redhead with spiky hair who thought he was funny. When they were introduced, Julie's expression shifted. She shot me a look, one eyebrow arched, then leaned in and whispered, "You're kidding, right? He's, like, five feet tall."

"Be nice," I murmured, biting back a grin as Joey and his friend wandered ahead of us, deep in conversation.

The afternoon passed in a happy blur. Laughter bounced off the walls as we darted between shops. Julie trailed behind, tossing out snarky comments that left Joey's friend visibly flustered.

At the music store, Joey and I messed around on a keyboard, our fingers brushing now and then, each touch sending a ripple through me. We kept stealing glances, both of us a little shy, a little charged.

Eventually, he drifted toward the back of the store, where rows of guitars lined the wall. Julie nudged me gently, her look unmistakable: Go.

So I did.

Joey turned and smiled. We looked at each other for a moment, then laughed at the awkwardness. I stepped closer, careful not to rush it. He moved toward me too, just as slow.

Then his lips met mine. The noise of the store melted away. The fluorescent lights blurred at the edges. And beneath it all, that low, electric hum curled under my skin.

Then the sharp honk of Molly's car split the air. But I barely heard it.

"I have to go," I said, looking into his big, doe-like eyes.

He nodded and let me go.

I saw the vision again. The same one that first came to me on that drive to Chatsworth two years earlier to the pool party. The hills. The sunset. The scattered houses dotting the curves of the land. Us at sixteen, the wind in our hair as we coasted down winding roads, his hand resting quietly on mine. In these daydreams, we'd pull up in a cherry-red car, its glossy surface catching the last light of day. He'd press me against the cool metal, pull me close, and kiss me until everything else blurred around us. We'd head to a party in the valley, some beautiful house tucked behind trees, laughter spilling out through open windows. I could see it so clearly: the music pulsing, the warmth of strangers, the clinking of glasses, his arm draped around my shoulders. This world would replay in my head hundreds of times.

Most nights, I stayed up until 4 am, hunched over the computer in the living room chatting with him. The only light came from the screen and I typed softly, careful not to make a sound. Molly and Slava thought I was asleep in my room.

Then came the days that stretched without a word from him, his silence gnawing at me. Still, I waited by the computer every night like clockwork, eyes scanning the screen for his name. And then one night, it appeared.

Hey.

My heart slammed against my ribs. I stared at the message, thumb hovering above the keyboard. Before I could type back, another one came.

I need to tell you something.

A pit opened in my stomach.

Then it hit: blunt, unvarnished.

I kissed someone else. I met her at the beach. I'm sorry.

My mind painted her clearly: a tanned blonde girl on the beach, her hair catching the sun like spun gold. She probably came from a perfect family, the kind that smiled in matching Christmas sweaters and sat down for dinner every night without fighting.

The words burned into the screen. I read them again and again, hoping they might somehow rearrange themselves into something softer, something survivable. But they didn't. And just like that, it was over. I couldn't understand how quickly it all unraveled. It wasn't supposed to end this way. What we had wasn't some fleeting teenage fling like adults loved to dismiss. It was real to me. It mattered. The kind of connection that felt untouchable, rooted in memories no one else could ever recreate.

But still, they all ended up leaving me. The darkness I feared had finally reached me.

The next day, Molly and Slava noticed my swollen eyes. I told them that Joey and I broke up. They exchanged a quick glance before quietly guiding me toward the car.

"Come on," Molly said gently. "Let's go get some ice cream."

She didn't wait for my response. They just drove, offering quiet reassurances along the way that everything would be okay, that I'd feel better soon.

Sometimes, they could be sweet. For all their edges and all the words that cut, moments like this reminded me that, beneath it all, they cared in their own complicated way.

As the sun slipped below the horizon, painting the rooftops in soft gold, I climbed out of my loft window onto the roof. My stomach churned from the bitter burn of the mouthwash I'd forced down moments before in the bathroom.

Standing at the edge, I felt the pull of the void beneath me, and when I stared straight ahead, into my future, I saw nothing but more of what I already experienced.

I imagined the fall. The rush of wind. The feeling of it all slipping away.

But just as the darkness seemed ready to swallow me, the sudden wail of sirens sliced through the stillness.

The noise jolted me back. I blinked, saw the steep drop below, and stumbled back through the window. I collapsed onto my bed, staring at the ceiling, pretending nothing was wrong while my stomach twisted with nausea.

Molly burst in moments later, her eyes wild, scanning mine with confusion and panic.

"What are you doing?" Her voice shaking.

She must've pieced it together: the aloofness, the mouthwash, the sound of the window opening. She'd called the police.

"What are you talking about?" I sat up calmly, hands folded in my lap, my face composed.

Inside, I was somewhere else entirely. I retreated to a place where nothing could reach me.

The pounding at the door shook the walls. Molly yanked it open with a sharp jerk, her voice tense and muffled as she exchanged hurried words with whoever stood on the other side.

A burst of static crackled from the officer's walkie-talkie as she stepped forward.

"We're here to speak with Tanja," she said.

I stepped hesitantly out of my room. "What's going on?" I asked.

The officer's eyes widened slightly across her otherwise stoic face as she took in my calm demeanor. Her gaze moved between Molly and me, as if trying to decide who the unstable one truly was. Molly stood stiffly beside me, arms crossed.

"She said you might be in danger," the officer said, her voice low but probing.

"She's been . . . emotional," Molly added quickly, as if that explained everything. "Over a boy," she tacked on, like everything I felt could be reduced to that alone.

The officer stepped forward.

"We need to hear what you have to say," she said, locking eyes with me like she could see straight through.

"Are you all right?"

"Yes," I said softly, offering a small smile.

She paused. "Do you often hurt yourself? Are you planning to hurt yourself again?"

"No. Of course not."

"You're too young for real love," she said after a beat. "Don't waste your life over a dumb boy."

I wanted to scream. To tell her how wrong she was about us.

But it wasn't just the breakup. It was the weight of something deeper; the quiet, grinding pain of knowing I was only loved when I performed. That no matter what I did, I was never enough. That even back in Germany, the kids had been right. Who I was didn't exist.

I was a ghost. A shell.

A corpse all along.

Knowing no one would ever truly understand, I just stared at her as her voice faded into a droning muffled blur. And as they left, the apartment, I wished—for just a fleeting moment—that I had let go quicker.

Couple months later, there was a knock at the door. I already knew who it was. Child Protective Services.

We were in a new place now, a studio apartment in West Hollywood, barely big enough to stretch without touching a wall. The ceilings were lower than the loft. We'd been evicted for missing payments, and this was all we could scrape together in Los Angeles.

The door creaked open. The caseworker stepped in with the same clipboard, the same sensible heels, the same look I was beginning to recognize; measured, professional, a little bored. Her footsteps clicked against the cheap tile.

These visits always came with rhythm. A phone call a few days before which always gave us time to prepare. She scanned the room, eyes pausing just long enough to register my new little corner. A twin mattress pressed against the fridge, a curtain dangling from a bent rod to simulate privacy. A wobbly desk shoved nearby.

No comment, just a faint nod. The kind that meant: This will do.

In reality, they probably saw a lot worse. Molly stayed out of the way, chirping something about how we were all "settling in." The caseworker scribbled something onto her clipboard. Molly would keep receiving her support checks. And the system would continue believing everything was under control. The backyard of this building was just a cracked patch of dirt. The only signs of life were a few brave weeds and, somehow, a goat. It wandered in slow, looping circles. The landlord was keeping it there, even though it was definitely illegal. Yet there was an unspoken understanding: everyone did what they had to to stay afloat in this city.

Things were better, in a strange way. Mostly because I was home alone.

It was the summer before freshman year, and I'd already made up my mind: I wanted to go to Fairfax High. It wasn't far from the studio, just a few blocks past the palm-lined streets and overpriced boutiques, where Russian restaurants sat on corners with velvet curtains and mirrored windows that reflected nothing back.

Molly and Slava were around less and less. Their voices, once loud and constant, had been replaced by the soft click of the front door shutting behind them. Another "errand." Another long stretch of silence. Sometimes they didn't come back for days. And I didn't mind.

With no one around to clock my comings and goings, I wandered. That's how I found the teen center tucked between a laundromat and a car wash, nearly hidden except for a sign and the occasional sound of laughter leaking through its doors.

Inside, the walls were cluttered with hand-drawn posters, event flyers, and old cast lists taped up with curling edges. I started showing up to their theater rehearsals. Just to sit. Just to watch.

But one day, I auditioned.

When I stepped onto that small stage under flickering lights, script in hand, and read lines that weren't mine, something shifted. I felt at home.

They cast me as one of the defiant teenagers. The role fit like a second skin of sharp edges, rolled eyes, a girl who asked too many questions and followed no one blindly. I didn't even have to act. I was purely myself.

Sheriff Shawn leaned casually against the edge of the theater room, his dark-circled light eyes following me. One afternoon, as I lingered by the doorway, dragging my feet before the long walk home, he stepped forward.

"Need a ride?" he asked.

I nodded.

Inside his car, he adjusted the radio, the crackle of static filling the brief silence. "Have you thought about joining our leadership program?" he asked, glancing at me. I'd seen the flyers taped to the bulletin board, pictures of camps, smiling teens, promise in every printout.

"That's not going to happen," I said. "My guardian would never say yes to me leaving for that long."

He tilted his head, considering. "I can talk to them."

I snorted. "Good luck with that. I'm not sure if they're even home."

When we pulled up to the apartment, he walked me to the door. The moment Molly opened it, I saw the flicker in her eyes. A uniformed officer at her doorstep was never good news. "Hello," he said, voice warm and easy. He extended his hand with the kind of practiced charm that made people forget their nerves. "You must be Tanja's guardian."

Molly hesitated, eyes flicking to the badge catching light under the overhang. Then, finally, she reached out, shaking his hand.

Slava appeared behind her, wiping his hands on a rag, eyebrows raised.

Shawn stood tall, calm. Confident. As he spoke about the program, I watched it happen, the way Molly 's suspicion ebbed, her shoulders lowering a fraction, her eyes drifting from guarded to curious. Slava gave a small nod. Something in their expressions shifted.

"I'm here to make sure she has the opportunity to participate," Shawn said.

"Well," Molly said, glancing back at me. "I suppose that'll be fine."

I blinked.

The next week, I found myself climbing into the sheriff's department van, surrounded by unfamiliar faces around my age. My afternoons shifted: organizing summer camp trips, sorting donated supplies, folding shirts into neat piles. In the hum of busy work, in the background laughter of kids who hadn't yet learned how hard life could be, something inside me began to soften. For the first time in a long time, I wasn't just surviving. I was contributing. And every now and then, when I'd glance up and catch Shawn watching us from across the room, I realized he was giving us the chance to find purpose before we even knew we were seeking it.

Meanwhile, Molly and Slava's absences stretched longer. They drifted in and out, just the creak of the front door in the early hours, the soft rustle of jackets, the quiet click of a cabinet closing. Their voices came in fragments, whispers behind bathroom doors, phrases cut off just before I could catch the meaning.

Receipts were scattered across the kitchen counter, some crumpled, others freshly printed and lined up like a trail. A clunky printer hummed in the corner, its green light blinking. I'd catch bits of conversation—state names, store chains, "make sure you use the right ink this time"—drifting past me like ghosts.

Then came the money. It showed up in quiet bursts: extra groceries, sudden new clothes, a wad of bills left carelessly on the desk.

I asked Molly once casually, over dishes.

"Where are you guys going so often?"

"Just handling some business," she said. "Better if you don't know."

But one night, while she was out on a run, Slava stayed behind.

He was at the desk, the room dim except for a lamp that buzzed quietly, casting uneven light across his face. He was hunched over something white in his hands, his fingers moving with quiet precision, like someone winding a watch.

"You want to know how it works?" he asked without looking up.

I hovered near the doorway, arms crossed. "Sure," I said, trying to sound casual.

He held up a roll of receipt paper, the kind I'd seen a hundred times curling from the edge of checkout counters. At the top, the logo of a major grocery chain gleamed faintly under the light. "Took this from the store," he said, his voice low, almost proud. "We buy a few beauty products, something cheap. Then we print a fake receipt, make it look like we spent triple. Return it somewhere else. Pocket the difference." He leaned back in the chair, and the shadows shifted over his features. The corners of his mouth lifted just slightly, that almost-smile he wore when he thought he was being clever.

To him, it wasn't just a scam, it was a strategy. A way to beat the system.

He didn't mention the risk. What would happen if they got caught. Maybe he didn't need to. Maybe when your entire existence in a place was a risk, this kind of thing didn't feel any different.

Something began gnawing at me from the inside like teeth dragging along the edges of my nerves. I could feel it, whatever it was, moving within me. My stomach twisted in ways that made it hard to eat, hard to sleep, hard to think. One evening, doubled over, I dragged myself to Slava and Molly, clutching my sides, trying to explain that something wasn't right.

"You're probably fine," Slava said, barely glancing at me.

"It could be something you ate," Molly called out from the kitchen. "Drink some water. Rest."

But days bled into weeks. My reflection in the mirror told the story they refused to hear: hollow cheeks, dark circles beneath my eyes, skin pale and too tight across bone.

We looked up the symptoms online and ways to take care of it. Slava handed me pumpkin seeds. "If it's a parasite," he said, "these'll take care of it."

The handful he offered smelled of raw earth. I stared at it, half-expecting him to laugh. He didn't. I chewed, swallowed, waited but nothing changed.

Meanwhile, Slava was unraveling in his own way. His face had begun to swell grotesquely, one side puffed and his jaw locked in a permanent grimace. He paced through the apartment in silence, cradling his cheek as if he could physically contain the infection pressing from within. When he spoke, it was through gritted teeth, each word jagged and soaked in pain.

"The dentist said I need surgery for this gum infection or I'll die," he muttered one night. "But what do dentists know? The body heals itself."

Eventually, the pacing stopped. He collapsed onto his bed, face down, unmoving.

Molly, who usually carried herself with that unshakeable holistic confidence began to fray at the edges. That night, she sat beside him, her hand resting on his back, drawing small, uncertain circles like she was searching for the right thing to say.

"We need to go back," she whispered. "This isn't going to heal on its own."

Slava didn't respond. He stayed buried in the pillow, breath shallow, body still. But in the morning, they went and the dentist cleared out his gums.

My issue turned out to be exactly what we suspected all along: a parasite, most likely something I picked up from the teen center or during one of those endless theater rehearsals. Molly and Slava finally gave in and we went to the doctor. The office was sterile and bright, humming with fluorescent lights and that faint antiseptic smell. The doctor barely glanced at my file before scribbling on a pad and handing me a single small white pill. "This should take care of it," she said, her tone flat, as if I hadn't been wasting away for weeks. I took the pill right there in the room. Within minutes, the symptoms began to fade. The strange movements in my stomach calmed, the tightness loosened, and for the first time in what felt like forever, I could breathe. I sat there stunned, the realization sinking in like a stone in water: weeks of pain, of raw pumpkin seeds and shrugged-off pleas, all because they didn't trust a doctor. And yet, sitting there in the passenger seat on our way home from the doctor's office, staring out the window, I couldn't shake the thought: even though Mother had left long ago, it was as if she were still here. Wired into our minds like faulty circuitry in an electric panel, shorting

191

out logic and replacing it with fear and folklore. She was still running the show.

After the final night of my theater show, applause still rang in my ears. I'd just peeled off my costume when the actors began trickling into the lobby, flowers cradled in their arms, cheeks flushed with adrenaline. The crowd was soft with post-show buzz, smiles, chatter of proud parents. And then I saw them.

Joey and his father walking straight toward me.

Joey, significantly taller. Hair too long, still falling into his eyes. Hands shoved into the pockets of his too-tight jeans like he was trying to fold himself inward and disappear. His father gave a polite nod, said something about seeing this event on my social media—maybe even a congratulations—but I couldn't meet his eyes.

There was an invisible wire strung between Joey and I, pulled tight, humming with everything unsaid. We hovered near each other like magnets; drawn in, pushed back, circling without touching.

And then after bidding me goodnight, they turned and walked away.

And I stood there, wondering when I'd see him again.

Molly and Slava were waiting outside the double doors.

"So," Slava started, dragging the word out like glue stretched thin between fingers.

"We're moving to Vegas," Molly cut in, breezy as ever, like she was announcing a trip to the store.

I blinked. "What?"

"In a couple days," Slava added.

My pulse stuttered. "You're joking."

Molly shook her head. "L.A.'s tapped out. Too expensive. We can't keep up. And the cops are locking up everyone in costume now—boulevard's a bust. The scams dried up too. People always catch on. We got lucky with the last close call."

"What about school?" I asked, though I already knew what she'd say.

Molly rolled her eyes. "You don't even want to be a kid anyway. In Vegas, you can work with me. No more teachers. Just real life. Freedom." Mina, her old Dutch roommate, had already made the leap, sending breathless updates about tourists with hundred-dollar bills and heatstroke, a city where you could sweat glitter and make a living off someone's fantasy.

We headed toward Molly 's car when I turned and ran—back through the building, past the smell of sweat and dusty costumes, to find the friends I hadn't even had time to say goodbye to.

Rachel's eyes widened when she saw me. "Wait—what do you mean you're leaving?" She held me in a tight, desperate hug. "You could stay with us. My mom already loves you. She'd take you in, no question."

I wanted to say yes. God, I wanted to say yes. But all I could do was shake my head.

"I'd lose my green card," I said quietly. "It would null my entire application process."

She looked at me with the saddest eyes and gave me one last hug.

Within days, our things were packed up in trunk.

I sat curled in the back seat, knees to my chest, forehead pressed against the window, watching the skyline of Los Angeles shrink behind us. Four years of life—of noise, of movement, of survival—receding like a tide behind me. Maybe it's okay to start over.

22

THE PRICE

The heater clicked off with a hollow clunk. I pulled the sleeves of my hoodie over my hands and leaned against the windowsill. It was snowing.

Not the kind that stuck, but the soft kind that vanished as soon as it touched the ground. Still, in the middle of the desert in Las Vegas, it felt like something out of a dream. The flakes spun under the streetlights like dust in a spotlight.

It reminded me of Germany. My birthdays there always came with snow, real snow, thick and heavy, blanketing the rooftops and turning the streets quiet. It felt like a piece of something I'd lost had drifted back to me on my fifteenth birthday.

I looked down at the envelope in my hand. My name sat cleanly under the plastic window. The green card inside caught the light when I tilted it open. For the first time in a long time, I felt it—I had a real chance at something.

When I was lying in bed in Mina's spare bedroom, imagining where life could take me, the visions started to come. Flashes that jolted through my brain like static from a busted TV screen. At first, I wondered if I had whatever Mother had. If I'd inherited it like her cheekbones or her strange ability to sense things before they happened. She always claimed she saw visions of the future. But the future I saw wasn't golden or cosmic. It was terrifying.

Everything around me was shifting—Molly , Slava, the people I depended on—they all seemed to change without warning. And somewhere in the middle of it, my brain decided that the darkness I saw in them could grow inside me too. That I could hurt people the way loved ones hurt me. I saw my hands, streaked with blood and trembling. I saw my own body, limp and pale, splayed across the floor in front of me. I couldn't even look at a knife without feeling like I'd simply go insane. I didn't want to hurt anyone. That much I knew. But then the voice would crawl in, slick and certain:

But you will.

The more I tried to push the thoughts away, the more they slipped beneath my skin, like glass splinters I couldn't tweeze out. They whispered the same thing over and over:

You have to stop it. You have to stop yourself before it's too late.

One night, that thought cornered me. It wrapped around my chest like a belt pulled too tight, stealing the air from my lungs. Out of sheer desperation I pulled Slava's laptop into bed with me, hands shaking as I typed into the search bar, not even sure what I was looking for. Just knowing I couldn't be the only one.

And I wasn't.

I found a forum. But it felt like salvation. These weren't strangers any more. They were me, in different fonts and usernames. One post after another, like buoys in a dark ocean:

I'm scared I'll hurt someone.

I can't trust my own brain.

I think I'm going crazy.

And there it was: obsessive-compulsive disorder. OCD. Not the scrub-your-hands-until-they-bleed kind. Not sitcom jokes or alphabetized DVDs. This was something else. Invisible chaos. Razor thoughts.

I actually laughed at myself. My brain wasn't showing me the future. It was showing me a glitch. A cruel trick of the mind, targeting the very thing I held dearest, my empathy, my restraint, my need to be good. That's what OCD does. It doesn't come for what you fear, it comes for what you value. It preys on the softest parts of you and tells you they're dangerous. I read until the sky outside turned pink and Vegas stumbled into morning. I learned that people with OCD aren't trying to control the world, they're trying to control certainty. To be sure they won't snap, won't lose it, won't become something monstrous. But certainty doesn't exist, and the more you chase it, the deeper you sink.

And that move to Las Vegas? The chaos, the noise, the strangeness of starting over in a city built on illusion, it had cracked something open in me. This, I realized, was my breaking point. The more I understood this, the more the thoughts began to lose their power. The alarms still sounded, but I could see them for what they were, misfires, not prophecies. And when those thoughts popped up, sudden as ever, I learned to name them: just a thought. The darkness that once felt suffocating began to loosen its grip.

At night, Molly and I became fantasies on the Las Vegas Strip to support ourselves, slipping into skimpy cop costumes; fishnets clinging to our legs, aviator sunglasses perched on our noses, padded bras fastened tight around our chests. We strutted the sidewalk like it was a stage, our confidence exaggerated and deliberately loud. Husbands laughed as we mock-arrested them, wrists cuffed in plastic restraints while their wives snapped photos, their faces glowing in the neon haze.

I leaned into the role, barking out fake violations and demanding fines— five, ten, sometimes twenty bucks for their "crimes." They handed over crumpled bills with drunk amusement, and for a brief, glittering moment, I felt powerful. In control.

When people asked how old I was, Molly told me to lie.

"Say you're nineteen," she whispered one night as she adjusted her bra in a convenience store window. "No one's gonna question it."

So I did. The money was good, no less than a hundred dollars a day. But it came at a cost.

Slava stood off to the side, watching it all unfold, his expression tight and unreadable. He couldn't look our way when a woman smacked my ass for the camera or when a random man would grab my face and kiss me. The catcalls bounced off me like rubber bullets, but I could see them hit him.

Dressed as Michael Jackson himself, he slid through the crowds with practiced rhythm, his white glove flashing under the streetlights. But the insults followed close behind, thrown like darts by strangers too entertained to care where they landed.

"Pedophile."

"Freak."

"Creep."

He tried to come up with new costumes once or twice. But he kept going back to the Jackson outfit. Maybe because he already had it. Maybe because it paid the most if you're a guy. Or maybe because when you've already been called that before growing up, it's easier to stick with the mask that fits. We paid for our job with a currency that nobody saw.

By the time we made it back to the apartment, the desert air had cooled, but I could still feel the grime of the night clinging to me; the sweat, the smoke, the touches I couldn't scrub away no matter how hard I tried. Our bags sagged with crumpled bills. Our cheeks were flushed, not just from the hustle, but from the cheap two-dollar wine Molly kept hidden in her car. She said we made more money drunk. She wasn't wrong.

But the control didn't stop when the heels came off.

Just because I was working again didn't mean I was free.

Molly had a way of managing everything, down to what we ate, how we moved, how we looked. She rationed our meals like a drill sergeant with a mission: half a granola bar in the morning, a spinach wrap for lunch with barely a smear of hummus, a single cup of juice. Nothing more. Every day, like clockwork, we'd lace up our sneakers.

"Come on," she'd say, already stretching. "Five miles. Gotta keep it tight."

I wasn't forced into it. It wasn't even a rule. It just became our rhythm. The kind of rhythm that forms when you're desperate to belong, when someone finally pulls you into their world and makes space for you in it. It gave me a sense of sisterhood.

But I knew this went deeper than that.

Especially after Slava's offhand comment, the one he barely remembered making, about Molly's legs being too heavy. I saw something go cold behind her eyes that night.

And I didn't want that happening to me either.

The whole diet felt good. It felt like control, like something in my life was finally mine.

Every skipped meal felt like progress. Every new bone I could see in the mirror felt like proof that I was doing something right. Seeing the scale numbers drop was addictive.

"You look great," Mina said one afternoon, her eyes sweeping over the thinner version of me like I was a piece of art finally coming into form.

But I knew the truth. I wasn't transforming. I was disappearing. Shrinking into a hollow shell, my reflection turning stranger by the day. Something lifeless stared back.

Like a corpse.

This was the mark that I wore.

During the spring, we had finally moved into our own two-bedroom apartment in Vegas, overlooking a man-made lake dyed a startling shade of blue. A paved trail wrapped around the water like a ribbon, and on quiet days you could see the reflection of palm trees ripple on its surface. I bought dark wood furniture for my room, pieces that made me feel grown up. I paid $500 of rent on time. I even had the time and desire to go to school.

But when we went to apply at the local high school, we hit a wall.

A woman at the front desk flipped through my papers and frowned. "Your guardianship is filed in California," she said. "If you enroll here, it'll alert the system. The checks Molly receives for you will stop."

I turned to her as we walked back to the car. "Did you know I wouldn't be able to go to school here?"

Molly glanced at me. "No," she said quickly. "I really didn't."

By then, things between Slava and Molly were unraveling. The fights got worse. I heard her crying through the thin drywall, her voice raw as she accused him of having sex with her in her sleep. The sound of her grief bled through to my bedroom, which sat just next to theirs. Some nights, objects hit the wall. Sometimes silence hit harder.

It was around then that Molly and I became closer. Maybe because she needed an ally. With Slava drifting away, she pulled me in tighter, and I let her. She started planning her return to Hollywood; said she needed distance from him and wanted to refocus on modeling and singing since Vegas was a dead end. She convinced me to get a second apartment with her in Los Angeles so I could go to school in California again. The thought of seeing my friends again excited me.

The new place was across from the motel my family had stayed in once, years ago, the motel from which Andy had been wheeled out in the ambulance. The building was old and beautiful, called La Leyenda, and it looked like something out of a forgotten Hollywood film, elegant and slightly haunted, with carved details that curled like lace across its façade.

Our studio apartment sat on one of the upper floors, tucked behind a heavy door and creaky wooden floorboards. We only had one air mattress on the floor. We alternated our stays there, trading off nights like some strange version of shared custody.

I signed up to an alternative school option in Burbank. Molly didn't want to drive me there once a week and, since I was an adult now in her eyes, I had to figure it out myself. That left me with no choice but to endure the grueling twelve-hour, one-way journeys from Las Vegas to Hollywood on my own on a slow shuttle bus. Slava walked me through the route once: a shuttle bus, subway, and two or three more city buses. My chest tightened just thinking about it. After that, I was left to navigate it alone.

Sunday nights after work became a ritual. I'd step onto the Greyhound half-exhausted, half-numb, the driver giving me a look that was too familiar now; the kind that hovered a second too long, like he was trying to figure out if I was a runaway. I just put on my headphones and disappeared to the back of the bus, avoiding everyone's eyes, shrinking into the corner seat.

Sometimes grandmothers would check in on me, kind faces leaning over with quiet worry in their voices: "You okay, sweetheart?"

I always nodded. Said I was fine.

That was enough for them.

As the bus rumbled out of the city, Vegas peeled away behind us, the neon lights blurring into streaks against the glass like melting candy. The city vanished quickly, swallowed by the vast desert that stretched out like a black ocean under the night.

I'd lean my head against the window, watching the emptiness roll past.

Above, the sky opened wide, quiet and endless, speckled with stars.

Around me, people had started to nod off with their heads tilted back, mouths open, the occasional soft snore rising above the hum of the bus. I unzipped my backpack and slipped on my headphones to create melodies on my iPad for hours to come.

By 4 am, East LA had transformed into a ghost town. The homeless moved like zombies beneath flickering streetlights, their faces obscured beneath tattered hoods, shadows dragging long across the concrete. Their eyes followed me as I stepped off the bus like they could see the fear I tried to hide. I turned back to the driver, trying to keep my voice steady.

"Is there a quicker way to get to Hollywood?"

He paused, then nodded. "We can take you to Hollywood," he said, pulling out his phone and dialing. No explanation, just the click of fingers on a touchscreen and a brief conversation I wasn't close enough to hear.

Then he stood and motioned for me to follow. "Come on. It's just in the lot over there."

My legs hesitated before my body did, but I followed with my brain fogged from the ride. The lot was mostly empty. That's when the van pulled in, a white one, windowless, coming in hot. Without thinking, I bolted.

The world blurred, and all I could hear was the sound of my feet slamming against the pavement, my heart pounding against my chest. I didn't look back.

I ran until the metro station came into view, glowing like a mirage.

This journey was supposed to be for a better future. But more and more, it felt like I was gambling with the one I already had.

The journey didn't end at dawn. Once I reached Hollywood, I still had another three-hour bus ride ahead of me to Burbank. By the time I finally walked through the school doors, it was 9 am, and I was running on nothing but adrenaline and sheer willpower.

I was supposed to be in class three days a week. Most weeks, I barely made it to one. But she never called me out. Just handed me a pencil, nodded toward the desk, and kept grading like she knew that just walking through the door had already taken everything I had. Most of the time I spent up to twelve hours in that classroom: testing, catching up, finishing assignments while my teacher stayed late.

"You should come to prom," my teacher said, her long black hair falling in a perfect sheet down her back. "It's this Friday." I shook my head. That was still my money-making day.

When I stepped outside, the sky was streaked pink and orange in the most beautiful ways, born from L.A.'s pollution. Palm trees swayed above me. I had the strangest feeling that someone was coming my way. I looked around, but it was just me and a line of traffic. Still, the feeling sat heavy in my chest. The same way I could sense the darkness buried at my core, I knew.

And sure enough, the next morning, back at the La Leyenda apartment, I was standing in the checkout line, the conveyor belt humming steadily beneath the weight of cheap fruit and boxed meals when he announced himself.

"Hey," a voice behind me said—low, familiar.

I froze. Slowly, I turned.

There he was.

Vincent Gallo, hands buried in the pockets of his perfectly worn jacket, like no time had passed at all. His eyes met mine, still holding that same mix of charm and mischief I remembered too well.

We ended up having dinner that night in a restaurant tucked inside a vintage railway car; one of those forgotten places wrapped in red velvet and tealight candles where you can hardly see anybody's faces. He lounged back in his seat, effortlessly composed, the way only men like him could be. He talked about his projects, his disdain for the industry, how Hollywood loved to chew people up and spit them out.

"They'll never give me an Academy Award," he said, slicing into his steak like it had offended him. "They don't give those to people who make real art. Just the ones who play the game."

I listened, half amused, half exhausted. But somewhere between the steak and the desert, something cracked open in me.

And when he paused long enough to actually look at me, I let it spill. The struggle. The nights I didn't sleep. The miles I traveled just to stay afloat. The weight of being a girl trying to survive a life she never asked for. He didn't interrupt. Just nodded slowly, like he understood something without needing to say it.

I told him how hard life had been, the words spilling out like water through a cracked dam. I told him how much I'd changed, how grown I was now. I needed him to see me, not as the girl he used to know, but as someone who had survived, who was still standing. To believe I could make something of myself too.

"Adopt me," I said.

The words tumbled out too fast, too raw. I heard myself say it, and in an instant, I was ten years old again.

"Take me away from my life. Please."

His eyes locked onto mine, but I couldn't read them. For a second, I thought maybe, just maybe, he would reach for my hand, say yes, say something.

But then his gaze shifted. Not far. Just enough.

He looked past me, his fingers moving absently over his napkin, folding and refolding it like he needed something to do with his hands.

He didn't say no. He didn't have to.

The silence was enough. The slight smile he gave me was pity dressed up as kindness.

I went home that night with a hollow ache lodged under my ribs, still holding on to the hope that he'd call. That maybe he'd show up. Maybe he'd do something.

But days turned to weeks. My phone stayed silent.

Vincent disappeared just as easily as he'd returned, fading out of my life like he was never really there to begin with.

The other invisible thread, the one that kept returning, no matter how many times we drifted apart, was Joey. After a few trips to L.A., I found myself dialing his number without hesitation. I didn't need to look it up. I'd known it by heart for years.

It rang once. Then his familiar voice answered and just like that, the thread pulled tight again, tugging us back together like no time had passed at all.

THE PRICE

Later that day, Joey and his dad pulled up in the same BMW I remembered from years ago. Joey leaned out of the passenger window, grinning like he always did, and waved me over.

"You ready?" he called, his voice still carrying that playful charm.

Joel sat behind the wheel. When I climbed into the back seat, he didn't ask how I'd been. Didn't mention what had happened all those years ago. It was like none of it existed.

If this was the only way to see Joey, I'd play along.

Even if my heart pounded at the sight of his father.

Only weeks ago, Joel had left a comment on one of my recent photos, something about how stunning a young girl I was. Joey didn't know.

At the museum, we wandered through the marble halls, our voices hushed but filled with stifled laughter. When we reached the gallery of Greek statues, we both froze, eyes locking on one particularly detailed figure.

"Nice," Joey whispered as he gestured toward the statue's anatomically accurate feature.

"Very artistic," I replied, my voice shaking with laughter. We tried to keep it together, but a snort escaped me, and that set him off. He bumped his shoulder into mine as we walked, the giggles spilling over uncontrollably until a nearby docent glanced at us with a stern expression. Joel walked ahead of us and muttered "Lovebirds" under his breath. He didn't glance back, but the rigid set of his shoulders and the way he was unusually quiet told me it bothered him more than he let on.

When I got back to Vegas and casually mentioned to Molly that Joey's dad had taken us to the museum, she went still. For a second, she just stared at me.

Then the storm hit.

"You let a pedophile drive you around?" she snapped. "Are you out of your mind?" Her hands found her hips, that familiar stance she used when she was about to tear into me. "Do you even think about the shit you do?"

I opened my mouth, but nothing came out.

"You're a child," she said, eyes wild. "You think you're grown, but you don't know anything. You think you deserve freedom? All you do is fuck up."

I stared past her and said nothing.

Joey's laugh was still in my ears. The way his shoulder bumped mine in the museum hallway. That was all I cared about.

Things got worse. Molly stormed into my room, holding something pinched between her fingers and tossed it onto my desk with a flick of her wrist.

A beer bottle cap that she found in the La Leyenda trashcan after I had my friends over.

"What the hell is this?"

Her eyes locked on mine, waiting, daring me to lie.

I didn't flinch. Just stared back. "A beer cap." She'd handed me worse at work. But now, suddenly, this was a problem.

"You think this is going to get you anywhere?"

"How is this a problem now?" I asked.

"You're coming back to Vegas the same day you leave for L.A.," she said, her voice low and final. "Or I'm done working with you."

I stared at the cap on the desk. My duffelbag sat half packed in the corner. None of it made any sense to me. The more she felt me pulling away and becoming my own person, the harder she clenched her fists around what little control she had left.

The timing couldn't have been worse. The last time I'd been in L.A., when I drank that beer, my friend Tatyana and I were outside a nightclub, the bass so loud it felt like it was trying to break through the concrete beneath our boots.

Taty clutched my arm. "This is crazy. The bouncer's not gonna let us in." She was eyeing the line snaking down the block.

I just smirked. "I always make things happen."

We reached the front, all nerves and fake confidence. "We lost our IDs," I said, like it wasn't something they heard from underage kids all the time.

The bouncer didn't even blink. "No." He folded his arms and looked past us like we were already gone.

Taty threw me a look; equal parts told you so and let's go before this gets embarrassing.

I was just about to turn away when the door opened and the owner stepped out, scanning the crowd. His eyes paused on us.

"You two," he called, nodding. "Let them in."

Taty froze. I grinned.

We slid past the velvet rope like we belonged there. Inside, the music wrapped around us in a full-body grip, neon lights flashing, bodies tangled in motion, the air thick with sweat, perfume, and tequila.

Later, he found me again, moving through the crowd like a man on a mission.

This time, he looked at me like he was trying to figure something out.

He leaned in, close enough that I could feel the heat of his breath over the beat. "So, what's your story?"

I hesitated, then pulled out my phone. I opened the music app and tapped play on one of the demos I'd recorded during the long, numbing rides between Vegas and L.A.

He listened, head tilted. Strobe lights flashed across his face, briefly illuminating the shift in his expression, thoughtful, focused. When the last track ended, he reached into his jacket and pulled out a sleek business card. Without a word, he placed it in my palm.

"You've got something," he said. "Come back next weekend. Open for our featured artist." I stared down at the card, its sharp edges digging into my fingertips.

Now, standing barefoot in the kitchen in Vegas, I chose my words carefully.

"Molly , can I go back to L.A. next weekend to perform?"

My voice was steady, but my stomach twisted tight. "It's important," I added. "This could be my big break."

She didn't even look up from the plate she was drying. "No."

I blinked. "You're joking." My voice rose without my permission. "You're such a hypocrite!"

Her head snapped toward me. "And you can't act like an adult, so your privileges are revoked!"

"But I pay rent here! I pay rent in L.A.!"

"As you should," she shot back. "I've done enough for you. You're ungrateful after everything I've done."

No matter how hard I tried, the road kept leading back to someone else's version of my life.

It was the summer of 2011, and I had just finished my freshman year. The air outside buzzed with heat, cicadas droning in the background. The thought crept in like morning light slipping through my drawn curtains.

What if I went back to Germany?

What if home still existed in the shape of people who remembered me before the bruises, before the pretending, before the fight to be seen? What if I didn't have to beg any more, or cling to people who only offered love in pieces?

What if I had real parents again?

The thought lodged itself somewhere behind my ribs and wouldn't leave.

I couldn't stand being near Molly any more. Even in silence, she filled the space with a sharpness that made my skin itch. Work had become a tightrope walk, strained smiles, clipped instructions, the dull throb of resentment pulsing beneath every shared task.

Slava was still around, orbiting us like a ghost of better times. We passed each other in hallways but the connection was long gone.

So I waited for the right moment, counted my crumpled bills and rolled quarters, and convinced Molly to book me a plane ticket to Germany to see family. I almost expected her to argue but she didn't disagree. Maybe she hoped I'd vanish.

Either way, I didn't care.

On the night before my flight, I stood at the kitchen sink staring out into the dark desert. The tile was cold beneath my feet. I imagined cobblestone streets and damp air. I imagined the church bells that used to ring through Regensburg in the morning, and the smell of fresh bread wafting from the bakery windows. I imagined people who might still remember my name.

Not the girl I'd become but the child I used to be.

I didn't know what I'd find there. But for the first time in a long time, I knew I had to go.

I found myself thinking about Andy and Dima. What time had done to them, how their faces might have changed. I hadn't seen Dima in five years, and Andy in a little over two.

Even Mother, complicated as she was, stirred something in me. Not forgiveness, not quite. But longing. I missed her, or maybe just the version of her I still held on to. The gentler one, the one that used to call me Nanya. Maybe they were all still there, buried beneath the dust of time, waiting for me to come home.

But it was my father I was most excited to see. The thought of him filled me with a mixture of nostalgia and anticipation. Memories of him, faded and fragmented, pulled at me even when I felt at my most happiest here.

When the plane landed in Munich, I stepped out into the gray morning light and saw Dima waiting by his car, arms crossed, a nervous smile tugging at his face.

He pulled me into the biggest hug, arms tight around me like no time had passed. He still looked the same but he blinked in surprise when he stepped back.

"Damn," he said, laughing a little. "You got tall."

He was living with our father now, and our stepmother. I could tell he wasn't sure where to take me, where I'd be welcome, or if I'd even want to go there.

So instead, he took me around town.

We drove through old neighborhoods, past bakeries and bus stops that felt familiar but distant, like seeing a dream from the outside. The windows were down. The air smelled like rain and pavement and something warm I hadn't felt in a long time.

Neither of us said much. But it was enough.

I stood in front of our old apartment building, and it was as if time had bled into the walls, staining everything it touched. Dark streaks ran down the facade like mascara on pale skin. The grass had grown wild, unruly, curling over the edges of cracked pavement. A new Russian family lived in our unit now. Bits of trash skittered across the ground in lazy circles. The memories I had of this place played back in slow motion, sunlight lingering on windowpanes, the clink of dishes in the kitchen, laughter echoing down the hallway like it was still chasing someone. Now, everything felt muted. Smaller. The playground my siblings and I spent time at was still there. The swings hung motionless, chains rusted and stiff, waiting for someone who never came. The streets, once wide and brimming with possibility, had narrowed. The magic had drained out slowly without anyone noticing. I wondered if the decay had always been there, hiding beneath the glow of childhood. Maybe it wasn't the place that had changed. Maybe it was just me. Older now, and finally seeing things as they really were.

Father lived only a five-minute walk from our old apartment, but as I approached his door, each step felt heavier than the last. When Dima first told him about my visit, his response had been immediate and firm: no. He had finally managed to rebuild his life, piece by piece, and leave behind everything that reminded him of his pain, including me.

"That's your only daughter," Dima had said. And now, standing beside him, I realized that if Dima hadn't stayed behind, we might not have had any family left at all. He had inadvertently kept us tethered, the last thread in something long unraveled. Father couldn't start a new life, a new family, not fully, not when Dima still occupied the only spare bedroom they had. Eventually, he agreed to see me, though whether it was guilt, obligation, or just a way to end the conversation, I couldn't be sure. Now I stood at his doorstep, Dima beside me, my hand hovering just above the doorbell. It was connected to a blinking panel, the kind used in deaf households to signal someone's arrival. I stared at it too long.

Then I took a breath and pressed the button.

A faint buzz echoed inside.

A pause.

Then the soft creak of the door opening.

There Father stood, framed by the doorway, his face worn by time. Lines carved around his mouth and eyes, more pronounced than I remembered. Gray streaked through his hair, stark against the dark strands that once made him seem unshakeable. His mustache, the feature that had once defined his face, was gone. Clean-shaven, he looked almost younger.

Even though he knew I was coming, his face froze as if he were seeing a ghost or someone who had risen from the dead.

He didn't seem to know what to do with himself. His hands hovered at his sides, twitching slightly, like they were searching for a gesture they had long forgotten. It was as if the simple act of embracing his daughter had slipped from his muscle memory.

THE PRICE

I wanted to break the moment. To raise my hands and sign, It's me—your daughter. Look, the birthmark's still here. But my fingers didn't move. I just stood there, hoping he'd remember me without needing to be reminded.

The realization hit like a wave: I had forgotten how to sign. I was holding back the sobs, the pain I stifled the past six years of being gone. The words I wanted to give him were trapped, tangled in years of distance and silence. His gaze searched mine, and for a fleeting second, it looked like he might say something, but instead, he stepped aside, holding the door open and waved his hand to step inside.

His new wife, my stepmother, appeared in the doorway, and to my surprise, I liked her immediately. There was no hesitation in her. She stepped forward and reached out, gently adjusting the collar of my jacket like it was the most natural thing in the world. That simple gesture, a quick, thoughtful tug carried a kind of motherly attention I hadn't realized I was starving for. You're beautiful, she signed, her smile spreading across her face. Her hands lingered for a beat before forming the next phrase: I'm so happy to meet you.

The emotion in her movements was unmistakable. It pulsed through every flick of her fingers, every shift of her palms. Her joy didn't need translation, it radiated from her, steady and sincere.

Father, though, was different. I could feel it in the way he moved around me. He was careful and measured, like I might shatter something if I stepped too close. There was a quiet fear that clung to him whenever Mother's name hovered in the air, even unspoken.

He had pieced his life back together after we left, building something new out of the wreckage Mother left behind. But standing in front of me, I could see it all rushing back to him, the memories he had tried so hard to bury. I wasn't just his daughter in that moment. I was a reminder of the past he was desperate to forget. He locked his bedroom door whenever I came over. As if I might be snooping for Mother. As if I might carry some residue of her, something poisonous I could leave behind.

And every now and then, he'd plead, Don't tell her. Don't tell her anything.

Mother's reaction to my return was warmer than I expected. Her face lit up, her eyes wide with disbelief, like she wasn't sure I was real.

"You're here!" she gasped, her voice trembling at the edges with excitement.

She rushed forward and pulled me into a hug, tight and desperate, like if she let go I might vanish again.

When she stepped back, her hands remained on my shoulders. She stared at me for a long while.

"Look at you," she whispered, her voice cracking. "You're all grown up."

Her joy spilled into everything; offering me food, anything I wanted, piling plates with care like it could make up for the time we lost. Their apartment was old and creaky. The bathroom floor dipped inward beneath my feet, soft and sagging, as if it might give way at any moment. They all shared one bed, and now I did too, curled in the middle, limbs tangled, Shayla wedged between our legs. The little dog growled every time we shifted in the night.

Late one night, after Andy had gone to bed and the apartment had quieted, she sat across from me at the kitchen table, fingers curled around her mug. Her smile faltered just slightly.

"I messed up," she said quietly. "Taking you all to America. It wasn't what I thought it would be."

She looked down, her thumb running along the rim of the cup. I didn't know what to say. But in that moment, I saw the weight she carried, not just the choices, but the regret too.

Monday through Friday, I stayed with her and Andy. Weekends were reserved for father. With Andy it was easy, I slipped back into old rhythms. We were the same height now and people thought we could pass as twins. We laughed at inside jokes and swapped stories late into the night like no time had passed. But Mother's warmth didn't last.

One afternoon, as I sank into the couch, the music in my headphones drowning out the world, they were suddenly ripped away. The sharp motion sent my heart racing as I looked up, startled, to find her face inches from mine. Her eyes were cold and unblinking.

"Bad things happen to bad girls who don't stand by their mother," she whispered, her breath hot against my ear. "You chose Molly over me."

"What?" I managed to ask, my voice thin, barely above a whisper.

But she didn't answer. Instead, she straightened, turned on her heel, and disappeared back into the kitchen.

Later, I told Andy about the strange interaction with Mother. His reaction was immediate, a roll of his eyes and a quick shake of his head.

"She's been doing that to me for years," he said. "Just ignore her. Mother's being . . . well, Mother."

She never once asked me about my life in the U.S.; where I worked, how I lived, what I'd been through. Not a single question. She only spoke about the U.S. to me when she could scold me. It wasn't her decision that failed, she said. It was us. If we had just tried harder. If we hadn't been such difficult children.

The blame came in casual remarks, sharp looks, and long monologues disguised as spiritual lessons. We were the reason for our downfall. Not her. Never her.

And just like that, the version of her I thought I might find, the one I remembered, the one I still hoped was buried underneath, was gone. I had nowhere to go. Unwelcome at my father's and trapped in Mother and Andy's cramped one-bedroom apartment. I was stuck. The lack of space, both physical and emotional, was suffocating. But I had no choice. My return flight wasn't until the end of summer, and I was only two months in.

Not that it mattered.

Because that's when Mother dropped it, the news landing like a hammer: I wasn't allowed to leave Germany until I turned eighteen.

"You're my daughter," she said, her voice final. "I won't let you run away again."

I felt it then—the darkness she carried. The way it wormed into rooms, into words, into me. I knew if I stayed, I'd become just like her.

I snapped.

Andy was the only one I thought might listen, the only one I believed could still recognize reason. I turned to him, my voice rising. "I'm done. I'm going back to the U.S.!"

His expression didn't change. "No, you're not," he said flatly.

"I will tell Molly and Slava! She's my legal guardian!"

Andy laughed. "It was their idea to leave you here."

I was stunned.

That was it. I couldn't hold it in any more. I bolted for the bathroom and slammed the door behind me. I crumbled, sobs tearing out of me, loud and uncontrollable.

Later that night, I was on the computer, lost in the digital haze, tuning out the world around me, when a strange sound pierced through—sharp, uneven gasps, like someone struggling for air. My heart lurched. I sprang from the chair and followed the noise into the bedroom.

Andy was on the bed, convulsing violently. His limbs flailed uncontrollably, his eyes wide and frantic with terror.

"Andy!" I cried, dropping to my knees beside him, but he didn't respond. His breath came in jagged, strangled bursts.

Mother's footsteps thundered through the apartment as she rushed in from the kitchen. "Andy!" she shouted, reaching for his shoulder.

But the moment her hand neared him, Andy recoiled with a force that made both of us flinch. "No!" he shrieked, the voice of a frightened child bursting out of an adult body. "Not you," he rasped, turning away from Mother. His eyes darted wildly before locking onto mine. "Her." His arm stretched toward me, shaking. His face was twisted with panic, his gaze pleading. Mother froze. Her hand hovered in the space between them.

I swallowed hard and moved closer, pressing my hand to his. His body eased, just slightly. The panic in his eyes dulled enough for his breathing to slow.

When the seizure finally passed, he looked up at me with unfocused eyes. His words slurred together.

"Don't leave me" he whispered, barely audible.

His grip tightened on my hand like I was the only thing tethering him to reality.

"I'm here," I murmured, again and again, until his body softened, and his eyelids dropped closed.

He woke up about thirty minutes later with no memory of what had happened.

The morning after was uncomfortable. "This is your fault," Mother said, glaring at me from across the room. "You stressed him out. That's why this happened."

I stared at her, stunned by how effortlessly she twisted the truth, how easily she shattered mental foundations and seized the control panels of the mind. And I knew then, without doubt, that she was dangerous.

I packed my things quietly and retreated to father's apartment.

Sitting on the edge of the couoch, I opened my social media, my hands trembling as I typed. The words spilled onto the screen raw and unfiltered, each sentence peeling back another layer of truth I had buried for too long.

I need help. I'm stranded in Germany. I don't have the money to buy a flight back to the U.S.

The vulnerability of it made my stomach churn. But I hit "post" anyway.

To my surprise, the response was immediate. Notifications started rolling in, messages, comments, donations. Some from people I hadn't spoken to in years, others from strangers I didn't even know. The staff from the teen center, who had barely remembered my name, donated what they could. I turned to Mark , my last hope, and sent him a message. The words poured out like a flood, raw and panicked, each one more frantic than the last.

I can't stay here. I won't. If I have to stay another month, I swear I'll kill myself. I mean it, Mark . I can't do this any more. I hate them. I hate everything here.

His reply came quickly, steady and clear, like someone tossing a rope into a storm.

We'll get you out of there. You're not alone.

Night after night, we sat at our keyboards, messages pinging back and forth in the quiet darkness of my corner of the world. Mark 's words were steady, unshakable, even as I came undone. He never dismissed my anger or tried to fix my hopelessness. He just stayed, listening, grounding me, offering flickers of light where I thought none existed.

He told me he would talk to Molly .

I don't know what he said to her. Maybe it was a scathing message that held up a mirror to her betrayal. Maybe he reminded her of everything I'd sacrificed, how hard I'd tried to adapt, to belong, only to be thrown aside like I'd never mattered. Maybe he sent money. I never asked, though the thought lingered at the edges of my mind.

What I do know is that, after days of silence, Molly finally called.

Her voice was clipped, her tone tight, the sound of someone forced into a corner but too proud to admit it.

"You can come back," she said flatly. "But only if you adhere to stricter rules."

Stricter rules. Whatever that meant, I didn't care. I nodded, agreeing to anything, everything.

That same night, I turned to father. "I need a flight," I said, making sure he could read my lips clearly. "Tonight. Before Mother finds out."

He hesitated, his brow furrowing as he weighed the request, but only for a moment. Then he gave a small nod. No argument. No questions. He knew better than anyone how hard it was to live with Mother. And he didn't want me staying with him either, not with Dima still occupying the only spare room.

I moved through the apartment like a whirlwind, yanking clothes from drawers in Dima's bedroom, stuffing them into my bag without folding. The sound of zippers, hangers clattering to the floor, and drawers slamming echoed through the space.

There were more of my things at Mother's. But I knew I had to leave them behind.

I couldn't give her a reason to stop me.

When the taxi arrived, Oma came with me. Her expression was soft but heavy. Just before we entered the Munich airport, she pressed a small wad of bills into my hand, her grip firm, but full of tenderness.

"Go," she said quietly, her voice laced with urgency. "Please be safe."

I nodded, unable to speak.

On the plane, I sank into my seat, the roar of the engines a dull hum beneath my thoughts.

As we lifted off, an elderly woman beside me leaned over, her eyes kind.

"Going home?" she asked, with the casual warmth of a stranger trying to soften the silence.

"Yeah," I said, forcing a smile, nodding once.

But the truth sat heavy in my chest. I didn't have one.

I turned toward the window, watching the clouds rise to swallow the last view of Germany until the land disappeared completely, and there was nothing left but the sky.

After a grueling twenty-six-hour journey and three exhausting layovers—the only available option on such short notice—a faded purple car finally rolled up late to the curb outside the Las Vegas airport. Molly and Slava stepped out.

They hugged me, quick and awkward.

"You know why we did it, right?" Molly asked.

"It was for your best interest," Slava added, his words sounding like they'd been rehearsed on the drive over. "We thought it was best for you to be with family in a normal environment."

The weight of what had been done pressed heavy against my chest, but I didn't dare say anything. One wrong word and I risked being kicked out again. So I nodded silently, their voices already fading as I climbed into the back seat.

The drive home was quiet. The only sound was the low hum of the engine and the occasional shuffle of movement from the front. I stared out the window, watching the blur of neon and desert stretch past, but none of it felt familiar any more. When we finally arrived, I stepped into the apartment and went straight to my room.

The door creaked open and I froze.

The walls were bare. The shelves empty.

The furniture I'd worked so hard to afford—the bedframe, the desk, the dresser—was gone. My eyes fell to the center of the room, where a bare mattress sat alone on the floor.

"We sold your things," Molly said, poking her head into the doorway. "We didn't think you'd be back."

I let my bag slide from my shoulder. It hit the floor with a dull thud.

For a long moment, I just stared at the mattress, at the emptiness of the room.

I knew where I was going next.

23

THE DELUSIONS

Mark nearly popped a blood vessel when I told him Molly wanted to shoot a police-themed photo set of me. In the shower. For a photographer she barely knew who had a wad of cash.

When I asked him to buy me a bottle of wine, told him I liked myself better after a drink, that people tipped me more when I was a little fuzzy around the edges, he stood up so fast the kitchen chair screeched across the linoleum.

"That's exploitation," he said, pacing across the cracked tile like he might wear a groove into it.

It was fall and I'd flown up to Washington to visit him. The air was colder than I remembered, brisk and pine-scented, with fog that curled like smoke around the edges of the trees. His town quieted early, the kind of place where time seemed to slow with the rain. It rained a lot. And as dusk settled in, porch lights flickered on one by one, like old war beacons.

That's when his plan began.

He took me to high school football games where the bleachers rattled with every stomp. He walked me past red-brick buildings and chain-link fences.

"You could stay here," he said it casually, eyes on the field. "Go to school. Start fresh. Make friends."

THE DELUSIONS

The thought had been in my mind before I ever boarded the plane. It didn't take much to convince me. When I missed my flight back to Vegas a week later, Molly's fury cracked like a whip through the phone. Her voice shook with rage as she screamed at Mark .

"She's a backstabber! Leaving me stuck with rent! That bitch!"

I didn't understand it at first. She was about to leave me in Germany. She'd still have been responsible for rent, with or without me.

But then it hit me.

The moment I enrolled in school here, the California child support would cease.

That's what she was really losing. Not me.

But the anger didn't stop there.

"I'll come up there with a knife and stab her myself."

And yet, every night since moving to Washington and turning sixteen years old, it felt like I was back on that old sunken couch, sinking into the nightmares of my childhood.

In the dark, I'd lurch out of my bed, disoriented, stumbling through my new bedroom, clawing at the walls like something was still chasing me. When I finally woke, the realization that I was safe came slow—my heartbeat still thrumming in my ears.

By morning, my nails were ragged.

The night terrors didn't fade. They only dug deeper, until even the thought of bedtime filled me with dread.

One night, I asked Mark if I could sleep in his bed.

He didn't argue. He just built a wall of pillows between us.

Still, by the middle of the night, I'd be curled at the edge of the mattress, knees pulled to my chest, shaking as the tears came.

"You're safe," he said once, voice low in the dark. "You're okay."

With dark circles under my eyes, I tried to adjust to my new high school life.

Eyes followed me through the hallways. They lingered too long, often paired with muffled laughter or whispers. A boy leaned against a locker, smirking as I walked by. "Fresh meat," he muttered, loud enough to make sure I heard.

I could tell the teachers didn't trust me.

Something about my file, the Vegas address, the foster system label put them on edge. My freshly dyed red hair and piercings didn't help.

They looked at me like I was already trouble.

But then they'd see my transcripts, scan the nearly perfect test scores and blink.

Always surprised.

The jazz choir was the one place where the constant noise in my head finally quieted. I hadn't planned on joining. But the moment my counselor found out I used to sing, she made it happen. Normally, there were requirements; auditions, evaluations, proof that you deserved a spot. She bypassed all of it, determined to give me something, anything, that might help me adjust to this new life. Our vocal group was a patchwork of strange and wonderful misfits, people who, like me, didn't quite fit anywhere else. With them, I didn't have to pretend. I didn't have to smooth out my rough edges or hide the parts of myself that made other people uncomfortable. They saw me exactly as I was and accepted me anyway.

And when we sang, our voices folded into one another, layering into something bigger than any of us.

At lunchtime students huddled in tight circles, whispering about who was dating who, who said what in the cafeteria line. Their voices blurred into static as I walked past, disconnected from the world they moved through so easily. I still didn't eat much. Most days, I skipped meals altogether. I tightened my grip on my backpack strap, grounding myself against the question that never left me: What happened to Mother? Her face surfaced without warning. When I was too small to help with the dough, she'd hand me a potato to knead, just to make me feel part of something. She smiled when I focused, hummed when she cooked. She cared for me. And no matter how much darkness came after, the part where she once loved me remained.

People who met Mother, even for a moment, never hesitated. "She's crazy," they'd say, like it was a fact, not an opinion. Maybe they were right. But I still remembered the way she'd tilt her head when she talked about energy fields, or how she'd clip pages from books and tape them to the walls. I'd grown up on her stories, how she wasn't insane, just tuned in to something the rest of us couldn't hear. A genius misunderstood by a world too dull to see it.

But even so, something kept tugging at the edges. The older I got, the more that story frayed. Just like I'd done with myself, naming the spirals, tracking the quiet compulsions, searching for why I counted things or checked locks three times, I felt the urge to unravel her. To pin the chaos to something solid. One evening after school, I opened my laptop and started typing. The memories came in fragments: her talking to the moon, the weeks she thought she was dying, the way her eyes glazed over whenever I spoke about anything that was mine—school, friends, music—to later use this information against me. I don't think she ever knew what I loved. I searched for answers—schizophrenia, narcissism—scrolling through symptom lists and forums filled with anonymous heartbreak. The words pulsed on the screen: delusions of grandeur, lack of empathy, emotional volatility. They weren't diagnoses. But they fit. She checked nearly every box. And somehow, that made the anger quieter. It gave it a container. A name. And in that container, something else floated to the surface: the realization that it had never been about me. She hadn't hated me.

It was impossible for her to love in the way I had needed her to.

I took screenshots of everything and attached them to an email. The subject line was "Mother". I just hoped Slava would see what I saw, that maybe, just maybe, this wasn't based in malice. Maybe it was something else entirely. And maybe that would be enough to loosen the chains pulling him under.

There was something jarring about realizing Mother wasn't all that different from the homeless people we used to pass on Hollywood Boulevard, shouting their gospel into the void. The strangest part was how obvious it seemed in hindsight. When you're in it, you can't see it. But everyone else can. And when the truth finally hits, it makes you feel stupid. Slava used to call himself that all the time, stupid. Like it was a scar he couldn't stop picking at. The loss of trust in our own instincts, our ability to see the obvious, wore us down in slow, invisible ways. It was in the quiet I was met with the aftershock.

As the house settled into silence, the hunger crept in, slow at first, then urgent. Barefoot, I padded into the kitchen, breath tight, ears straining for footsteps that never came. The cabinet door creaked as I opened it. My fingers trembled as I reached inside, pulling out crinkled bags, torn boxes; chips, cookies, whatever was left. I stacked them high on a plate.

Back in my room, I sat cross-legged on the floor in my underwear and ate. Quick, greedy bites. Crumbs scattered down my chest, breath heavy between mouthfuls, heart pounding. The plate emptied faster than I meant it to. When it was gone, I just stared at the wrapper in my lap, wondering if I wanted more. I kept eating until I felt sick, until the pressure swelled in my belly and I had to move. Fast. I barely made it to the bathroom in time. Locked the door behind me. The tile chilled my feet. I knelt beside the toilet. One hand gripped the seat. The other shook as I pressed my fingers to the back of my throat. My body lurched.

Afterward, I stayed there. Knees pressed to the floor, forehead resting against the cool wall. The air tasted like acid and something worse. I didn't cry. I didn't move. But there was a strange sense of relief like I'd emptied something heavier than food. I got a rush from eating until I felt terrible and another from undoing the damage. A high and its erasure, back to back. It started happening every day.

Eventually, Mark noticed. I'd forgotten to wipe down the rim leaving a faint trace behind. He found it that morning. I heard the pause in his footsteps. The bathroom door left open just a crack. A long silence. Then the slow creak of the kitchen stool as he sat back down.

When I came in, he didn't yell. Didn't even look startled. He just lifted his eyes from the history book splayed across the counter and met mine.

"You okay?" he asked, his voice low.

I didn't bother lying. "I'm purging," I said flatly. Like I was saying I'd missed the bus.

Mark was quiet for a beat, fingers still resting on the pages. Then he exhaled, slow and steady, like letting air out of a tire. He turned back to his book.

"You gotta stop," he said. Not harsh. Not tender. Just distant. "I don't know . . . maybe find a therapist." And that was it. Just a sigh and the sound of pages turning.

I didn't know who to talk to or who might understand me best, so I called Slava. He was the only person who ever came close. But my calls went unanswered. My messages sat unread. Days passed. Then weeks.

And then, out of nowhere, a message appeared—but not from him. It came from a stranger, someone I'd never met: a family member of another inmate who had found me through social media. Her words hit like a gut punch. Slava was in jail. One of the worst jails in Oakland, California.

He'd been accused of holding a new girlfriend hostage during a camping trip. But according to the message, she was the one unraveling—driven by obsession, by some festering need for revenge. She'd broken down his apartment door more than once. Her fixation had spiraled out of control. And yet it was Slava who ended up behind bars, charged and cornered because in stories like these, a woman's word is often all it takes.

Knowing his history with Molly , and the long, bruising trail of controlling women that followed, I didn't hesitate to believe it. But the charges were serious. Felonies. Ones you don't just walk away from.

I waited weeks for another update. Then, out of the blue, my phone rang. It was Slava.

"The situation got bad," he said, voice rough around the edges. He walked me through the mess, how everything had spiraled, how he'd refused every plea deal, every offer.

"I wasn't going to take it," he said. "I didn't do what they said. Even when they tortured me with cold rooms." Then came the twist. A clerical error, small, easy to miss surfaced in the paperwork. Something even the prosecution couldn't ignore. That, paired with his ex's failure to show up in court and the prosecutor's own lateness, shifted everything.

Slava walked out with a misdemeanor.

The relief in his voice was palpable, even over the phone. But he downplayed it with a dry laugh. "Close call," he said. I could tell he liked beating the system, being the smarter one, the one who saw the loophole before anyone else did. Something told me this wasn't going to end here. This was his control.The Heartbreak

FAME OR DEAD

The Hollywood life still followed me, even after I'd left the boulevard behind. The pressure to be extraordinary didn't vanish, it just shifted. If anything, it deepened. I still aimed to be exceptional at everything: perfect grades, flawless performances, the image of a girl who had her life together, even when I didn't.

By junior year, I was still searching for a place to belong. I slipped in and out of identities like costumes, trying them on to see which one fit. I went to teenage parties filled with cheap liquor and pulsing music. I'd linger in the corners with a red cup in hand, watching other kids laugh with an ease I couldn't replicate. I kissed boys. I sent photos. I was searching for attention, for affirmation, for something. One afternoon, Mark mentioned he'd seen one of the photos on my tablet. He said it so casually, like he was commenting on the weather. "You have nice breasts," he said, as if I should be flattered. But the words hit like a heavy stone dropped into deep water. Something inside me sank with it.

Mark often bragged about me to other parents. They'd nod, compare grades and performances with their own children as if we were trophies polished for display. I joined sports, signed up for theater, packed my schedule tight so I wouldn't have to sit with the silence. I was busy from morning to night, practices, rehearsals, homework, meetings, more homework. I told myself even if I wasn't going to become rich, at least I was going to be successful here.

Then I turned seventeen.

One night, around 1 am, I jolted awake and knew instantly something was wrong. The heartbeat inside me had become the only thing I could feel. It beat unevenly, skipping in strange patterns, pausing just long enough to leave a silence in my chest before slamming back into rhythm with a force that made me cough. I tried to breathe deep, but my lungs refused to expand. The air wouldn't come in all the way. It felt like I was being suffocated from the inside.

Panic took over. I climbed out of bed, legs shaky, and stumbled down the hall to wake Mark . I shook him gently, my voice small and breathless.

"I think something's wrong. I need to go to the hospital."

He stirred, squinting at me through half-closed eyes. "You're overreacting," he mumbled. "If it's still happening in the morning, I'll take you."

Then he rolled over and pulled the blanket tighter around himself.

I flashed back to Mother, clutching her chest, eyes wild, gasping for air that never seemed to reach her.

I'm not like her, I thought.

I'm not like her.

I grabbed my phone and texted Jenny, my friend who was a year older, already eighteen, and had a car. Within minutes she responded, saying she'd be right over and to stay put until she arrived. As I started gathering my things, trying to steady my breathing, Mark stirred, his voice breaking through the crack of his door.

"Where are you going?" he asked, with a mix of confusion and irritation, as if I were causing a scene over nothing.

"Jenny's taking me to the hospital," I said firmly, not caring if he believed me or not. The urgency in my voice must've caught his attention, though. He sat up, rubbing his eyes. "Really?" Mark sighed, tossing the blanket aside.

"All right," he said, resigned. "I'll take you."

When I got to the emergency room, they barely asked my name before taking my temperature. The nurse's eyes widened, her expression shifting from neutral to urgent. She turned to someone behind the desk.

"We need a wheelchair over here. Now."

"I'm fine, I can walk," I protested.

"You're not fine," the nurse said firmly, crouching to meet my eyes as another nurse wheeled the chair into place. "Your fever is dangerously high. Sit down."

I hesitated, but the pounding in my chest made it impossible to argue. I sank into the chair, gripping the armrests as they whisked me through the hallway.

In the room, separated by thin curtains, a doctor appeared almost immediately. "What's going on?" she asked.

"She came in with a fever of 104.4," the nurse said, glancing at her clipboard. "She's complaining of heart palpitations."

The doctor knelt beside me, her eyes scanning my face. "Do you feel lightheaded? Dizzy? Any pain in your chest?"

I nodded. "It's like my heart stops and then restarts again," I said. "I can feel the irregular pounding."

The doctor nodded. "We'll take care of you," she said. "Let's get an EKG and start fluids. And call for a chest X-ray."

I blinked, the words blurring together. "Am I going to be okay?"

"We're going to figure out what's going on." She shot me a smile.

The nurse reached for my arm, sliding a blood pressure cuff into place. "Try to relax," she said softly, though her hands moved with urgency. "We've got you."

I was told to strip out of my clothes and into a hospital gown. Even though my fever ran high, I couldn't stop shivering. The nurse moved quickly, attaching sticky pads to my chest, connecting me to a heart monitor. The machine came to life with a sharp beep, then another, chaotic spikes lighting up the screen, perfectly matching the erratic thudding inside my chest. When the doctor glanced at the monitor, her brow furrowed. Without a word, she turned and called for a cardiologist. Time stretched painfully thin. Each beep of the machine felt like a countdown. Hot tears slid down my cheeks. I didn't want to die—not like this, not now. Not in a paper gown under fluorescent lights.

I don't even know who I am yet.

The cardiologist finally arrived, barely acknowledging me as she moved toward the monitor. Her fingers flew across the keys, scrolling through data, flipping between screens. I watched her face, searching for something, but all I saw was the same tight-lipped confusion I'd seen in the doctor before her.

She lingered for a moment longer, her eyes narrowing as she studied the chaotic spikes dancing across the screen.

"Am I going to be okay?" I asked, my voice thin.

She hesitated. Her gaze softened, but remained unreadable.

"I don't have all the answers yet," she said quietly, then turned and walked out of the room.

It wasn't long before the nurse returned. "We're transferring you to a children's hospital," she said. "They have specialists there."

Within minutes, I was being loaded into an ambulance. The stretcher rocked gently as the wheels clicked into place. The paramedic beside me adjusted the IV and glanced down with a small, practiced smile.

"You're in good hands now," he said.

The paramedic leaned closer, eyes flicking between me and the monitor. "Let me know the second it happens," he said. I waited, breath shallow, until the now-familiar jolt hit.

"There," I whispered, pointing weakly. He watched the screen and nodded. "Yeah. I see it." A wave of relief washed over me. I wasn't crazy. Someone else saw it too.

We arrived at the children's hospital. It was warmer than the emergency room, which had felt like being trapped inside a refrigerator. Here, the walls were painted in soft pastels; warm wooden cabinets lined the room, and stuffed animals perched patiently on every shelf, watching like quiet guardians. The nurses were kind. They invited me to movie nights and let me pick chocolate from the basket they passed around. When Mark was finally allowed to visit, he walked in with an apologetic smile, the weight of realization hanging in his eyes. "I'm sorry, honey," he said gently. "I didn't know you were being serious."

The sun was starting to rise when a doctor pulled up a stool beside my bed, her movements deliberate and calm. "Hello, Tanja," she said, offering a reassuring smile. "I'm Doctor Reagan. How are you feeling this morning?"

I hesitated. "I don't know," I said, "everything feels off."

She nodded, her expression softening. "That's understandable. You've been through a lot, and it looks like your body is fighting off an infection in your throat. We're keeping a close eye on you."

There was a pause as she glanced at her clipboard, flipping through the pages. Then she looked back at me, her tone shifting slightly. "Can I ask you a few questions? Just to get a clearer picture of things."

I nodded.

"How are things at home?" she asked, her voice gentle, leaving plenty of space for me to decide how much to share.

"All right, I guess," I answered.

"You live with your father?" she asked.

I recoiled slightly, shaking my head. "He's not my father," I corrected her quickly. "He's just my guardian." I wondered if he told them that he was my parent.

Her pen paused briefly, then resumed its quiet scratching on the paper. She didn't press further, but the shift in her posture told me she was paying even closer attention now.

When she asked, "Do you use drugs?" her gaze stayed on me.

"No," I replied quickly.

"We're still figuring things out," she said. "Right now, we're looking at a few possibilities. The tests should give us more clarity."

Every few hours through the night, the door would creak open and a nurse would appear, silhouette glowing under the dim corridor light. Without a word, he'd inject another round of antibiotics into the IV line taped to my arm. My male nurse, soft-spoken with kind eyes, always brought me the same thing: a peanut butter sandwich cut neatly with my initials, and an extra pudding cup balanced on top.

Three days later, the door to my hospital room swung open, and the familiar hum of jazz choir voices spilled in. Before I could process it, they were on me—flinging themselves onto the bed in a tangle of hugs and laughter. "Careful, careful!" a nurse called from the hallway, but I couldn't stop laughing as their arms wrapped around me from every angle. When they finally pulled back, their hands were weighed down with bags of chocolate and handmade cards, their faces split with grins though I could still see the worry flickering behind their eyes.

Rachel held up a glitter-covered card featuring a snail with a tiny Hitler mustache. "Too much?" she asked, barely suppressing a laugh. I laughed harder than I had in days, wiping tears from my cheeks.

"You're terrible," I said. But it was Brianna's eyes I kept returning to watching me through the noise, through the joy. She had been the one I called in the worst moments over the past few months, when the urge to binge and purge wrapped around my throat like a fist. Her voice on the other end was often the only thing keeping me tethered, even as I trembled. And somewhere in that stillness, I realized I was withdrawing just like an addict. But I knew it had to stop. The damage was starting to show: throat polyps had begun to form, which made my voice hoarser than it used to be. And though no one had said it out loud, I had a feeling that whatever brought me to the hospital now was connected.

On the fifth day, Doctor Reagan walked in and took a seat.

"Well, you definitely have arrhythmia," she said. "There's a good chance it's linked to your workouts and eating habits" she continued, her tone shifting slightly, as though trying to soften the blow. Mark must've told her. "It can also be stress induced."

I hesitated before speaking. "I did take a quarter of a pre-workout supplement," I admitted, avoiding her gaze. "One of those big-name brands. It was before my last session."

"That could definitely be a factor." She nodded as if the puzzle had finally come together. It wasn't just the supplement, it was the price of years of overdrive.

She looked up, her gaze softening but still firm. "We're assigning you to a counselor," she said. "And no exercise for three months. Your body needs time to recover."

"And what about the infection?" I asked.

"It's clearing up," she said. "Your body's been through a lot, though. Your immune system is really low."

When the time came for discharge, I didn't want to go home.

"I'm not ready to leave," I insisted. "Can I stay just a little longer?"

She looked surprised as she studied me. Here, I felt safe, warm, and cared for. The doctor sighed softly, setting her pen down. "One more day," she said after a pause and relief flooded through me.

When Mark picked me up, I stared out the window, letting the blur of traffic and sunlight soften the edges of my thoughts. The hum of the engine filled the silence between us. We drove straight to the counseling appointment the doctor had insisted on, no music, no words. In the therapist's office, I sank into the chair. The fabric was rough, like it wasn't meant to be comforting. Mark sat a few feet away. The therapist barely looked up, her voice flat. "How are you feeling about everything that's happened?"

"I don't know," I said, matching her disinterest with my own.

She leaned in slightly, pen poised over her clipboard like a blade. "Can you tell me what's been on your mind? What's been weighing on you?"

I glanced at Mark . He was watching me.

I didn't know how to say this makes me uncomfortable without lighting a match I couldn't put out. The one time I tried to tell Mark , barely even a suggestion of my own physical boundaries, he reacted as if I'd accused him of something unspeakable. He disappeared into his bedroom, sealed himself behind closed doors and drawn curtains, swallowing the light with him. For days, the apartment held its breath. No footsteps. No cough. No flicker of a lamp beneath the door. I began to wonder if he'd died in there.

I still don't know if raising girls—me being the fourth—was Mark 's way of finding purpose, or if there was something darker at play. I couldn't tell where his tenderness ended and something else began, something watchful, invasive, quietly wrong. Maybe he didn't know how to love without hovering. Or maybe I'd just spent so long rationalizing the unease in the name of having a normal life that I forgot how to hear my own alarm bells at all. I knew that saying the truth would break his heart, maybe even break him entirely. So I swallowed the words.

"I'm just tired," I said, looking away.

The therapist paused, pen frozen midair. "Anything specific making you feel that way?"

I gave a shrug I barely meant. "Not really."

The session crawled by. I watched the clock more than the therapist. And when we left, stepping back into the too-bright afternoon, I knew one thing for certain: I wouldn't be coming back.

When Mark was away for work, I invited a few friends over. It was supposed to be a quiet night, just music, drinks, nothing loud. But like most things do at that age, it got out of hand fast. By midnight, someone was passed out by the staircase inside the barn. Robert, Mark 's brother, showed up before I had a chance to clean anything up. He found the kid slumped over and his face shifted from surprise to rage in a breath. Things went flying and glass shattered. Mark called that night, and the night after. And the one after that. "You know Robert's gonna want me off the property for this," he said. "Or he'll make damn sure you're the one who goes." But after a while, his voice just became noise and I stopped caring.

Molly showed up shortly after. I had just stepped out of my friend Rachel's car when I saw her marching across the driveway, eyes sharp with fury. She didn't waste time on greetings.

"How dare you disrespect the person who took you in," she snapped.

Without warning, she raised her hand and struck me across the face. My head snapped sideways. Rachel gasped, her breath catching in her throat.

I gave her a look—go. She fumbled for the door handle, climbed in, and sped off without another word.

I laughed and turned toward the house.

"Don't you dare walk away from me!" Molly's voice cracked behind me like a whip.

Minutes later, the pulsing red and blue of police lights lit up the walls. Rachel must've called them. Through the window, I saw Molly dart across the backyard, slipping into the overgrowth. I sat on the edge of my bed, frozen, listening to the murmur of voices outside the window. "Don't say anything," Mark murmured. "I'll tell them it was a misunderstanding." Outside, Mark 's voice rose, smooth and practiced, weaving some half-truth I couldn't make out. The police seemed to buy it. After a few tense minutes, the footsteps retreated. The porch door creaked shut.

The streetlights outside Jenny's house flickered dim between the trees, casting broken pools of amber along the endless stretch of road. I stood at the edge of her driveway, watching moths slam themselves into the glow like they couldn't help it—drawn in, destroyed, repeat. Somewhere two doors down, someone was grilling, charcoal smoke drifting over the scent of cut grass. Inside, the house was quiet. The television spilled soft light across the living room walls. Her dad was on the couch with a bottle of beer. I'd been staying there for weeks. Her parents didn't say much, but I could feel their wariness of me.

I padded down the hallway in a pair of borrowed socks. Outside Jenny's door, I paused. It was cracked just enough to see her, curled beneath a mess of blankets, her bedside lamp still on, casting soft gold over the paperback splayed open on her stomach.

She looked up and smiled. "Hey," she whispered, patting the bed beside her. "You okay?"

I wanted to lie. I wanted to pretend it was just another night, that I hadn't planned this.

I stared at the soft place she'd made for me in this borrowed life that wasn't mine.

"I think I have to go," I said.

Her smile faltered. "Now?"

"I have to leave town." I said. "I can't keep doing this. I can't look the other way and pretend things are fine."

She didn't say anything. Her body tensed, not from surprise, but from understanding.

She didn't know everything, but she knew enough. She'd heard the stories—about Molly , about the night I called and asked her to take me to the hospital, about the strange comments that didn't sit right. Even though, on paper, I had a home. Even though people called it a second chance.

She didn't hesitate. She slipped off the bed, padded quietly downstairs in bare feet, and pleaded with her father. I lay on her bed, frozen, the hum of the air conditioning blending with the muffled sound of her voice rising, cracking, falling into silence.

"Please," she begged. "She can't go back there."

"She is not our responsibility." I heard her father say.

When the refusal sank in, Jenny broke.

She came back upstairs in pieces, her face crumpled, eyes shining. She collapsed next to me and sobbed, her whole body shaking under the weight of what she couldn't fix.

"How can anyone be so heartless?" she choked. "How can they see what's happening to you and just do nothing?"

I didn't know what to say. I wanted to comfort her, but I didn't know how to reach her without unraveling myself. Her pain mirrored mine.

So I didn't speak.

I just reached for her hand, gently, and held it.

"It's okay," I whispered. "I'll find a home for myself."

24

THE RUNAWAY

My heels were too tight, clicking too loud on the marble floors of hotel lobbies in Los Angeles. I'd just finished taking new head shots in the photographer's hotel room for a pyramid scheme. I stood there in the lobby filling my second cup of coffee, telling strangers nearby I was building something big. But underneath the blazer and borrowed confidence, I was still just a seventeen-year-old runaway and high-school dropout barely out of the Pacific Northwest a few months ago.

When I got back to my bedroom, I packed everything into a single suitcase. Nobody was home. I didn't leave a note.

Slava had set me up with a group of people he knew, strangers to me, but not to the world we were about to enter. They'd just come down from a weekend seminar in Portland, high on motivational jargon and dreams too big to fit in their matching tote bags. People who needed something to believe in.

I climbed into the van with them and didn't look back. Mark called not long after, once he realized I hadn't just run off to a friend's house. That I was really gone. His voice on the other end was calm. Strangely calm. "I get it," he said. "And if you want to come back, I'll be here honey." There was no anger, no guilt trip, just this eerie softness. Supportive, almost. Like he didn't know whether to let go or keep holding space just in case I turned around.

We drove south for twenty hours. Windows cracked, music loud, adrenaline masking the fear of not knowing where I'd land. Slava was part of it now, too. After jail, he needed a clean slate, some kind of rebirth, and this scheme, like all the others, promised just that. His hair was neat and short now. He looked like a true professional.

I told them stories and bits and pieces of my life, spilled across the long stretches of highway. I didn't mean to be impressive, just honest. But they listened. They asked questions. And somewhere near the California border, one of them turned around in their seat, smiled, and said, "You should write a book."

I laughed at the time. But later, when I had to pick a dream to chase, when someone asked me what I really wanted, I remembered how much I liked writing. How natural it felt to put things into words. How I used to fill notebooks as a kid, long before the world told me what was realistic. "I'm going to write a book," I said. And it was funny, almost embarrassing in its simplicity. After everything I'd tried to become, it turned out the thing I was always meant to do was the thing I'd loved all along. Sometimes, you just have to reach back to your roots to find your calling again. It was there, tucked into childhood, waiting for me.

And yet, I liked the pyramid scheme, too. I liked the way people clapped when I said I wanted to be a writer. I liked hearing "you're a leader" from someone wearing a Rolex and standing in front of a laminated dream board like it was a portal. I liked that no one laughed when I said I wanted more, the way they had when I was back in Washington.

After Hollywood, after chasing dreams that twisted into something hollow, I didn't even know what I wanted any more. I didn't trust wanting. I didn't trust the part of me that once believed I was meant for something bigger, something bright.

But standing in those hotel lobbies, in heels that cut into my ankles and a blazer that didn't belong to me, I felt something shift.

It was through a girl named Brandee who had sharp eyeliner and sharper instincts, that Slava and I stumbled into promotional modeling. We'd met in the orbit of the pyramid scheme, one of those fast-talking women who always seemed to know where the next opportunity was, even if she had to invent it herself. She told me the secret plainly, like it was obvious. "If you're attractive and can fake a resume, you're in."

So we did.

We pulled together a list of imagined gigs, polished the words to sound legitimate, just enough industry gloss to pass, and suddenly I was being hired. $25 an hour to smile in heels, to hand out samples and pitch products in branded crop tops and tooth-whitened charm.

Photos of me working these events began to surface on social media as they tagged me, the lighting flattering, my expressions poised. The notifications rolled in, and among them, Mark 's private messages arrived like clockwork.

His words blinked onto the screen: "I will make all my comments discreetly in this manner so you can reserve your page for your peers." I paused. He always chose his words carefully, but now, they felt like they carried more weight, as if he were tiptoeing around something.

"I have seldom commented on your pictures because the qualities I admire in you are your spirit, your brains, and your courage. I don't so much see you as feel you."

A second notification followed: "That being said, you look jaw-droppingly stunning in your newest posts. They are some of the best you have ever posted."

"Thank you, Mark ," I typed back, hesitating for a moment before hitting send.

The last message landed like a weight: "Don't worry. You are unforgettable. The imprints you have made are indelible. Your eyes look incredible. You also look thinner."

Was I reading something into this that wasn't there? Was I overreacting? The questions circled in my mind but I was too busy to keep ruminating.

Soon, I was working convention centers in Las Vegas and Los Angeles, giant halls lit in migraine white, full of noise and artificial enthusiasm.

I moved back and forth between cities, a suitcase always half-packed. In

Vegas, I stayed with Slava, who was still chasing reinvention in desert heat. He worked under a different name now—Mark to everyone who knew him in the promotional industry. A fake social security card folded neatly behind a wad of cash in his wallet. And when I was in L.A., I was staying in Joey's bedroom.

The house Joel rented now looked like it belonged in a horror movie. Its creaky floors, shadowy corners, and dark, weathered wood gave it an unsettling feeling. Gang members loitered on the lower floor, drawn in by a roommate who rented the room downstairs, while upstairs a yogi practiced silent meditation. The house was filled with ghost-like roommates, faces I'd glimpse once, then never see again. Though we all lived under the same roof, no one really knew each other. That was the home Joel had created. And despite everyone paying their rent, Joel was always behind on the payments.

There were many midnight drives with Joey to get some alone time. Windows rolled down, wind tangling my hair. The air in his cadillac he couldn't afford was thick with marijuana and coconut air freshener, the scent of recklessness wrapped in something almost sweet.

I looked at him focused on the road and thought how funny life is. A few weeks ago, he asked me to come to his eighteenth birthday, and by midnight we had drifted away from the noise and chaos of the party. We climbed the stairs in silence. The upstairs bathroom was small, dimly lit, a forgotten corner of the night. It smelled faintly of old soap and cologne.

Joey leaned back against the sink, his hair brushing the edges of his shirt collar, eyes locked on mine. Brown and steady, but searching.

And then the distance between us disappeared.

The kiss was sudden, electric. A collision years in the making.

But then, the door creaked open.

Bree, Joey's best friend stood there, frozen. Her gaze flicked between us, disbelief giving way to something deeper. Something raw. She didn't say my name, or his. Just—

"It's always been her."

And then she turned.

Her words had come months before, tucked into late-night messages that lit up my phone in the quiet. "He hasn't been the same without you." "You should talk to him. I think he still cares." Back then, I thought Bree was being kind. Thought she was trying to mend what had been broken between Joey and me by distance.

But this told me otherwise.

Joey blinked. "What . . .?" He took a step back, as if the air had shifted, as if he wasn't sure where he stood any more.

He didn't get it.

But I did.

The way Bree hovered by his side at the party, the way her eyes tracked his movements like she was memorizing them. The way she looked at me when I showed up that night, tight-lipped and unreadable. The messages. The timing. She'd been waiting. Not for me to come back but to see if I'd stay gone.

Joey looked at me then, really looked. His hand brushed my arm, tentative at first. His touch lingered, like a question that had waited too long for an answer.

"It's always been you."

My trips to L.A. became more frequent. Longer stays. Slower goodbyes. And with each return to Vegas by the shuttle bus I knew so well, the air between Slava and me grew thinner. It wasn't just the miles, though they didn't help, it was the shift. The quiet misalignment of two people who once ran in the same direction and now kept drifting toward different exits.

We tried to play music together again, like we used to. We dusted off old chords, pulled out the keyboard, opened Logic Pro. But it never stuck. Slava's patience had shortened, his irritation seeping through in clipped sighs and barely veiled jabs. At first, he tried to swallow it, bury the sharpness in his tone. But one night, after I got back from another weekend with Joey, it all spilled out.

"You don't care about the business any more," he snapped. "Or the music. You're too busy crushing on some guy to even think about what we're trying to build here."

I froze.

He stood across from me, fists clenched at his sides, jaw tight.

He'd thought having me here would mean purpose again. That I'd be his tether back to music, back to drive, back to meaning. That the pyramid scheme would somehow bloom into something real if we were in it together. But it wasn't. We weren't making money. The dream was slipping through his fingers again, and this time, I was standing too close not to blame. I could see it—behind the fury, beneath the accusations—what he really felt.

Abandoned. The same look from years ago, when I left him behind in Washington.

"I'm finally eighteen now and I'm living my own life. I am done playing the savior in this family," I said. Looking back, it was the single most important decision I ever made, even if I didn't realize it at the time.

25

THE WARNING

Rain streaked the glass as I stood by the large window overlooking the Pacific Northwest's lush pine trees. The backyard, overgrown and alive with spider nests was a wilderness I admired only from a distance. My laptop sat open on the desk, the manuscript on the screen, the blinking cursor pulsing like it was waiting on me to say something, but I had nothing. I was stuck. Joey poked his head into our bedroom, and I couldn't help but memorize him quietly before it all slipped away,

We were both twenty-two now, and he had grown into his looks: muscular, handsome, and effortlessly magnetic. Somehow, we made it this far together.

We moved and built a life in someone else's backyard unit that became our sanctuary. Late nights curled up on the threadbare couch, the hum of old heaters, the quiet comfort of being broke but together. We did wild things just to get by, once stealing a turkey from the grocery store so we could throw a Thanksgiving dinner for our friends.

I spent hours as an intern at a recording studio in Portland, learning the language of sound, growing into myself through music. But mostly, we worked in promotional marketing, long shifts, loud venues, cheap energy drinks, always side by side.

People saw us so often together they stopped saying our names separately. We were a unit. Inseparable. For better or worse.

We'd drink cheap wine, our laughter filling the room as he brushed my hair back behind my ear, his touch tender. "You're the most beautiful girl I've ever seen," he'd whisper. I'd never been looked at like that before: like I was made of glass, not fragile, but crystal clear and I suddenly became very aware of my soul, which I met for the first time in the reflection of his eyes.

But the truth lingered beneath the surface:

He didn't want to leave me, even though I knew—deep down—he wasn't happy.

He craved solitude, a chance to rediscover who he was outside the shadow of his father, who still lingered at the edges of our lives.

And through me, that shadow never really left.

Being with him was like being gently negotiated by a car salesman who wouldn't take a hint. He didn't have bad intentions, but it was done in persistent in a way that made "no" feel like a delay, not an answer. Sometimes, I'd catch Joel in the corners of his face, a flash of expression, and I'd flinch, my fear visible before I could stop it. It made Joey feel like I despised him and maybe in those moments, I did. When he saw how much it affected me, he began to believe he was no different from his father. That thought hollowed him out and the realization of his mistakes came too late.

As much as we loved each other, we had become mirrors for each other's wounds; reflecting, triggering, spiraling. The doubt between us grew roots, showing up in every fight. He'd go cold, pretend I didn't exist, and I'd explode—screaming, throwing whatever was closest, desperate to be seen again. The love we had curdled.

When our eyes met as I stood by the window, he quickly looked away, the warmth in his gaze replaced by something I couldn't quite name. I followed him as he moved toward the front door but stopped cold when I saw my brother standing on the other side. Slava looked wrecked, the sharp lines of his face carved deep and I knew this wasn't just a casual visit. Lucas, his business partner was in the hospital with brain damage.

"They think he was pushed off." Slava's eyes flicked up, dark and hollow.

"I'm a suspect." Lucas had gone on a date that night. The girl led him to the dimly lit parking lot, her laughter fading as shadows closed in. Before he could react, figures emerged from the dark, rough hands shoved him to the ground. The world went black. He was found a few stories below.

"The cops didn't find his phone. I did," Slava continued. "It was stashed in some crack in the parking lot, hidden, like they didn't want it found." His gaze shifted to the floor. "I even went to the casino, tried to get the footage . . . but they shut me down. Wouldn't let me see anything."

Slava told me that for days he had been at the hospital, watching over Lucas to see if he might make a recovery, even though the doctors said he would not. Lucas's mother arrived, her voice cold and brittle. "You did this," she said with a thick Spanish accent. "You wanted him dead because he owed you money." The weight of his criminal record pressed down on him like an invisible chain.

"I didn't do it. I would never," he said, his voice cracking. "I was just trying to help."

Slava crashed on my couch for weeks, sprawled out like he belonged there. Even when the heat died, he didn't leave. Empty soda cans and half-eaten chip bags piled up next to him, but he didn't seem to notice or care. Joey and Slava were thick as thieves, whispering about plans to make it big. It wasn't long before they started actually being thieves and stealing supplies. Taking massive loans. Stealing wood panels, insulation, fabric to build a soundproof booth for their music in the corner of our tiny one-bedroom apartment.

For a while, it felt like things might actually take off. But then, late one night, Slava's voice cut through the low hum of the apartment.

He paced back and forth, agitated.

"You're lazy, man! I've put thousands into this, and you just sit there," he snapped, his glare fixed on Joey , who sat rigid at the desk, jaw clenched, saying nothing.

He stepped closer, looming over the computer like it owed him something, his fingers twitching with impatience.

"Give me the password," he demanded.

Joey pulled the laptop toward him, his voice sharp. "No. You're drugged out."

"I'm not!" Slava barked.

"Dude," Joey said, locking eyes with him, "I can see it in your eyes."

A few days after, I flew back to Germany to visit family.

Dima was getting married to a warm, grounded woman named Victoria.

The wedding was set in a countryside hall just outside Regensburg, the kind with creaky wood floors, ivy climbing up the stone exterior, and string lights zigzagging overhead. The air smelled like grilled meat and wildflowers, and old Russian songs poured out of the speakers while cousins spun each other in crooked circles. Plates clinked. Beer foamed over the edges of tall glasses.

Between laughter and champagne toasts, I initiated a video chat with Slava.

His face lit up when he saw me, but there was a weight behind his smile. A kind of homesickness that had nowhere to land.

I could see it in his eyes, the ache of not being there, of maybe never seeing them again in person. "It's funny," he said, after a long pause. "Everyone used to think Dima was the hooligan, the one who'd never settle down."

He looked away, his voice quieter now. "But now it's me."

It had been over ten years since he had seen Dima or Father.

Andy was flushed and smiling, his arm slung over my shoulder as we swayed side to side. He looked so happy and riled up that the moment lodged itself in my brain. Then he asked, "Don't you feel sad sometimes? That our childhood is gone forever? The way we were always together?"

I looked out across the room and saw Father spinning our stepmother across the dance floor, his hand steady at her waist. He glanced over at me mid-turn, his smile soft and almost boyish.

"No," I said.

But the truth lodged in my throat. I didn't want to name the ache.

At the end of the night, we took a taxi cab home together and agreed to see each other more often during my visit.

That's when it happened. We were at a restaurant sitting at the patio when Andy made a bitter joke about Joey—something small but cutting. I drew a line, gentle but firm and he didn't like that. The warmth drained from his face. His eyes narrowed, his posture stiffened. "You're just like everyone else," he said. "I believed in you to get us there. And for what? You've become ordinary. You're an alcoholic and turned me into one. You sided with Father." The words hit like a slap, but it wasn't just what he said, it was the way he said it.

"You're thirty, Andy . Nobody can make you drink and I certainly didn't. I'm not responsible for your life. I make my own decisions and so should you."

But I realized he couldn't make his own. I saw her. Not Andy. Her.

His face molded into Mother's bitterness, her need to punish, to control. It had seeped into him. I stood frozen, gravel crunching beneath my shoes, the cold cutting into my skin.

He kept talking, but I wasn't listening any more. I turned and walked.

I had seen enough.

Andy messaged me like nothing had happened. A half-hearted joke. A link to some meme. I stared at the screen, felt my stomach twist, and set the phone face down. The silence between us was no longer something I wanted to fill. I saw Mother for a brief moment, knowing it had to be the last time. The grip she had over the psyche of my family was dangerous. On the last day, she showed me an old piece of artwork I'd made when I was about seven, stick figures with me and a boy, and above him the word Joey written in big, uneven letters. I vaguely remember this drawing. My breath caught.

"You always knew the way." Mother said. And I took it as a sign.

I didn't say goodbye with a grand speech. Just a glance. She looked through me like she always had.

The call came in just after sundown. The light outside had turned a dull blue, and the bathroom tiles pressed cold against my bare legs. I answered anyway.

Dima didn't say hello. His voice cut straight through, tight and sharp, like he was already annoyed.

"You need to stop," he said. "You're being childish and need to make up with Andy . . . Every time you're here, it's pure stress."

I hung up. My chest rose too fast, too hard. The corners of the room blurred.

I curled forward, fists clutched into the towel I'd used that morning, and screamed.

I didn't want to lose my Andy or Mother, not again. But I knew what it would cost to keep them. I lay back, the towel twisted beneath me, the ceiling swaying overhead like water. My heart, the one that had stuttered again and again since the hospital visit, held steady. For the first time in five years, it didn't miss a single beat.

All of the understanding came after I wrote the first draft of my manuscript in the late nights of my bedroom. That version was raw, full of pain, full of blame. I had pointed the finger squarely at Mother, laying out every moment she disregarded me.

The second version shifted. I tried to include her perspective alongside mine. But it was still tinted by the lens of my own pain, and in doing so, I warped the person I was writing about. So, I tried something else. I pretended I was a writer named Joel with glasses, notebooks, fiction. He wasn't writing a memoir. He was writing a story. And from that distance, I could finally move through the plot. The third version was stripped down. Just how it happened. I let the reader decide how they felt about it. And that was the version that set something free inside me. It was therapeutic in a way I hadn't expected. I had to ask myself, over and over: Why did this happen? Not to me—but in general. I had to remove myself from the scene enough to understand the characters' motives. To process the reality without taking it as a personal attack. Because what happened was real. And it was painful. But in writing it this way, I began to shed the identity I had built around that pain, the belief I had clung to my whole life:

Bad girls have bad things happen to them.

That I deserved it. That I was marked. That I'd live a life full of pain.

Something shifted.

I began to see my family as they were, not as I needed them to be. I saw their patterns. Their limitations. I saw the pain they would keep causing me, not out of malice, but because they would never heal their own pain. Through the writing, I made a decision: to save myself. It didn't happen all at once. It was a slow boil, so slow I almost didn't notice it.

I didn't know, then, that the childhood dream I'd always carried—to be a writer—would end up being the very thing that saved my life.

When I returned to the U.S., that first night back, I found Slava's marijuana stash on the kitchen counter. I didn't hesitate. I lit it and let the smoke fill my lungs, hoping it would dull the gnawing anxiety that had started crawling up my spine.

Slava glanced over from the couch, his eyes unusually serious.

"I don't think that's a good idea," he said. "That stuff messes with your head. It's a weird batch."

I laughed, exhaling a cloud of smoke, convinced he was being dramatic.

But later, under the harsh fluorescent lights of the grocery store, everything shifted.

One moment I was reaching for canned food, and the next, it felt like the floor had dropped out from beneath me. The lights overhead burned too bright, warping the aisles into endless tunnels. Everything stretched away from me. My heart pounded faster, then faster still. My breath came in short, sharp bursts. My skin tingled like ants were crawling just beneath the surface. My hands trembled as I gripped the shopping basket but it felt foreign, like it didn't belong to me.

And neither did the rest of my body.

I was watching myself from somewhere outside, floating above my own skin. The panic surged higher, throat tightening, legs unsteady. I could still hear the store around me, the low hum of refrigeration, footsteps, voices but it was all underwater now. Muffled. Distant.

I dropped the basket. Groceries spilled across the floor, and I didn't care. I stumbled toward the exit. The cold night air hit me like a slap, but the tightness in my chest didn't ease. It felt like I left my body behind in the isle.

At home, I collapsed into bed, convincing myself it was just the weed. It had been bought legally in Oregon, so surely it was just that. I told myself it would pass. I just needed to sleep it off.

But when I woke up, the world still felt wrong.

For the next seven months, reality warped into a waking nightmare. The trees outside, once vibrant and full of life, now looked like flimsy cutouts pasted against a painted sky. Everything felt artificial, hollow. People moved and spoke, but their voices were muffled, their gestures robotic, like actors performing for an audience I couldn't see in a play I no longer understood. I wandered through my days in a haze.

Nights were worse. My body would tremble uncontrollably, the violent shaking rattling the bed frame. Tears soaked into my pillow, hot, relentless. Joey would wrap his arms around me, trying to hold me together. His grip was tight, desperate, but no matter how close he held me, I kept drifting further away.

"What is the point of life?" I asked one night. "Why are we here spinning on a ball through the universe just to suffer? It doesnt make sense. "

Joey didn't know how to answer my relentless questions. The bluish dawn filtered through the curtains, casting a pale glow across his face. He didn't know how to help me.

"Maybe it's time to see someone," he said eventually, his voice low, like he'd rehearsed the line for days before saying it out loud.

I stared up at the ceiling. "With what money?" I whispered.

I wasn't working right now. My bank account was empty. I had no health insurance.

But even I got tired of my own excuses. One morning, I sat at the edge of the bed, holding my credit card in one hand and my phone in the other, like I was disarming a bomb.

The first session didn't fix anything. But it stopped me from unraveling entirely.

Week after week, I returned, swiping my card, watching the balance climb while hoping for some kind of relief.

"Am I going crazy?" I asked during one of those sessions. The psychologist's office was quiet, still. He adjusted his glasses, considered me for a long moment.

"It doesn't seem so," he said. "You're aware of what's happening. It sounds like an intense version of derealization or maybe an existential crisis."

I thought of Germany. Not the country itself, but that trip, the way it cracked something open in me. I wasn't sure when the unraveling began, only that afterward, everything felt different. As if the scaffolding of my beliefs had quietly collapsed, thread by thread, until I was left with nothing but a blank slate—raw, exposed, uncertain of what to trust any more.

We kept going with the therapy. Week after week, I followed the pendulum with my eyes, breathing through the nausea that came with remembering. Rapid eye movement, they called it, a way to retrace the past without being consumed by it. I replayed the same memories again and again, except now, I was allowed to change the endings.

Not to what they were, but to what I needed them to be.

This time, someone stepped in. Someone said stop. Someone saw me.

Mother hugged me in these versions. She called me Nanya.

It wasn't about rewriting the past. It was about giving my nervous system a new story to hold on to. One where I wasn't trapped. One where I wasn't voiceless.

The memory remained but the wound around it started to close.

"You're doing great. My therapist leaned forward slightly. "Start small. Try going outside again. Ground yourself. Meditation can help. The hurt and anger you've been carrying, they're coming to the surface now. You have to let them come through."

The suggestion lingered, unspoken but loud. Don't run, face it.

At first, it was unbearable. The sunlight felt too sharp, the world too loud, like stepping into a crowded room after being locked away for years. I would sit in the park, legs crossed, staring at the grass until the green began to blur. I practiced breathing slowly, as if I could coax my mind to stay in my body. The meditation felt futile at first, but over time it anchored me in ways I didn't understand.

I started collecting the books without really meaning to, titles passed to me by my psychologist, friends, even near-strangers who had clawed their way out of their own darkness. I didn't know what I was searching for, but maybe a way to create meaning out of my life. My desk disappeared beneath the mess. Stacks of paperbacks with cracked spines, post-it notes jutting out like thorns. Spirals of half-filled journals, highlighters, underlines, circles around phrases that made something in my chest ache. Pages marked up like I was trying to track down some hidden map of myself to a version of God. I learned that not all darkness is cruel. When everything fades to black, even the faintest flicker of light becomes easier to find and sometimes, it's only in the dark that you learn how much you need it.

I started to notice the way I laughed when I was uncomfortable, the way I said "it's fine" when it wasn't. The way I smiled—Mother's smile—even when something inside me screamed no. I learned how to say the truth.

Books kept piling up, but the weight in my chest started to lift. Slowly, quietly.

And then one morning, sunlight filtered in through the window just right. I sat up in bed, stretched, blinked at the ceiling.

And I realized:

I felt . . . normal. Like a person again.

I had one last vivid dream during those nights and it's stayed with me ever since.

We were at the docks on a stormy night, the sky bruised with dark clouds, the wind howling like it was mourning something. The water below surged like a living, furious thing. Slava stood at the edge, rain pouring down his face, his jacket soaked, lit in bursts by flashes of lightning.

Without a word, without hesitation, he dove into the black water and vanished beneath the churning waves.

Joey followed without thinking, laughing. His silhouette disappeared into the darkness after Slava, swallowed by the night.

I stood frozen, my hands gripping a weathered wooden bollard, its splinters digging deep into my palms.

"Come back!" I screamed, my voice shredded by the wind.

Joey's laughter faltered. He turned, eyes wide with panic, as the weight of it all hit him like a wave. He fought his way back to the dock, clawing at the slick wood and lifting himself up.

But Slava . . . Slava was gone.

The ocean had taken him. Swallowed him whole.

I screamed his name again and again, but the storm drowned me out.

All that remained was the endless, empty sea.

I jolted awake, heart pounding. I knew it wasn't just a dream. It was a warning.

26

THE HOUSE

There was a grand house tucked deep in the Oregon woods, at the end of a cul-de-sac where lanterns glowed amber in the mist. Towering evergreens lined the road, their silhouettes stretching high into the sky, and behind the house, the mossy forest sprawled endlessly.

I stepped onto the porch and knocked on the heavy wooden door.

A blonde girl opened the door a moment later and a husky burst through, its paws thudding against the boards as it bounded toward me, tail wagging like it had been waiting all day. It looked like a movie set; the curated version of a perfect American life.

And the strangest part was . . . it belonged to Slava.

"Hi! You must be Tanja."

She stepped forward, extending a hand with a soft smile that didn't quite hide her nerves. "I'm Melanie. Slava's told me so much about you."

She looked to be about a year younger than me, round-faced, kind-eyed, the kind of beautiful that came from how she carried herself. Not like the others he used to date. There was no performance in her. She was a little overweight, with clear blue eyes and an energy that immediately felt warm, like stepping into sunlight after a long shadow. I liked her instantly. "That's

Amy," she added, gesturing toward the husky who was spinning in circles. "She's kind of the boss around here."

I laughed.

Melanie and Slava had met by chance. Joey had posted on social media looking for someone to record background vocals on his tracks, something soulful and R&B-influenced. Melanie replied. She showed up while I was away for Dima's wedding.

And the rest, as they say, was history.

While a new love was forming in that makeshift studio, Joey and mine came quietly to an end. We finally made the decision—the one we'd been circling for months—to let go of what no longer worked, even though I didn't want it to end. Leaving wasn't easy for me. It was the only thing I had left that still felt like home. I had put my entire self into that relationship, all the versions of me, from the girl I used to be to the one still trying to find her shape. Walking away from him felt like peeling off my own skin.

I believed love was worth saving. It was the thread that made everything bearable. And for a while, our love put a bandage over a pain I couldn't name. It made the world feel survivable.

But deep down, I knew it wasn't fair. Not to him. Not to me.

Being alone in the world again was terrifying. "I'm scared," I admitted one night as I was packing up my belongings, my voice barely above a whisper. "I don't think anyone will ever love me the way you did."

Joey looked at me, and for a moment, I saw the boy who used to climb cherry trees.

"The way you saw me as a kid," I said, tears burning at the edges of my voice. "What I went through. What I survived. You know me. Nobody will ever know me like that."

He held my gaze, quiet for a long moment. Then he said,

"Maybe that's the point."

His voice was gentle, but certain.

"Maybe it's time for someone to love you for who you are today."

But even after we agreed to part and my friends helped me move out, I didn't let go easily. I screamed into pillows when no one was around. I cried so hard my body ached. I left voicemails, too many, full of things I never said when it mattered. Desperate, messy confessions. Half-apologies. Half-hope. I just wanted him to say something. Anything. Something that would make it make sense. But my friend Amanda, who I moved in with, told me I needed to move on. Eventually, I stopped calling.

During this time, I started a new job, one I never could've predicted would change everything. I auditioned to host my own online talk show as a livestreamer through a promotional agency I already had rapport with. It felt almost like a scam at first, but the opportunity was real. And somehow, it fit. I remembered Andy telling me years ago, "You'd be great at that." Back then, I didn't believe him because I am shy and quiet. But now? I had nothing to lose. And after three months, it took off.

I was unhinged in the best way; bold, outrageous, especially in the wake of the breakup. I cracked jokes that made people spit out their drinks, I overshared, I acted out. And they loved it. They kept coming back.

My fanbase grew to 300,000 strong. Suddenly, I was making a living just by being myself.

For the first time, I didn't feel like I had to be chosen to matter. I didn't need a relationship to feel seen. The spotlight, oddly enough, made me feel seen and understood. It pulled me out of my shell and held up a mirror. I liked what I saw.

And Joey ? He watched me. He'd join my streams under anonymous usernames, hiding in the scroll of the chat. But I knew it was him. He was watching the version of me that bloomed without him. And part of me hoped he was proud, part of me hoped he regretted everything.

While I was moving out and trying to find my footing in the world, Slava was doing the same after finally deciding that Joey wasn't worth working with any more after a few physical altercations. I first heard about this house through Dima and Father. They couldn't believe Slava lived somewhere so beautiful. He'd sent them photos, the view of the evergreen forest stretching endlessly from the back deck, the private sauna in the basement glowing amber under soft lights. But stepping inside told a different story.

In the middle of the living room sat a massive bean bag, large enough to swallow three people whole. An old piano, left behind by the previous owners, rested against the far wall. Melanie sat at it, her fingers gliding effortlessly over the keys. Her music filled the space, soft and moody, as rain streaked down the tall windows behind her. Upstairs, the house opened into at least three bedrooms, all empty.

Slava stood at the window. "You could hide a body outside and no one would find it," he said, laughing. I shook my head, laughing too.

"We can have parties here once I get a real dining table," Slava said, leading me through the hallway. He held up a cardboard box. "Look— cocktail shakers. You can make your fancy drinks again."

Downstairs, he showed me his office. A sleek gaming setup took up all of the room. On his monitor, a flurry of Adobe Photoshop files were open, all layered and chaotic. My eyes drifted to the corner of his desk. A stack of envelopes from the bank. Thick. Official. I leaned closer. The numbers were staggering. Hundreds of thousands in loans.

"Slava, this is a terrible idea," I said, pointing at the letters.

He grabbed a folder and slapped it over them like he could make them disappear. "The less you know, the better . . . if it all goes south."

I turned to him, frowning. "How are you planning to make this work?"

"I'm day trading," he said with a shrug. "Lost ten grand today."

He laughed, but there was no joy in it. I stared at him, my mouth falling open. His forehead was lined deep with worry, aging him by years. He looked like someone who hadn't slept properly in weeks.

"This is so risky."

"All or nothing, baby," he said, flashing a forced grin. "If I don't make it rich fast, it's over for me."

That's when it clicked. He'd backed himself into a corner to gamble everything on the belief that stress would turn into fuel, that collapse would somehow birth success.

"What do you mean, 'it's over'?"

He looked me dead in the eye. "If I don't make it by thirty-five, I'll kill myself."

"You're joking."

But he didn't flinch.

He was thirty-three.

"But you're not going to make it like this," I said. "It's not the way to do it."

"Yeah, but I'm not going to make it through music," he said. "I haven't yet."

"You haven't even done anything yet," I shot back. "You haven't recorded, submitted, performed—nothing. Not in the last ten years. Of course you haven't made it."

"We performed for three years in Hollywood," he argued.

"You and I both know that wasn't the way to go," I said. "But to call it failure before you've even tried properly? That's crazy."

"Well . . . it's too late now."

He said it with finality. Like he'd already decided the outcome.

He'd said outrageous things before—about moving to China to live in a monastery, about robbing a bank just to see if he could get away with it. So part of me wanted to chalk it up to Slava being Slava. But something in his voice didn't feel like a joke this time.

At night, he sat by the window, fingers clenched around his phone as he spoke to our mother. He'd pause mid-sentence, his eyes dimming with frustration. Then he'd try again, softer and gentler this time, as if he could still break through the wall she'd spent years building. Sometimes he read to her from his own self-help books. But she twisted the words, bending the lessons until they served her. She'd talk and talk, her voice filling every pause. She once even admitted, offhandedly, like it was nothing, that the séances, the spirits, had all been lies. Just tools to control us.

And when he brought it up again, she denied ever saying it. Eventually, he'd mute the call and walk away. Her voice kept going, spilling into the room, completely unaware that no one was listening any more.

"You know it's no use," I said quietly.

He didn't look up.

"You need to let her go."

Now he sat in this hollow house, still pretending he'd made it. In some way, he was still appeasing her, still performing the version of success she always wanted to see.

Maybe he just needed to know what it felt like, whatever it was he'd spent so long chasing. To finally have it, only to realize it wasn't what he thought.

And maybe what made it worse was the silence; the empty rooms, the oversized furniture, the echo of his own footsteps. A house this big, and no one came to visit but me.

Maybe that was the cruelest part: realizing that what mattered most was the thing he'd given up to get here.

Family. Connection. Us.

Slava disappeared into the basement office for days at a time, hidden beneath the house like a ghost. The rest of the house stayed dark.

Then Mel texted me, her concern bleeding through the screen.

I'm worried about him, she wrote. I found a medication that pulled me out of my depression. It's unconventional, but it filled a void I didn't even know I had. I told him about it, and he wanted to try. The change was immediate. He's brighter now, optimistic, engaged. The darkness isn't consuming him any more. He can think clearly, logically. He's open. He's honest. It feels like he is a new person.

She paused, then added:

He says I saved him. And maybe I did. But really, it was all him. He let me in. He chose to try. He saved himself.

Mel's words radiated hope.

There's nothing I want more than for him to be happy, she wrote. This is just the beginning, but I hope it stays this way.

So did I.

Slava had vanished into the basement again, according to Melanie.

Days passed without a word. The only sign of life was the faint hum of the computer below and the flicker of blue light bleeding through the cracks in the door at night. The rest of the house stayed quiet like it was holding its breath, waiting for him to resurface.

I could imagine him down there, hunched over the desk, eyes bloodshot, the glow of the monitor casting sharp shadows across his face. Half-empty energy drinks crowding the corners. Then my phone buzzed. Her message came in fragmented bursts, like she didn't know where to start.

I'm worried about him.

There was a pause. Then the typing dots returned.

I found a medication that pulled me out of my depression. It's unconventional, but it filled a void I didn't even know I had.

I leaned against the kitchen counter, reading her words.

I told him about it, she continued. And he wanted to try. The change was immediate. He's brighter now. Optimistic and engaged. The darkness isn't consuming him any more. He can think clearly, logically. He's open. He's honest. It feels like a new dawn.

I could almost picture it, he version of Slava that existed in her eyes. One I hadn't seen in years.

He says I saved him, she wrote. And maybe I did. But really, it was all him. He let me in. He chose to try. He saved himself.

My fingers hovered above the screen, unsure what to say.

Mel's last message came through a minute later.

There's nothing I want more than for him to be happy. This is just the beginning, but I hope it stays this way.

So did I.

27

THE STRANGERS

The sky over LAX was pale and washed out, the kind of gray that made everything feel suspended. Planes dipped low over the city, their engines a dull roar overhead. We waited outside the arrivals terminal, where the air buzzed with the chaos of reunions; crying children, arms flung around necks, the clatter of suitcases dragging across concrete.

And then I saw them.

After weeks of persuasion, I had finally convinced Father and our stepmother, Irene, to visit the United States in the Summer of 2019. It hadn't been easy. Father was cautious by nature, and even more so with the language barrier; he and Irene were both deaf, and the thought of navigating a new country made him tense. But I knew what this trip could mean. For Slava, it was everything. He couldn't leave the country, so bringing Father to him felt like the only way to give him that flicker of connection—patch of home planted on unfamiliar soil.

The heat hit us in waves, bouncing off the blacktop. I could see the tension in Father's shoulders even as he waved. Slava and Father gave each other a brief, slightly awkward embrace. But there was something in it, a flicker of recognition, of grief, of love trying to remember its shape. We packed into a rental vehicle, Slava driving, Melanie beside him, and me in the back seat with Father and Irene.

Father sat rigidly, his hands clasped tightly in his lap. Though Slava was his son, he seemed nervous, almost formal. Father kept glancing over, studying him in small, quiet moments. I could see it, the way he was trying to connect the grown man in the driver's seat with the little boy he once tucked into bed. Irene, on the other hand, was radiant. She couldn't stop staring at him. "He looks just like your father," she signed to me. "It's uncanny."

And it was. The resemblance was undeniable, from the sharp jawline to the quiet, watchful eyes. They were strangers with matching features.

Slava didn't say much. He kept his focus on the road, hands tight on the wheel, face unreadable. But I could feel it, the weight of what he wanted this to be, and the fear that it wouldn't be enough. Outside the window, L.A. unspooled in flashes: strip malls, freeways, gas stations, palm trees. It made you feel small and enormous all at once.

Father was wide-eyed the moment we parked on Sunset Boulevard, near our private homestay. Helicopters hovered overhead like mechanical vultures, circling slowly as searchlights carved pale arcs into the sky.

Even though Father couldn't hear, he felt L.A.—the bass thrumming up through the pavement, the vibration of sirens pounding in his chest like war drums. His eyes darted from one light to the next, alert to every flash, every movement. It was overwhelming, electric, a sensory overload compared to the quiet rhythm of Regensburg.

Slava watched him, hands stuffed in his hoodie pockets, eyes locked on Father like he might vanish if he blinked.

"He looks so old," he murmured.

I looked at Father, his hair thinner, skin loose at the jawline. Slava had imagined time would be kind—or at least paused until he made it successful—like thirteen years in America might somehow only equal one in Germany. But time had moved on. Now he had to measure the cost of his choices in the lines on our father's face.

The shame lived just under Slava's skin. It always had. He'd been the one to agree to the divorce that day, back when we were just kids. The one who told Father to leave. And though Father never said it out loud, I knew he resented him for it. It hung in the air between them.

Inside the apartment, they began to sign to each other.

Slava's hands moved slowly at first, hesitant, clumsy in places. The language he hadn't used in years sat just beneath the surface, like something buried but not forgotten. When he couldn't remember the right signs, he pantomimed—wide gestures, exaggerated expressions—and somehow, it worked. And Father smiled. Not with his mouth, but with his whole body; the way he leaned in, the way his eyes softened, the way he responded without correcting. Then, without warning, they sat down at the kitchen table and locked arms, a playful, silent challenge. An arm wrestle.

They laughed. A full-bodied, boyish kind of laughter.

And Father won. His hand slammed Slava's knuckles to the table with a thud.

Slava shook his head, grinning through the sting.

During our roadtrip and long drives to surrounding states, Slava confessed to Father that he'd never really wanted to be with Mel. He criticized her weight, said she wasn't the model-perfect partner he had always imagined. Mel sat beside him, oblivious. She didn't know sign language. She had no idea what he was saying, though, painfully, I knew he'd told her these things before. They were together, but he was never truly in it.

I found myself mentally drifting throughout the trip, constantly trying to recalibrate around Slava's moods. He'd be up at 4 am to go swimming, then return and sleep through noon while the rest of us waited, dressed and ready. When we planned outings for our parents, he brushed them off.

"I've already done all that," he'd say, waving a hand dismissively.

"It's their first time," I'd reply, trying to keep the peace. "Can you please just come along—for them?"

He'd sigh, roll his eyes. "I don't need to sit through some lame tour just because they haven't." Despite his resistance, he spent lavishly on dinners for them, only to complain about it later, cornering me in private.

"You need to pay me back what you owe," he'd snap. "Or I'm not covering any more of this trip." Slava tried to charge me for the toilet paper he bought and I used during this stay, calculating it down to the number of days, the number of sheets. He scribbled numbers into a spreadsheet on his phone.

"I'm using my credit card just to keep up," I'd say, trying to stay calm. "I accumulated a lot of debt with all the therapy sessions I had."

But he was already spiraling, arguing over sunscreen, of all things.

"Why didn't you let me use the nice one?" he demanded. "Instead of that cheap spare?"

"Because I need it to last the whole trip," I said, exasperated, walking that familiar tightrope around him.

But something darker was surfacing.

One night, I noticed Melanie shaking; pale, sweating, her hands trembling uncontrollably. She was going through withdrawal. And when I looked at Slava, I saw the same signs. Whatever new antidepressants they'd picked up in Mexico, they were now trying to go without. And it was going badly.

I did my best to distract my parents, filling our days with conversations, sights, anything to keep them from noticing what was unraveling behind the scenes.

That evening, as we sat outside under the flicker of city lights, I signed to Father quietly.

"There's something you should know about Slava," I said.

He turned to me, concern etched in his eyes.

"What's going on?" he signed back.

"He's struggling," I signed. "I think he's dependent on something. It's affecting everything, his moods, his anger. It's not just stress. I don't think he's himself any more."

Father's face tightened. He searched mine for the truth.

"I'll talk to him," he signed.

I nodded, unsure. Their relationship was fragile and newly reformed.

The next morning, Slava stormed into my room, eyes wild, cheeks flushed.

"You told Dad about me?" he hissed. "About my problems? Who gave you the right?"

"Slava, I was worried. You're scaring them. You're scaring me—"

"You're unbelievable," he snapped. "And don't worry. I told him something about you, too."

His voice dropped, venomous.

"I told him Joey 'raped' you. I told him Joey cheated. I told him everything."

I froze, the blood draining from my face. "Slava, that's not even true. You had no right—"

"I don't care," he said. "Now the family knows exactly who Joey is. You'll never get close to him again."

Hot tears welled in my eyes.

He shrugged, a bitter smile crawling onto his face. "Now everyone knows who Joey really is."

I had a flashback to Joey telling me, "If Slava never moved in with us, we'd still be together."

At the time, I didn't understand it.

But now . . . now I saw it clearly.

He had chipped away at us slowly, strategically, subtle undermining, whispered chaos, truths bent out of shape and slipped between us like poison. He'd said one thing to Joey, then come to me and ask, "Do you really trust him?" I didn't see it at the time. But now it was suddenly clear.

Just like that, he drove the final stake into any reconciliation I'd still been secretly hoping for. And into my trust in him—whatever was left of it. The entire end of the trip, we spoke when we had to: polite, clipped exchanges over coffee or keys or the last clean towel. Mostly, we just stayed out of each other's way.

After Father and Irene left back for Germany, Slava and I maintained a cool distance. We still tried to see each other on important holidays. I was the only family he had here, and no matter how bad things got, I worried what would become of him without me.

On Christmas Eve, the car hummed softly as Slava and I drove through the dimly lit streets, the glow of holiday lights flickering across windshields and storefronts.

When he popped the trunk to stow my presents on the way home, a chill swept through me. I caught a glimpse of something that didn't belong: a coil of rope, a shovel, and a rubber mask that looked disturbingly real. Human, almost.

"What is that?" I asked.

He shrugged. "A magic trick."

But something in his tone sent a shiver down my spine.

The road stretched endlessly ahead, flanked by dark, empty fields.

We talked. We laughed. For a moment, it almost felt normal.

Then, without warning, Slava said,

"I think I'm going to kill three people."

I turned, stunned. "What?"

"Yeah," he said, eyes locked on the road. "I'm taking three motherfuckers with me—the guy who raped Melanie, Joey for what he did to you, and Joel's dad for being a pedophile. Then, I will kill myself."

My heart stopped. "What the fuck is wrong with you?" I gasped. "You can't play karma and kill people! Seriously? This is a Christmas conversation?" My voice cracked. I searched his face for some hint of a joke, but there was nothing. "What about your family? What about Father? What about me? That would destroy us. I can't live without you. I'll come right with you."

"You'll be fine," he said. Cold. Distant. "Everyone dies. Everyone moves on."

My hands trembled in my lap. "You can't throw your life away like that. You have so much ahead of you."

He shook his head.

My voice broke. "Slava, please. You need help. See my therapist. I'll pay for it. I'll go with you—just please."

Weirdly enough, he agreed.

And for a second, I believed he meant it.

I thought maybe—just maybe—he was ready to try.

But a few days later, during my own session, my psychologist pulled me aside. His expression was grave.

"I'm sorry," he said. "Slava can't come back here."

I stared at him, confused. "Why?"

He sighed. "He spent the session tearing apart my methods, mocked the process, demanded a refund, and left after ten minutes."

I pressed my fingers against my eyelids, trying to hold myself together.

On my twenty-fourth birthday, just a week later, I found myself in Texas, battling through the relentless icy wind as I pushed my body through a full marathon. My breath came in sharp bursts, my muscles burning with each step. I was focused, determined until my phone buzzed in my pocket.

I checked it without thinking.

Slava.

His message lit up the screen, stark and jarring:

You can't stop me. I'm going to kill Joey.

My stomach dropped. The cold that had wrapped around me from the wind was nothing compared to the chill that ran down my spine.

My fingers trembled as I typed back, each word laced with panic and disbelief.

If you do that, I'll report you. You'll be deported before it ever happens.

Then I fired off a message to Joey, short, frantic, desperate.

Please stay away from home. Go somewhere safe. Now.

His threats echoed in my mind as I kept running, my legs moving on autopilot, my thoughts spiraling into places I didn't want to go. The what if clung to me like a shadow but deep down, I didn't believe he'd do it. He wasn't a psychopath.

And yet . . . if I called the police, he might actually go through with killing himself. He'd told me before he'd rather die than go back to jail.

I knew Slava was using this. Weaponizing fear.

Because he knew exactly where to hit me. Because threatening Joey was just another way of hurting me. And that night, I made a decision: I cut off contact with him. Not because I didn't care, but because I'd reached the edge of what I could carry. I hoped the silence would quiet whatever need he had to pull me back into his chaos. I hoped his depressive cycle would settle and he would return to his normal self for awhile, like he had before.

28

THE ARIZONA

The late afternoon sun in Phoenix hit my face like the blast from an open oven door. Heat shimmered off the asphalt, warping the air in waves, even as the day began to cool. In the distance, the mountains stood silhouetted against a sky that was fading into soft purples.

After COVID hit and restrictions were put into place, my roommate decided to move to Arizona. Within five hours, I had packed my life into boxes and jumped into the car with her. I did not overthink it. I just wanted a fresh start.

I got a two-bedroom apartment in a small complex just outside Old Town Scottsdale. The building was low and white, a mid-century holdout with updated landscaping, raised wooden planters, gravel-lined paths, and a central pergola. I adopted two cats, who followed me from room to room and slept curled at my side at night. I started dating Miguel, a new boyfriend who made me laugh so hard my head would snap back. I kept livestreaming, the glow of my setup casting soft colors against the walls, and the income stayed steady. I enrolled in yoga school too, chasing the idea of becoming a certified teacher. Yoga did something to me. It slowed the static that used to rattle under my skin, taught me how to breathe through the fear instead of running from it. For the first time, my body didn't feel like something I had to escape. And when I sat at the central pagoda after class, drinking wine with my friends, it finally hit me. Somewhere along the way, without even realizing it, I had built everything I used to wish for. A stable home. My own space. A life that was completely mine. And then, out of nowhere, Slava's message lit up my phone:

I miss you.

It had been a year since we last spoke—my twenty-fourth birthday—and now I was twenty-five. I missed him more than I wanted to admit. So I called.

His voice crackled through the speaker, familiar and jumpy. The camera tilted as he walked me through the shed he now lived in behind Mel's parents' house; a cramped space lit by a single bare bulb, walls cluttered with storage bins and salvaged junk. He looked thinner, unshaven. Thirty-five, though he somehow seemed both older and younger than that number.

"Still breathing," he said with a crooked smile, when I asked how he'd been. "Had a rough spell . . . but I'm out of it now. You know the kind."

I nodded. I did.

He launched into his latest project with the same manic edge I remembered—fingers darting into the frame to show me a closet lined with reflective foil. Shelves of microgreens, heat lamps, jars labeled in marker. "Gonna sell them out of the van," he said, panning to a beat-up white van parked outside that he'd bought with the last of his money. "Organic. Local. Sustainable."

Then came the maggots, a writhing large box of them.

"Protein," he grinned. "Cheap and efficient. Nothing goes to waste."

I laughed, uneasy. "That's disgusting."

"They eat everything," he added. "Even bodies. Leave no trace."

He glanced at the screen to catch my reaction.

"Oh god," I said, half-laughing, half-frozen.

"I'm joking," he smirked. "C'mon. I knew that would freak you out."

Not long after, he asked me for money.

"For an apartment," he said. "I'll have Melanie sign for it since I can't have my name on a lease right now. I'm laying low, hiding from the banks."

"Where should I send it?" I asked.

"Melanie," he finally said. "Send it to her."

I told Miguel, my boyfriend about Slava; about the shed, the microgreens, the life that had shrunk down to a backyard corner. Miguel set his beer down and leaned back against the couch.

"You should bring your brother out here," he said. "Give him a different perspective."

I thought about it for a long time after he said it. And eventually, I bought Slava a plane ticket.

Miguel and I had first crossed paths in a seedy bar in Portland with sticky floors awhile ago. He slid up next to me, offered to buy me a drink. I smiled, shook my head. I was still with Joey. That was that. Or so I thought.

Two years later, his name popped up in the chat of a livestream I was hosting. He was supporting a friend's stream when he recognized my photo. You probably don't remember me, he typed. But I met you before.

I did remember.

We ended up talking in messages and it grew into a deeper connection.

He lived in L.A., but that didn't stop him. Every Friday after work, he'd make the long drive to see me. He'd show up tired, hands stained from the shop, but smiling like it was the best part of his week. Miguel wasn't what anyone expected.

He had that L.A.-style script tattooed down his forearm and a past most people would run from. A felony, a few hard years, stories he never glamorized. He was rough around the edges, but he was hardworking—a mechanic by trade—and despite everything that might have made people second-guess him, he was gentle in ways that completely disarmed me. His hands, calloused from years of turning wrenches and fixing engines, would cradle my face like he was afraid I'd break any moment. Where I used to have to beg Joey to close the closet door at night—an old habit, a fear that never quite left me—Miguel just did it. Every night. No questions, no smirks. He'd open the door, peek inside, and say softly, "See? No monsters in here." Then he'd lock it, climb into bed, and pull me close.

When Slava arrived looking like his normal self, we took a walk around my block, the sun dipping behind rooftops, washing the neighborhood in gentle amber. The soft, sweet scent of white blossoms drifted on the warm Scottsdale breeze. We moved quietly at first before I finally broke the silence.

"You know," I said softly, turning to him, "it's because of you that I found one of my callings. You got me into promotional marketing. Without that, I'd never have found live streaming."

Slava raised an eyebrow, his shoulders shifting uncomfortably.

"Seriously," I continued, smiling, "livestreaming is basically street busking, just online. I still sing, still dance, still tell awful jokes. It's just that now I have an audience of thousands that tip me."

Slava looked away, startled. He seemed touched, almost confused, like he'd never imagined I could see anything good coming from him.

"Nah," he muttered quietly, shrugging it off. "That was all you."

But his eyes softened, and I knew my words had landed. He carried a burden, that he'd caused me pain, that the damage he left outweighed anything else. Yet, in that quiet moment, on a street far from where we'd started, I caught a glimpse of something rare: pride. A flicker of peace. And as we walked together beneath the fading daylight, I hoped he felt even a fraction of the hope and possibility I had finally found.

As we walked the quiet streets, shadows lengthened under the fading sun, and Slava's voice broke the comfortable silence. "You know why I invested in Joey's music?" he said quietly, his eyes fixed on the sidewalk. "It wasn't because I believed in him. I always believed in you. But I was upset that you didn't want to work with me, so I invested in him just to show you what could've been." He paused, his shoulders dropping. "But it was a mistake." His voice softened, thick with a regret I hadn't expected. "I should've been supporting you all along."

"I forgive you," I said gently.

He nodded slowly, then glanced over his shoulder before leaning in closer, his voice suddenly low and tense. "Listen," he whispered. "How well do you know Miguel?"

"Well enough," I answered, confused.

"I think Miguel is here to kidnap you."

I stopped walking, caught completely off guard. "What?"

"I think he's cartel," he said quietly, dead serious. "Undercover."

I almost laughed. The absurdity hit me so unexpectedly that a smile pulled at the corners of my mouth. Miguel, a cartel agent? Warm, steady Miguel who checked closets for monsters every night?

But one look at Slava's eyes silenced me. He was genuinely afraid.

"I've been watching videos," he continued, "on the dark web. Real footage. Cartel killings. You have no idea what these people are capable of. I came out here to see for myself—to make sure you're safe."

I felt my heart twist. This wasn't just a visit. Slava hadn't come to see my new life or meet my boyfriend; the darkness brought him all the way here. When we returned, Miguel was already asleep. I slipped quietly into the room, careful not to disturb him. Before climbing into bed, I gently closed the door and placed my twenty-five-pound kettlebell against it. I paused for a moment, staring down at the dark shape on the floor, unsure why I was doing it. Just in case, I thought.

It was as if we'd never had that conversation. Slava and Miguel grew closer by the day, filling the apartment with laughter as they watched comedy shows, tossed quotes back and forth, and invented inside jokes that drifted into the next room where I worked. They were such different people, but somehow they fit; often locked in animated conversations about jail, dissolving into easy laughter like they'd known each other for years.

One night, after finishing my live stream, I found them sitting quietly on the couch, snacks scattered between them. Slava was leaned back, uncharacteristically quiet, while Miguel nodded, his expression serious.

Later, when I asked, Miguel told me their conversation had shifted from jokes to something heavier.

"Slava talked about jail?" I asked, surprised. It was a subject he rarely touched, even with me.

Miguel nodded. "Not much," he said. "But he hinted at some pretty rough stuff. He said he saw things that would 'mess anyone up.' After that . . . he just shut down. Wouldn't say more."

Whatever had happened to him in there, it was locked so deep inside him he could barely even brush against it. When we went out to my favorite restaurants, Slava would try to slip me a crumpled twenty-dollar bill under the table. "I'm sorry," he'd say quietly. "It's all I have."

"No, Slava," I said every time. "You already paid for me so many times. It's my turn now."

I saw the way his eyes shifted around the room when we were out, how he seemed to flinch under the simple weight of being seen. Like he didn't quite know how to sit still near a table where people were laughing freely, where no one was watching their back.

At these places, we often talked about Slava's future, too, his plans, his dreams, and what moving to Arizona could look like for him. I even tried to get him excited about getting a green card, hoping to give him more options. "I can help you," I'd say, pulling up application forms, suggesting jobs he might enjoy, even imagining a place of his own. We even talked about locations in a different country if he couldn't move past his loans. But every time we got close to making concrete plans, he'd brush it off, claiming it wasn't the right time or he wasn't ready. His eyes would drift, his body shifting uncomfortably, and the topic would evaporate. Part of me wondered if he actually believed any of it was possible. Deep down, maybe he felt stuck, trapped in the shadow of whatever he'd experienced, unable or unwilling to reach for something better, as if he didn't truly believe he deserved it.

At night and early mornings, Slava had started taking long walks, something he'd never really done before. He'd slip quietly out the door, returning with an expression I couldn't read, eyes distant. Sometimes, I'd catch him muttering under his breath, words just out of earshot. "What was that?" I asked him gently one afternoon, trying to mask my concern.

He blinked, startled, as if only just noticing I was there. "Nothing," he said quickly. "I didn't say anything."

"Oh, never mind," I said, brushing it off. "Wanna see what I'm working on?"

He walked over and I sat him down to hand him the first page of this memoir.

"It's not finished yet," I said, my voice wavering slightly as he took the paper from me.

He read in silence, eyes tracking carefully down the page. When he finally looked up, a genuine smile spread across his face. "This is so cool," he said softly. "You need to finish this."

Encouraged by his reaction, I felt brave enough to press further. I started asking questions about our past, especially about certain moments with Mother, hoping to fill in the gaps. But as I spoke, I watched the color slowly drain from his face, his jaw visibly tightening with every word.

My voice trailed off mid-sentence as the weight of his discomfort sank in. "You can read the rest later," I said quickly, forcing lightness into my tone, gently steering the conversation elsewhere. "You know, once it's actually finished."

The day Slava left, he pulled me into a long hug. His arms tightened around me, the tension in his grip saying everything he couldn't. When he finally let go, he turned to Miguel.

"Take care of her," he said, his voice low but steady. "Watch over her, no matter what."

There was a strange finality to his words, something that settled heavily in the air between us. Then, without looking back, he walked away.

The Last Five Days

My phone buzzed on the kitchen table. Mel's name flashed across the screen.

I opened it and a long text unfurled:

Things here have been chaotic. Slava seemed better after he returned from Arizona a few months back, but everything spiraled after my stepdad told him he couldn't grow weed in the shed. Slava muttered about "no one telling him what to do," started pacing like a caged animal. My stepdad called the cops, but they said it was legal. After that, it was a war zone.

We tried to rekindle things, but he was just using me to avoid eviction by my parents. Now he's holed up with junk food and weed, lost in his own world. I'm scared, Tanja. He's not coming back.

Another message popped in:

He got abusive again. Said it was his right. I told him we needed to go to therapy or nothing but of course he refused. I left. He's spiraling now, making up stories, vandalizing, stalking. He even hears voices now and says that your mother is controlling his brain. It's terrifying.

Miguel came in, kicking off his shoes, freezing when he saw my face. "What's wrong?"

I just handed him the phone.

He read silently, then said, "You might have to get him committed."

A few hours later, another message arrived, but this time with a video.

I tapped play.

Mel's stepdad stood his ground, chest puffed out, hands open like he was daring Slava forward.

"Go on, then!" Mel's stepdad roared. "Do it!"

Slava's hand moved. The gun came up, steady and terrifying.

Then his eyes shifted, flicking toward Mel's camera. And slowly, he lowered the gun before running off.

I stared at the frozen screen.

The money I had sent him, it hadn't been for rent. He used it to buy gun parts.

Mel said, I loved him once. I really tried. But he's unfixable now. His brain's trapped in the trauma. It's heartbreaking.

I understood. It was hard to let go, even when you knew you should.

Another text followed:

He told me once he'd kill everyone and then himself. Can you help me with the restraining order? Did he ever say anything about hurting us?

No, I texted back. He was careful.

Mel responded:

I'm sorry he hurt you when you were a child. He showed so much remorse . . . I wanted to believe he changed. I should've run.

The memory came rushing back, like a flood bursting through a dam Melanie had just cracked: Slava, sitting in the bathtub with me. Even then, even as a small child, I knew something was off. I felt it in the pit of my stomach, a twisting wrongness I didn't have words for yet. "What are you doing?" I asked. "Nothing," he said quickly, brushing it off like it was no big deal. He apologized later and I forgave him. That was the end of that. I sat there, staring into the muted light of the room, wondering. Was he always like that? Or did Mother tap it into him like a curse she spelled out over years, taping mittens on his hands, calling him things no child should ever hear? They say a young brain is soft, malleable, like clay. Belief alone can shape it. Press it down hard enough, repeat it often enough, and the mind will start to fold itself around the story it's been told. Maybe he wasn't born broken. Maybe he just believed he was. And maybe that was enough to make it true.

Slava tried calling me twice from jail. I let it ring both times.

I knew what he would ask, to bail him out, and I couldn't do it. Not any more.

Later, I found out the charges were dropped.

Self-defense, they said. The video showed him panicking just enough to pass as a victim.

He was free again.

Anger shook through me. This had been their one chance, a hospital stay, stabilization, maybe even a way back for him. Now there was no proof left to get him admitted.

My mind spun with options. I could call the police, tell them everything. But Slava's voice echoed in my head: If the cops ever come for me again, I'll kill myself.

I thought about telling my family. But what could they really do from across the world?

The last time I spoke up, told Father about Slava's drug use, it had exploded in my face. Slava had torn into me, furious, accusing me of betrayal. The others had pulled back, awkward and unsure. Even now, no one would believe me, not when Slava could laugh and smile and look so normal. Not even after he'd called Dima from his van a few weeks back, bragging about spying on Joey with binoculars and Dima had just hung up, uncomfortable but not alarmed.

It was never shocking enough. Not after growing up with a mother who blurred every line between strange and normal until none of us could tell the difference any more.

I pressed my hands against my thighs, forcing myself to breathe.

If I said something now, would it save him or destroy whatever was left?

Not yet, I thought.

Not yet.

Then my phone buzzed.

A new text from Mel lit up the screen:

He's going after my brother. He texted him today, threatened to shoot him, then unsent the message. All it said was: "You loot, I shoot." He's furious we took his gun and bullets. He's packing up now, hiding at the neighbors' while we finish filing the restraining orders. Hopefully he'll be served today.

Slava reached out a few more times after he was released. I knew deep down it was only a matter of time before he tried to find his way back to me. Maybe even show up at my door.

And even though I hated admitting it, I was scared. Scared of what he might do to me.

Scared of what he might do to Miguel. I knew nothing was going to change.

But I could protect the life I'd built. And I could keep us safe.

Miguel noticed before I even said a word.

"You don't look so good," he said softly one night, studying my face. "You're pale."

I sat down at the table, the screen glowing in front of me, and typed the message.

I tried to be kind. I tried to be careful. But I was tired—tired of suppressing the way I felt to make room for someone else's chaos.

I've thought deeply about our connection and realized I don't want to continue it. It no longer feels healthy and our lifestyles are just too different.

A few minutes later, his reply came:

We're family, but okay. Is there anything specific I could work on for the future?

The words felt hollow, like something he'd picked up from a self-help book without really understanding it.

I answered:

I know. But honestly, I don't want to be associated with your lifestyle. It reminds me too much of how Mother used to harass people she stayed with. I want to build my life with people who come from healthier places, people who aren't caught up in toxicity, drama, or substance dependency.

He pushed back:

Where is this coming from? Why are my struggles affecting you? Do you know something I don't?

I closed my eyes for a second before replying:

You don't believe in taking care of yourself or seeking therapy, even though you need it more than anyone I know. Your view of the world, your distrust, it's not something I agree with. If we met as strangers, I wouldn't choose to keep you in my life.

I hesitated.

Then I added:

And I can't forget what happened to me as a child. I don't know the full extent of it, but I know there was harm. Your text message during the summer when you called me sexy doesn't sit right with me. It made me realize I can't trust someone who could even think that way, especially toward their own sister.

My fingers hovered over the screen, heart pounding, but I kept going:

I know it's hard to hear. But I can't be around the life you're choosing. I respect your right to live it but I'm choosing my health. This isn't easy. I know we're family. I still want the best for you. But actions have consequences. And family isn't an excuse to look the other way any more.

His reply came through in a long burst, and I sat there reading it, my stomach knotting tighter with every line.

You're incredibly smart. Smarter than me. Don't insult your intelligence by pretending you don't remember. We were both kids with a bad mom. I never saw you that way. Maybe I was curious, maybe I misunderstood things because of poor parenting. But there was never any intent.

This lifestyle isn't a choice, it's forced on me. I'm a drifter, depending on people just to get by. I can't have a normal life like you. But I don't pretend you're a stranger.

When I said you were 'sexy,' I meant you're an attractive woman. I see now how it came across.

There was a beat, a pause where I could feel him pulling on that last thread between us.

You already forgave me once. And now you're taking it back.

But I'm still here, if you ever need something. That's who I am. Family first.

If you'd told me earlier this was building up, I would've kept things 'happy-friendly' in my texts.

A notification popped up.

He unsent a message. I unsent one too.

The next morning, my phone buzzed again. The cops still haven't found him to serve him, Mel wrote. Do you have any idea where he is? Or how to find him?

Slava did call Dima, I texted back. Asked him for a plane ticket. Dima asked me if I could cover it, but he said Slava would have to stay with our mother. And I'm like no way. He might kill her.

There was a pause, then Mel responded quickly:

He abandoned Amy at a vet clinic yesterday. I'm picking her up now. Not even a twenty-four-hour place. Just left her. How much is a one-way ticket to Germany? I'll pay it. If you can work it out so his family will help get him treatment once he's there, I'll buy the ticket. My mom and I just want him gone. We're so tired of living in fear.

I'll call Dima and see, I promised.

Awesome. Thank you, she wrote back almost immediately.

And hey, good news. I found Amy a perfect home. A full family. People who'll love her. It's with one of my coworkers, so I'll still be able to keep tabs on her. She'll go with them tomorrow, maybe a few days tops. So at least something good is happening.

I let out a breath I hadn't realized I was holding.

One tiny piece of this wreckage was finally being set right.

When I called Dima, my hands were trembling. Father was about to send money to bring Slava home to Germany, but they had no idea what was waiting for them.

I thought about my niece, only two years old, defenseless, trusting, and my stomach twisted. It hit me, clear as day: it was my responsibility now. I had to make them understand. No matter the consequences.

"Where?" Dima had asked him repeatedly, but Slava was so paranoid he wouldn't tell Dima how to send the money.

"It's . . . strange," Dima said, frowning through the video call.

I took a sharp breath. "You can't let him come back."

He looked at me, puzzled. Vika sat beside him, my two-year-old niece asleep in the next room. I'd never shared any of this before out of shame. But now there was no choice.

"He's dangerous, Dima. He's not the Slava you remember," I said.

Confusion clouded his face. I knew what he saw when he thought of Slava—the funny, impulsive nineteen-year-old who had left for America, full of dreams.

I pushed forward. "He planned on killing people."

"He's just saying that." Dima said dismissively.

I shook my head. "That's what I thought too, but he is not."

I took a breath and continued on, "During our last call, he told me he thought you were molesting your own daughter."

The color drained from Dima's face. "He actually said that?"

"Yes."

"In what way?"

"Calmly," I said. "Like we were talking about the weather."

Dima sat back, stunned. "Why didn't you tell me?"

I hesitated, guilt clawing at my chest. "How could I?" My voice broke. "I knew if I said that, he would never have a chance of building familial relationships again."

Tears blurred my vision. "But there's more." I took a deep breath. "He can't be around the little one. It's not safe."

"What? How do you know?" His voice was rising.

I swallowed hard. "Because it happened to me."

For a long moment, Dima said nothing. His mouth opened, closed.

"Why didn't you tell me sooner?" he finally choked out.

Vika reached for his hand, trying to ground him.

"I couldn't," I said. "It would have destroyed everything. It would've shattered any hope he had of a life, of redemption. And part of me . . . part of me hoped it would get better. That he would find a way back."

I wiped at my face. "But now . . . it's too late. You have to keep him away or get him hospitalized."

"I have to call him," Dima said.

Before I could stop him, the screen went dark.

As soon as Dima confronted him, Slava's voice shifted, higher, defensive, almost mimicking Mother's.

He insisted he'd never said anything like that, never done anything wrong to me.

Then, exasperated, he snapped, "Are you gonna help me or not? Otherwise, I'll die."

Dima felt the pressure tightening, an emotional chokehold.

"You can do whatever you want, Slava," he said, the sharpness creeping into his voice. "But if you're serious about coming, we'll send the money. I have heard this too many times from you and you always change your mind about coming home."

But then, out of nowhere, Slava's tone changed again.

"What was that?" he asked sharply. His voice was tight, suspicious.

Confused, Dima asked what he meant.

"Are the cops there?" Slava said, panic bleeding through every word.

He sounded convinced now, convinced the line was tapped, that Dima was working with someone, that it was all a setup to get him arrested.

The plan was simple:

Dima would call back after collecting the money from Father to buy Slava's plane ticket.

But when he called, again and again, Slava never picked up.

Instead, Slava messaged me:

Can you please, please help me?

A few minutes later, another text:

Do you want my iMac? I don't need it.

I just bought a new computer, I replied.

You should sell it.

The next day, December 9th, 2021, at 11:33 am, another message came through:

You were right. I'm sorry for my lifestyle. But I love you though.

That evening, at 7:04 pm, I typed back,

FAME OR DEAD

I love you too.
He never read it.

29

THE FINALE

December 10th slipped into the still hours past midnight.

Miguel lay beside me, his breathing shallow and uneven. I could hear it, the quiet catch in his lungs, while my own chest fought against a different kind of tightness. We had both tested positive for COVID-19 a few days before, and the virus pressed against our bodies like an invisible weight.

The room felt too warm, stifling, but I shivered anyway, curling deeper into the blankets.

A strange sensation came over me. It floated toward me, pressing into my chest, seeping into the deepest folds of my heart. For a fleeting moment, I felt it—warmth, sadness, love—so familiar it made my ribs ache. And then, just as suddenly, it tore through me, slicing out of my back like a cold knife, vanishing into the dark room, leaving me hollow.

Tears welled up before I could stop them. Hot, heavy, spilling silently across the bridge of my nose, soaking into the pillow.

"We don't have much time," I said out loud, the words escaping before I could catch them. My voice cracked on the last syllable. "We need to love each other more. Tell each other more before it's gone."

Miguel stirred beside me, turning toward me, his brow furrowing in the dim light.

He reached out instinctively, pulling me against him.

I closed my eyes against the tears still falling. My body knew something before my mind did.

The next morning, the calls kept coming. Each one an unanswered plea buzzing against my pocket, a growing weight gnawing at me with every ring.

Hello, Miss Ross, this is Detective Hermenez calling about your brother, Slava . . .

The voice on the voicemail was monotonous.

I clicked pause before he could say more. They're onto him, I thought. Again.

I couldn't bring myself to listen to the rest. I tucked the phone away and told myself I would wait until I was emotionally ready. But there was no such thing as ready for this.

After finally testing negative for any illness, Miguel and I ventured out of our home. Our bodies still moved like they were underwater, slowed down by the lingering weight of the virus. My lungs felt leaden. My limbs dragged as if they had forgotten how to carry me.

But when we stepped outside, the cold winter air filled my chest, shocking me awake. I closed my eyes, savoring the sharpness, hoping it would cut through the fog in my mind. We went grocery shopping, a mundane task that somehow felt sacred, picking apples, comparing loaves of bread, Miguel tossing a bag of chips into the cart.

We had just stepped back into my apartment when my phone buzzed again.

"Miguel," I said, "They keep calling me about Slava."

He froze. "Who's calling?"

I checked the latest notification, my thumb trembling over the screen. "The medical examiner's office."

Miguel's face shifted instantly. "You need to call them. Now."

"What if they're just trying to find him?" I blurted, the words coming out too fast. "What if he hurt someone? What if they found someone he killed?"

"You can't avoid this one." He said it calmly, but his face told me that this was bad.

I didn't know what the medical examiner's office even really meant. I didn't understand, and some part of me desperately wanted not to.

The air in the apartment felt thin. My chest tightened as I pressed the call button, each ring slicing deeper into the silence.

When the line picked up, the man who answered spoke softly, his voice professional, almost too kind. I introduced myself, barely managing to say my name.

"Miss Ross, how are you related to Slava Ross?" the man asked.

His voice was steady and formal, but underneath it, there was something else. A softness trying to brace me for what was coming.

"I'm his sister," I whispered.

The line went still.

I heard the faint intake of his breath, the way someone breathes when they have to say something unbearable.

The seconds stretched, unbearably long.

"Miss Ross," he said at last, each word deliberate, almost gentle. "I'm very sorry to inform you that your brother was found deceased."

Sound collapsed around me, folding inward, until all I could hear was the pounding rush in my ears, like I had been dropped underwater.

"What?"

"Yes," he said, his voice unwavering, a tether trying to keep me anchored.

"He was recovered from the water near San Francisco's China Beach around 3 pm on December 9th."

They have the wrong person, I thought. But then the man on the phone mentioned the tattoo, the one etched onto Slava's neck, just below his ear, that said "Process".

The floor seemed to tilt under me.

I gripped the edge of the kitchen counter to stay upright.

Miguel was still standing there, watching, but his face blurred at the edges of my vision.

All I could hear was that word, echoing over and over, until it didn't even sound like a word any more:

Deceased.

China Beach.

It was where my brother's body had been pulled from the cold, unyielding sea.

My vision tunneled, the walls of our small kitchen seeming to press in, closer and closer, until I could barely see or hear anything but the quiet, merciless facts I'd just learned.

"No, no, no," I screamed, my voice cracking, my hands reaching out blindly, searching for something solid to hold me up.

On the other end of the line, the man's voice stayed steady, calm.

"I know this is overwhelming, Miss Ross, but you'll need to make arrangements. The body will need to be transported . . ."

My body shook. The tremors wouldn't stop.

My knees gave out, and I sank to the floor, gripping the edge of the stovetop, my fingers digging into the cold metal as if it might somehow keep me from dissolving completely.

Across the room, Miguel stood frozen, the color drained from his face, watching me with wide, helpless eyes. The grocery bags lay forgotten at his feet.

When I finally hung up, a scream tore out of me that didn't even feel like it belonged to me. It bounced off the walls, rattling down the empty hallways of our building, vibrating through every nerve in my body.

"He's dead!" I screamed. "He fucking killed himself. I failed him. It's all my fault."

I must've been screaming the entire time, because Miguel was begging now, his voice breaking.

"Please stop," he said, reaching toward me.

But I flinched back hard, wrapping my arms around myself like I could hold myself together.

"Don't touch me!" I shouted, pushing him away as he hovered, helpless, not knowing what to do, not knowing how to reach me.

For a long time, we just sat there on the floor as I bawled.

Grief wound around us like barbed wire, tight and cutting. My world had been altered in a way I couldn't undo. There was no fixing this, no saving him, no redo of any sorts.

And eventually all I could do was cling to Miguel, hoping it could give me the strength to keep going. But I wanted to die too.

The next morning, after sleeping for a total of two hours, I woke with a start, my heart pounding as if it could somehow outrun the truth. In those first few seconds, I would forget. For a fleeting moment, he was still out there somewhere. Then the memories would come crashing back. The world around me dulled. Colors faded to muted shades of gray. Food tasted like dust. But the worst part was telling my family. Making that call was like climbing a jagged mountain with no end in sight. There were no soft words to offer. No way to cushion the fall. When my parents' faces appeared on the screen, blurry through my tears, I forced the words out.

Slava is dead, I signed.

My stepmother's scream ripped through the air. My father, just stood there, frozen.

The silence that poured out of him was deafening. It said everything.

Telling Dima was no easier. I felt myself slipping deeper into numbness, detaching from my own body as I forced the words out again. Each time I said it, it felt less real.

On the other end of the line, I could hear Dima breathing heavily.

With Andy, it was the same.

"You need to wake Mother and tell her," I murmured.

It felt like I was passing on an impossible burden.

When I told Mel, she collapsed. I could hear it over the phone, the sharp, broken sobs, the way her breath hitched and caught in her throat. I knew, without seeing, that her hands were pressed to her heart, trying to hold the pieces together, trying to keep it from breaking open completely. Her true love, her awful love.

Gone.

Just a day later, the newspaper covered it with a single, detached line:

Body found near China Beach.

Slava was found nearby Deadmen's Cliff, a jagged, desolate stretch known for its suicides, where the violent ocean churned endlessly below. Maybe he thought the waves would erase him completely, that we'd be left to reach me one last time?

If I had stayed quiet, buried my pain, would he have stayed and turned his life around?

The maybes stacked on my chest like stones, heavy and merciless, and I didn't know how to put them down.

Miguel grew increasingly worried. He would sit next to me, talking, trying to pull me back, but I barely heard him.

"It's traumatizing," he said one night, his voice raw with hurt. "You don't even know I'm here." He was right. I wasn't there.

I was somewhere else, combing through the wreckage, trying to solve a puzzle that no longer had any pieces left.

Through every agonizing step of the funeral, Miguel held my hand when the shaking wouldn't stop and sat with me in silence when words failed. He had planned to leave for L.A. before Thanksgiving to see his family. But then we both caught COVID again. He missed his flight, and we ended up quarantining together for the weeks to come. I don't know what would have happened to me without him. "It's fate," he said softly, standing over the stove, stirring a pot. "I'm here for you."

He placed a plate of food in front of me, food I wouldn't have eaten otherwise, and encouraged me to eat.

Father wanted to fly out and be there for me. But I told him no. I couldn't handle his presence, couldn't let him see me like this. I needed to protect him from my pain, to keep him at a distance, where he wouldn't have to witness the depth of it.

Mother reached out as well. A year ago, she had dialed by accident, muttered it was a mistake when I answered, then hung up. She did that often, even with Slava. Sometimes I wondered if she wanted to hear our voices. But this time, it was intentional.

"You need to go to the spot," she said. "Where he jumped. Scatter his ashes there. Let his spirit go." The words poured out in a frantic rush. "If we don't, he'll be stuck wandering. He won't move on."

I gripped the phone tighter. "You want me to go to the edge of a cliff that's closed to the public? Where people go to jump?"

"Yes," she whispered.

"And what if I fall? Is that what you want?"

The thought alone, the screaming wind, the dizzying drop, made my stomach turn.

"You should've been there," she said flatly. "You should've forgiven him. You should've given him love. That's all he needed."

A bitter laugh escaped me. "He hurt me, Mother. I did the best I could."

"No," she said, her voice cracking. "You don't understand. He needed you. He always loved you. Always protected you . . ."

Each word a knife.

"Where were you?" I shouted. "You're his mother. Where were you when he was struggling?"

A long pause.

"Do what you want with the funeral," she said coldly. "It's on you."

I hung up.

I thought about bringing my brother's body back to Germany.

But Mother refused outright.

"I can't have him buried here," she told Dima. "I can't live with the graveyard so close, knowing he's there. I couldn't bear it."

She wanted him laid to rest with me in America.

"Slava never wanted to come back to Germany," Dima said quietly. "Every time we asked, every time we pleaded, he turned us down. Even when he said he might, he always changed his mind. He wanted to stay in America, right up to the end. All or nothing, he'd say."

Slava had chosen America over his family, even in death.

In the middle of all the logistics, a message lit up on my phone.

It was from Lucas, Slava's old friend, the one who'd been pushed off the parking garage years ago and somehow survived. I guessed this meant that he didn't believe it was Slava who did it all along.

I have Slava's passport and documents, he wrote.

My heart thudded.

Maybe that's why Slava was in San Francisco—to reach the German embassy.

Maybe he tried to get a temporary passport, only to realize he couldn't, not without anything to prove who he was.

Whether it was building a life in the U.S. or coming home, neither had been an option any more.

Please send them to me, I replied immediately. We need them to bring him home.

But then—nothing.

Days stretched out and Lucas left all my messages on seen.

As I was scrolling, without warning, all of Slava's profiles vanished from social media.

One day, his face still flickered back at me through old posts, old memories frozen in time. The next, they were gone. It was a setting you could arrange on social media to erase your digital footprint when you die.

It was like losing him all over again.

I could no longer turn to his page and see him smiling, hear his voice echo through old captions, trace the strange, scattered constellation of his life online.

The last fragments of him had slipped away, just like that.

The blame ricocheted through my family like a cruel game of ping pong, each of us swatting it away, desperate not to hold it.

Mother pointed at Dima for not helping Slava fast enough.

Dima turned on Father, saying he should have fought harder during the divorce, should have kept us from ever leaving for America.

Father, disabled and isolated, said it was unfair, that he was left playing a game he never stood a chance of winning.

Then he turned the blame back on Mother, who finally landed it squarely on me for sending that final message to Slava.

But none of them wanted to confront the darker truths, his violent fantasies, his depression, the drugs. When I tried to explain, to show them what he had been up against, they accused me of tarnishing his memory.

They simply couldn't, or wouldn't, see him for who he had become.

And maybe, in a way, I was glad they couldn't.

Better for them to remember the boy they loved than the man who had with nothing but questions about his disappearance and an empty, gnawing ache. But fate had other plans, and it saved our remaining sanity.

A swimmer found him in the ice-cold waters, risking their own life to drag him to shore.

His final act was as dramatic as his life had been. And when the police found his white van, it sat there quietly, the tank bled dry, zero miles left. Just like him.

I'd imagine my brother standing there, toes curled over the edge, the ocean stretching dark and endless below him.

I could almost see him, tears streaming down his face, the wind tearing at his hair, his shoulders sagging under the unbearable weight of his final choice.

Sometimes, in those dark imaginings, I pictured myself running toward him, heart pounding, screaming for him to stop. Begging him to turn around, to come back, to let me reach him. But every time, just as my fingers stretched out to grab his sleeve, he was gone.

And the scene would replay, over and over, a relentless loop that clawed at my sanity.

I wondered what he was listening to in those final moments—his earbuds still on him when they found him. Was it one of his favorite songs? I pictured him in his favorite sweater I gave him on Christmas, though it was never recovered, probably swallowed by the waves.

Just a few days before, he had liked some of my songs on SoundCloud.

I wondered where he was now, if he was trapped somewhere dark, or if, somehow, he was somewhere beautiful.

If he could, I knew he would haunt me, just for a laugh. But as I sat and waited for a sign, the silence stretched on. The thoughts became a trap, looping endlessly, pulling me deeper each time.

I'd sit for hours, staring at nothing, lost in the replays.

What was he thinking?

What was he feeling?

What could I have done differently?

Would he still be alive if I had answered his message sooner?

When he offered me his computer, was it a goodbye, a desperate attempt already been lost long before he hit the water.

The blame ricocheted through the family like a frantic game of hot potato.

Mother jabbed a trembling finger at Dima: "You should have sent the money sooner."

Dima turned on Father, his voice cracking with old wounds: "You should have fought harder in court. You should have never let us leave for America."

Father, shoulders hunched and eyes hollow, only shook his head, the words piling up behind the wall of his disability.

Finally, Mother turned on me.

"If you hadn't sent that message and lied, he'd still be alive."

Then I remembered, Bad things happen to bad girls.

No one wanted to talk about the other things.

The dark fantasies. The days lost to drugs and depression.

The strange, terrifying things he said in the end.

When I tried to bring them up, they'd stop me.

"You're tarnishing his memory," they said. But I knew the truth.

And maybe, just maybe, it was better that they didn't.

Better for them to remember him in golden flashes—the boy they loved—than the hollow man he had become.

At his desk, Dima hunched over a scattering of papers and news clippings.

"You don't get it," he said, "Slava didn't kill himself. Something happened. Maybe it was Melanie's family that had him killed."

He called the detective again and again, voice rising from pleading to demanding.

The final time, the detective's voice hardened. "Stop calling," he said. "There's nothing more we can tell you. All the signs are there."

They were all grieving, blaming, grasping for a story that made sense.

And I thought of my niece, asleep in her little bed.

Small hands curled into fists, eyelashes fluttering against her cheeks.

If I could go back, I wouldn't change a thing.

I pictured her, safe and unaware, her breath steady in the dark only because I dragged the truth into the light. There are choices you make knowing no one will ever thank you for them. I would carry their resentment. I would carry their blame.

But I would not carry the guilt of what could have happened if I had stayed quiet.

Seeing my family unravel over it unfurled something darker inside me.

I hated him.

I hated him for every ounce of torment he had dragged me through, for making me wait endlessly in fear and hope, for leaving me to wrestle with the wreckage he left behind.

I hated him for making me love him so deeply that even now, even after everything, there was still a part of me that would live through it all over again if it meant he was still alive.

Every time I reached out to someone about Slava, I was met with empty promises.

There was no circle of friends willing to step up, no community to mourn him, even though they all said wonderful things once he was gone. How he stood up for them, how he helped them when no one did, how funny he was.

But no one gathered. No one showed up.

When Mel reached out to Joey to let him know what happened, he said he'd sell his computer to help with the funeral costs. Even though Joey and I didn't speak any more, part of me wanted to believe he meant it.

But like so many others, it was just another let-down in the hardest time of my life.

It was the day before Christmas Eve when we arrived in Oregon.

Outside the window, snowflakes drifted lazily, casting a soft glow over the disordered shed where Slava had lived. His essence clung to every corner, as if he had just stepped out for a moment, as if he might walk through the door at any second.

I moved through the space, picking up pieces of him.

Notebooks lay scattered across the desk, their edges worn thin from restless handling.

I flipped through them, skimming page after page of scribbled affirmations and meticulously written goals, the words pressed so deeply into the paper it was like he had tried to carve them into reality.

Then I stopped.

One page stood out.

Line after line, filling the paper with a single, brutal phrase:

I want to die.

And the word "Scum" spray painted on his sweater. It struck me then how difficult it must have been for him: to be so painfully self-aware, so intelligent, and yet so tormented by the parts of himself he couldn't fix.

At his computer, I found what looked like a wiped drive. But fragments remained.

Search histories for group therapy programs and options he never took.

Strange videos, too: grainy clips of him pacing back and forth between the main house where Mel lived with her family and the shed where he stayed.

Email drafts and lawyer correspondence, filled with talk of suing her family, trying to take their house.

I drank an entire bottle of red wine by the fire with Miguel and Mel, piecing through the wreckage, trying to pinpoint where it all went wrong.

Every theory, every memory, every desperate what-if led us back to the same place of grief. Everything that could have saved him, he refused. And we realized tragedy looks preventable when you're not the one going through it.

Sleeping at Mel's place triggered dreams of him.

In them, he would appear in the corners of rooms, standing quietly, his face clouded with confusion and sorrow, as if he were only now realizing he was gone.

His "broken" body, as he used to call it, seemed to fall away in these visions, revealing a softer, more vulnerable spirit, lost, bewildered, still searching for a peace he hadn't found in life. In the dreams, I would run to him, overwhelmed with relief.

"Call Dima," I would plead, grabbing his hand. "Let him know you're alive."

He would only smile, soft and sad, and then—

I would wake up.

When Christmas Eve arrived—the only day they had an opening for his burial—instead of gathering with family to unwrap presents, I found myself staring at the box that held my brother's body.

All that was missing was a bow on top.

"You motherfucker," I muttered. "Worst present in the entire world."

Mel and I had chosen the place ourselves: a stretch of towering trees and silent groves, where he could be absorbed back into the earth, his body feeding the roots, merging into the ancient fungal network that whispered beneath the soil.

His life would become part of the forest, something enduring, something still alive, long after the rest of us were gone.

Miguel stood beside me, his breath fogging in the air, his eyes wide with a kind of quiet awe as he pointed out icicles clinging to the bare branches. He was trying, in his tender way, to pull me out of myself, to anchor me in something small and beautiful. Mel stood a few feet away, her knuckles white with tension.

I clutched my phone tightly, ready to video chat my family after they lowered my brother into the earth.

The forest workers, bundled in heavy coats and boots, moved with quiet care, guiding his body down into the earth.

I couldn't watch.

A sudden, overwhelming urge clawed at me, to run to him, to cover his naked body, still held together by ropes after the autopsy like a puppet, with a blanket.

He's going to get cold, my mind cried over and over, even though I knew he wouldn't feel it any more. Just then, a single beam of sunlight pierced through the dense canopy, casting long, soft shadows across the snow and warming the frozen air around us.

The forest fell silent. Even the wind held its breath, as if the world had paused just for him. In that hush, something within me shifted. A quiet calm settled into my bones, deeper than grief, older than words.

The snow glittered like crushed crystals, and the sunlight touched my skin with unexpected warmth. For the first time in what felt like forever, the weight began to lift.

I knew then he was finally at peace.

30

THE BUCKWHEAT

The tiny Christmas tree in my apartment leaned slightly to one side, its twinkling lights casting soft, uneven patterns across the walls. My cats circled it, one of them crouching low before swiping at a fragile, low-hanging ornament.

A year.

A whole year had passed since Slava's death.

I told myself, over and over, that I was okay. That time had softened the edges, dulled the pain. But my body knew better. On the worst days, without thinking, I still dialed his number, pressing the phone to my ear, listening to the endless ringing, holding on to the silence like somehow, if I waited long enough, he'd pick up and say, "I've returned! It was all a part of my new magic trick."

I spent the whole year staring at the wall, just gone, lost in a world where Slava still physically existed. In that version of reality, he'd text me out of nowhere, sending unfinished thoughts and absurd videos. He'd walk through my door uninvited, crash on my couch, laugh too loud at his own jokes. He'd ask for a ride, ask for money, ask for forgiveness without ever saying the word. In that world, I could still save him.

It wasn't long before Miguel stood in the doorway, jacket in hand, eyes tired in that way people get when they've held on too long. The apartment was dim except for the flicker of the TV I wasn't watching. I sat curled on the couch, a blanket draped over my legs, a half-eaten bowl of soup on the table beside me.

He lingered there for a moment, just watching me. Then quietly, he said, "You need to see someone. This is getting bad."

I didn't move. Didn't blink. Just stared at the spot on the wall I'd been staring at for days, maybe weeks.

He crossed the room and knelt in front of me, his hands hovering just above my knees like he wasn't sure if he was still allowed to touch me.

"I love you, Tanja. But I don't think you're here with me any more. I think you left a long time ago."

The words didn't even sting.

He reached up to brush a piece of hair from my face, and I flinched without meaning to. His hand dropped.

"I feel like I'm dating a ghost," he whispered.

That made something inside me twitch, but I couldn't find the energy to follow it. I wanted to tell him I was trying. That I wasn't doing this on purpose. That I used to be full of warmth, too.

But all I could manage was, "I know."

I looked at him then, really looked, and saw the hurt beneath the patience, the fatigue of someone trying to love someone who couldn't meet them there. I opened my mouth, and for the first time, said the truth out loud.

"I just . . . can't be with anyone right now," I said. "The version of me you knew, she's been gone for a while."

He waited. For what, I don't know. A promise? A plea? I didn't have either.

So he stood. Looked around the room like he might be forgetting something. Paused, just long enough to see if I'd stop him. Then nodded again, as if to himself, and left.

I knew he was right. I stood at a crossroad, split wide open: stay buried in the darkness, or gather what strength I had left and wrestle my life back from the grief.

The next morning, I made the call.

I don't remember what I said when the receptionist picked up, something about needing help, about things getting bad. My voice sounded flat, unfamiliar. She offered an appointment for the following week, but I must've said something right, because she paused, then asked, "Can you see me tomorrow?"

And I did.

When I sat down for my first therapy session, I had to fill out a PTSD questionnaire. I stared at it, unsure how to even put this feeling, this thing swallowing me, into words. But I answered honestly.

My score was double.

For reference, the therapist explained, a score of thirty qualified someone for intensive cognitive processing therapy, the kind designed for soldiers returning from war.

I sat there, holding that number in my hands like it was something fragile and damning all at once. But all it really did was confirm what I already knew: I couldn't go on without receiving help.

Sleep had turned against me. When I managed to drift off, it was only to be pulled into nightmares, visions of myself unraveling, losing touch with reality, just like my brother. It felt like his pain had seeped into my bloodstream, as if madness was something you could inherit. I couldn't shake the thought that I had failed him. That my love hadn't been enough to tether him to this world.

"It's not your fault," my therapist said one afternoon, her voice steady, almost shamanic in its calm. She stared into me, past the surface, with her dark eyes, as if she could see the places even I couldn't reach. "You did everything you could. If love or words were enough to save him, they would've worked long ago. But this was deeper. You can't force someone to heal."

"Maybe if I hadn't said anything, if I'd just kept quiet about his behavior, he would've gone home," I whispered.

"He never wanted to return before. You don't know what harm might've come if you'd stayed silent. He wasn't in a state of mind where anyone was safe, especially your niece. If something had happened to her, you would've never forgiven yourself. Not saying something . . . that would've made you part of the problem. You shed the light on it because he left you no choice. It was the truth."

Her patience seemed infinite, even as I kept circling the same pain, like an animal returning to its own trap.

"But how do you love someone who hurt you so much?" I asked, ashamed of the question even as I spoke it.

Her gaze softened.

"He wasn't himself at the end, Tanja. But he was still your brother," she said gently. "Of course you loved him. You always will."

"Why did he start acting so inappropriate toward me all of a sudden?" I asked. "It was normal for so long. Then . . . it wasn't."

She paused, choosing her words carefully. "It's not uncommon with illnesses like schizophrenia. Sometimes it manifests in inappropriate behavior. Sudden sexual disinhibition. It's part of the disease."

As the sessions wore on, my trembling hands and bloodshot eyes didn't go unnoticed. She eventually suggested medication, antidepressants, or even an in-patient program.

I recoiled, fear catching in my chest. What would medication do to my brain? What would my family think?

To them, needing help meant weakness. Failure stamped across your forehead.

But then I thought about Slava, how that same fear might have stopped him from reaching out, from saving himself.

Hesitantly, I agreed.

The first dose of fluoxetine didn't fix everything, but it cracked the door open.

A few days in, my body started moving differently. Slower, but with less drag, like walking through shallow water instead of cement. I could get up without thinking about it for an hour first. Brush my teeth.

Then came the colors.

One afternoon, I looked up and realized the sky was blue. Just . . . blue. Not threatening or irrelevant. Just there.

And I smiled. Not because anything was better.

But because I noticed.

I had to get out of the sweatpants I'd been wearing for days on end. I walked over to my closet and creaked the door open. The air inside was still, like a sealed vault.

I stepped in and grabbed the first thing I saw—a wrinkled black sweater—and pulled it over my head. Then jeans that barely fit me any more.

But something was rising in me. A pressure that had been building for months.

And then, without warning, I snapped.

I grabbed the first handful of shirts I could reach and I shoved them to my face.

I screamed. The clothes clung to my face, muffling it, swallowing it whole.

Somewhere between the screaming and the silence that followed, I felt it:

That I was still here. In this body. In this life. If I was still here, then I had to be here.

I wanted to want things again. Not in some grand, sweeping way. Just in small moments. To care if the coffee tasted good. To answer a text. To hear music and not flinch.

It felt like life had been stolen from me twice, once when I was a child, again when Slava died. But now, something was shifting. Not peace. Not forgiveness. Just the smallest, sharpest thought: No. I leaned back against the closet wall, surrounded by everything I used to wear, the life I used to fit into.

And I whispered to the darkness that still lingered around me:

You don't get to take me, too. I'm not a fucking corpse.

I was so desperate to rewrite the neural pathways of my brain that I started small.

I took walks outside, every step feeling foreign, like I was relearning how to exist among the living. I kept my head down, sunglasses on, earbuds tucked in even when the music wasn't playing. I flinched when people brushed past me. I timed my walks for odd hours when the sidewalks were emptier, when the sun hung lower and the world felt quieter.

I forced myself to take one photo a day that I printed and hung on my wall for me to see.

THE BUCKWHEAT

The steam curling off a cup of coffee.

A shard of sunlight cutting across the floorboards.

The crinkle of a friend's smile, caught mid-laughter.

At first, they felt like nothing, tiny, weightless fragments scattered across my life.

But day by day, they grew. One image. Then another. Then another.

Until, almost without realizing it, they began to stitch themselves together.

A mosaic of quiet moments. Proof that joy hadn't vanished, rather it was waiting for me to notice. A reminder that the world hadn't ended with him.

I just had to remember how to see them.

There were months when I couldn't even meet my own eyes in the mirror, weighed down by the shame of being me, of where I came from.

Now, when I look, I still see traces of Mother in the high cheekbones, the dimple at the tip of my nose. I see her, ruthlessly determined, who survived the only way she knew how. In my blue eyes, I catch glimpses of my father's quiet humor, his stubborn, unwavering kindness.

And in the rest of me, I no longer see the girl they once called Corpse.

I no longer see a bad girl.

She's gone now, buried with everything I had to leave behind.

What remains is simple me.

A woman who clawed her way out of the dark and built a life on the other side. And despite it all, despite the chaos and madness, I'm proud to be my parents' daughter.

Because it took all of it to become who I am now.

My father called more often now; sometimes it felt excessive, but I understood he needed the reassurance. When I arrived in Germany for a visit, he hugged me at every chance, gripping tighter than he ever had before.

"You should move back," he signed, pointing toward an apartment complex near his home.

I shook my head, smiling softly. "I like America," I signed back. "I like the home I've built for myself."

Dima changed as well. He was softer, more attentive than ever before. He took me out for breakfast, asked about my projects, made quiet plans to spend time together. The sharp edges of our old arguments had worn down, replaced by an unspoken understanding: we were all we had left now.

"How do you live so normally?" he asked one afternoon as we sat in his car, the pale spring light leaking through the windshield. "Do you still think about him?"

I let out a soft laugh, thin, brittle. There was no such thing as normal any more. Not after something like this. The wound never closed; it just stopped bleeding me out.

"I think about him every day," I said, my eyes fixed on the window, watching the world smear by in muted streaks of color.

"I'd give anything to have him back . . ." I said. "Healthy. Happy."

Dima was silent for a long while, then asked, almost in a whisper, "Are you relieved?"

I glanced at the photo of his daughter clipped to the dashboard, her small face frozen in a smile untouched by all of this.

"Yes," I said. Then, after a breath, "And no. Relieved the pain is over. Heartbroken that he's gone."

The words felt heavy in the small space between us, but honest.

From the corner of my eye, the photo blurred. And for a moment, I didn't see his daughter at all. I saw myself, small, bright-eyed and unprotected.

Maybe the tragedies would never fully leave me and just trail behind like a shadow, a silent companion at the edge of every sunrise, every small beginning.

When we returned to my father and Irene's apartment, I wandered to the window and looked out at the neighborhood I grew up in. And there he was.

Sixteen-year-old Slava, caught in the amber of memory. At the ping pong table, his laugh drifting through the summer air. On the old bench, elbows on knees, watching me dig in the sandbox like I was searching for treasure. In the grass after soccer, mud on his shins, cheeks flushed, smiling like he was the happiest boy alive.

And everything stood still, just long enough to believe he might look up and wave.

Father laid a hand on my shoulder, and I turned, startled.

THE BUCKWHEAT

When I looked up, he smiled at me. Then he signed, Food is ready.

We stood there for a moment as if he could see Slava too before he motioned for me to join them at the dinner table. The food was simple, laid out under the warm kitchen lights. Everything passed with impeccable manners. Father launched into one of his wild stories again, his hands flying, his face animated. My stepmother looked at him wide-eyed, full of love.

My niece darted in circles around the table, clutching a stuffed animal I gave her.

Dima and Victoria leaned back in their chairs, laughing.

And just like a small flashlight in the dark, the beautiful moments of my current life began to flicker through and something softer bloomed inside me; a fragile, stubborn kind of hope. And as I let it all sink in: the clatter of dishes, the murmur of conversation, the hum of life that had found a way to keep going, I realized it wasn't perfect.

It wasn't a million-dollar home.

It wasn't fame under the flashing lights of Hollywood.

It was buckwheat. Ground beef. A child's laughter.

And somehow, after everything . . .

It was, in the end, the only dream that mattered.

I would like to thank Thomas Ocovos for the design work and for bringing my vision to life on a short deadline; my editors Margaret Diehl, Edward Wall, Caroline Leavitt, and Michael S.; my brother, Dietrich Ross, for his design input; photographer Jeff Points for capturing my portrait that serves as the cover of Part III. I am also deeply grateful to my English teacher, Kevin Erickson, who generously took the time to review my earliest - and admittedly quite terrible - first draft, despite his already demanding teaching schedule. Finally, I wish to thank Brew & Brew for providing a space where I could complete my final draft, and my friends whose encouragement sustained me throughout this journey.

SLAWA ROSS

1985 - 2021